AN LEABHARLANN
COLÁISTE NA hOLLSCOILE, CORCAIGH

Níl sé ceaduithe an leabhar seo a choimead thar an dáta is déanaí atá luaite thíos.
This book must be returned not later than the last date stamped below.

1 5 MAR 1994		
1 5 JAN 1996		
2 4 JAN 1996		

The Library, University College, Cork

CHARLES J. KICKHAM (1828-82)
A study in Irish nationalism and literature

Yours faithfully
Charles J. Kickham

CHARLES J.
KICKHAM

A study in Irish nationalism and literature

R.V. Comerford

WOLFHOUND PRESS

Published by Wolfhound Press
98 Ardilaun, Portmarnock, County Dublin.
Phone 452162

ISBN 0 905473 14 0

Printed in the Republic of Ireland by Folens Printing Co., Ltd.,

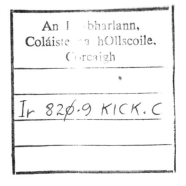

CONTENTS

LIST OF ILLUSTRATIONS

ACKNOWLEDGEMENTS

My research on Kickham began under the supervision of the then Professor of History at Maynooth and now Archbishop of Armagh, His Eminence Cardinal Tomás Ó Fiaich. Professor R. Dudley Edwards was the first to suggest publication and he has been generous with help and encouragement from start to finish. Much of what I know about fenianism was learned under the guidance of Professor T. W. Moody. Dr Donal McCartney kindly undertook the task of reading most of the final draft. He made valuable suggestions, as did Rev Professor P. J. Corish and Rev Professor Peter Connolly, each of whom cast an expert eye over sections of the manuscript. I am grateful to them all.

James Maher of Mullinahone who died in 1977 worked devotedly for many years at rescuing, collecting and publishing Kickham material, some of which would now be untraceable but for his efforts. Anyone coming to the study of Kickham after him inevitably owes him a large debt. I am indebted, too, to his brothers, Richard and Thomas A., who have given me permission to use material from his books. Others who have allowed me to make use of items in their possession, or over which they have rights, include the following: Patrick Murphy, Alexander Swaine, Anthony Twomey (of George Fottrell and Sons) and John Elliott, all of Dublin; Dr Thomas Morris, Archbishop of Cashel; James Cusack and the Misses Myles of Clonmel; Benedict Kiely; Miss Nora Norton of Mullinahone; Miss Mary Keating of Ballinard; Mrs Hanrahan of Ballycurkeen; Mrs Bradshaw of Drangan. Miss Mary Leo, Fr Christopher O'Dwyer and Dr David Leonard kindly allowed me to read their unpublished theses and helped in other ways.

I am indebted to the proprietors and staffs of the following libraries and archival institutions for the opportunity to consult sources (and in some instances for permission to quote or reproduce material): National Library of Ireland, Public

8

Record Office of Ireland; State Paper Office, Dublin Castle; Registry of Deeds; Royal Irish Academy; Trinity College Library, Dublin; Maynooth College Library; British Library; Public Record Office, London; Broadlands Archives Trust; National Register of Archives (Royal Commission on Historical Manuscripts); Tipperary County Library; Cashel Diocesan Archives, Thurles; O'Connell's School Library, Dublin.

Of the many who have answered queries, given advice or made helpful suggestions I owe special thanks to Marcus Bourke, the biographer of John O'Leary; he has placed his extensive knowledge and expertise at my disposal on many occasions over a number of years. I am also indebted to Dr Leon Ó Broin, Dr F. S. L. Lyons, Fr James Ryan, Mme Godeleine Carpentier, Michael Gill, Ulick O'Connor, Dr P. C. Power, Peadar O'Dwyer, Frank and Raymond Murphy, Monsignor Maurice Browne, Máire Cruise O'Brien, Hugh Ryan Michael Coady, Br W. P. Allen, the late Mrs Nora Egan; and to Jacinta de Paor of the Geography Department at Maynooth who prepared the map on page 12. The Maynooth Scholastic Trust helped generously with my typing expenses.

Sheila and Denis Foley have taken exceptional trouble to help me and I cannot hope to thank them adequately. Of the many other Mullinahone people who have given assistance I shall mention two: Dan Hogan and Joe Lawrence.

I feel that I have been especially fortunate in my publisher Seamus Cashman who has been a model of patience and understanding.

My greatest debt is to my wife, to whom the book is dedicated.

PREFACE

Owing to unusual personal and domestic circumstances, Charles J. Kickham, unlike the majority of nineteenth-century literary men, has not left behind a hoard of private papers, or a large volume of correspondence with contemporaries that would facilitate the work of a biographer. On the contrary, much of his career is very thinly documented, so that preparing his life story has involved an extensive search in many places for any and every scrap of enlightenment. Information on some areas is still not abundant, but it is now possible for the first time to present a rounded account of Kickham's life and work. Over and above the necessary elucidation of his career in some detail, his biography has to fill the obvious need for a clarification of his political and social views and an assessment of his place in political and literary history. He is generally recognised as an important figure in the fenian story and is known as the author of *Knocknagow*, but otherwise his image, even in the eyes of well-read students of Irish history and literature, is enveloped in haze. My hope is that this book will succeed in sharpening the focus.

An enduring feature of the political culture of nationalist Ireland is a tendency to accept that the extravagant, romantic response to problems is morally superior to moderation and compromise — no matter to what extent compromise may prevail in practice. The translation of this attitude from pages of the *Nation* to the realms of popular sensibility was the work of many individuals, of whom Kickham was one of the most important.

For many older people mention of *Knocknagow* evokes the ethos of the Ireland of their youth. Though he died in 1882, Kickham's work exudes the spirit of the rural-oriented majority in southern Irish society in the first half of this century. That 'mentality' has been largely superseded, but it still has not been adequately investigated. A biography of the author of *Knocknagow*, will, I hope, make some contribution to the understanding of it: Kickham is of relevance to more than the political and conspiratorial aspects of Irish nationality.

ABBREVIATIONS

N.L.I.	National Library of Ireland
S.P.O.	State Paper Office, Dublin Castle
Devoy, *Recollections*	John Devoy, *Recollections of an Irish rebel* (New York, 1929)
Kickham, 'Young Ireland'	C. J. Kickham, 'Notes on Young Ireland' in *Irishman* (Dublin), 26 Mar.—5 Nov. 1881.
O'Leary, *Recollections*	John O'Leary, *Recollections of fenians and fenianism* (2 vols, London, 1896)
Valley nr. Slievenamon	James Maher (ed.), *The Valley near Slievenamon: a Kickham anthology* (Mullinahone, 1942)

for PHIL

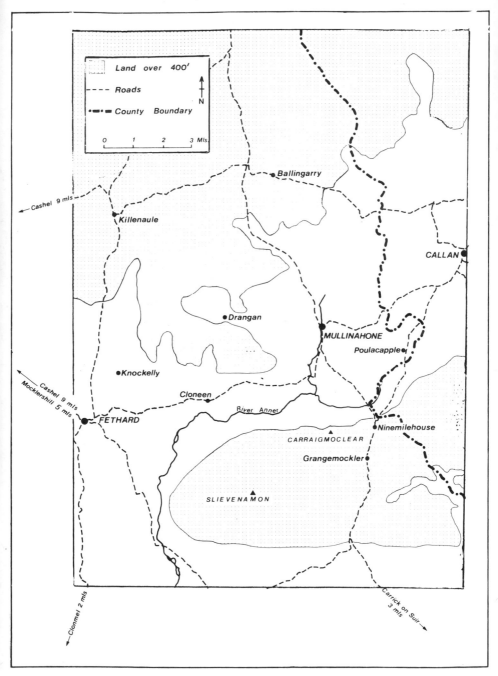

A map of the Kickham country

Chapter One

BACKGROUND AND EARLY YEARS

Family and local tradition and other sources agree that the Kickhams[1] of Mullinahone and district in County Tipperary owed their origins to an English settler of Cromwellian times, reputedly a military farrier. That was an important position involving responsibility for the welfare of the horses in a cavalry regiment, but it was not sufficiently prestigious to ensure admission to the ranks of the colonial gentry. The Kickhams never became large-scale territorial landlords, though in time some of them acquired the tenancy of gentlemen's holdings such as Knockelly Castle near Fethard. However, the tradition of the professional horse-handler survived in the family for a surprisingly long time.

Charles Kickham (1752-1815), grandfather of Charles J. Kickham, was described as a blacksmith in a legal document dated 1796, which also provided evidence that he was well on his way to becoming something else, for it recorded an extended lease to him of land and houses in Mullinahone village.[2] In the papers dealing with his next recorded property transaction, in 1810, he was described as a shopkeeper. He was then purchasing the freehold of his own premises and an interest in three neighbouring properties.[3] His last major business coup came in May 1815, months before his death, when he made terms with a local landlord who had run up debts with him to the impressive sum of £537. The settlement was for an annuity of over £50 payable to Kickham and his heirs out of the rents of extensive property in the village.[4]

Just as Charles Kickham's career placed his branch of the family in a new economic and social setting, it also witnessed a change in religious affiliation. Though information on this question is scanty and vague, we can conclude, with some confidence, that he himself belonged to the established church in his early years, and, with certainty, that long before his death his children were catholics.[5] Two of his sons, Charles and Roger, studied at Maynooth, entering in 1817 and 1827 respectively.[6] Charles later served as a priest in the archdiocese of Cashel and died in 1844. Roger, after his ordination in 1834, joined a small group of priests formed the previous year which was to become the first Irish province of the Congregation of the Mission (Vincentian fathers), and he was on the staff of Castleknock College when it opened in 1835 and for many years afterwards.[7]

Handsome provision was made for the other sons. James, the eldest, inherited his father's business premises on the Square in Mullinahone; Thomas acquired a farm at Clonagoose just outside the village; John (father of Charles J.) was enabled to establish a retail business in Fethard Street, Mullinahone.[8] All three (and at least one sister) married into farming families, two of them into the same family. Thomas married Mary Mahony (subsequently rendered as O'Mahony) from near Cashel, and on 16 July 1827 John married her sister Anne. Their first son was born in the early days of May 1828 at the residence of his maternal grandparents. At baptism this child was given the name Charles; later, possibly at confirmation, the middle name Joseph was added. He was to have three brothers — Alexander, Thomas and James (who died in infancy) — and four sisters — Maria, Bridget, Elizabeth and Anne.

Although he was born at or near Cashel (see Appendix Two) and visited there in his childhood, Charles J. Kickham's home was in Mullinahone. The village, which has the Slievardagh hills to the north and Slievenamon with its foothills to the south, is situated in a flattish valley linking the lowlands of south-central Tipperary with those of central Kilkenny. The land is good and capable of producing high agricultural yields, although the flat terrain gives rise to a drainage problem in places.

By the early nineteenth century Mullinahone had risen from being a mere adjunct of the nearby Killahy Castle to the status of a market and service centre catering for the growing needs of the surrounding countryside. It became the location of an important weekly butter market frequented by merchants from Kilkenny, Clonmel and Carrick-on-Suir. Two fairs were held annually.[9] Shops and public houses proliferated; nailors, bakers, harnessmakers, cordwainers and tradesmen of every description opened up businesses. For a few years in the 1830s there was a military garrison in residence; a constabulary barracks was established; the fabric of the catholic church was greatly improved and enlarged, and in 1842 a new protestant church was opened on the outskirts of the village, involving a removal from the old headquarters of the parish at Kilvemnon. With a maximum recorded population of 1,306 (at the 1841 census) Mullinahone was never very large, but in the decades before the great famine, when Charles J. Kickham was growing up there, it was a thriving, lively place.

The nearest town was Callan, County Kilkenny, six miles away, where Humphrey O'Sullivan was writing his remarkable diary from 1827 to 1835.[10] An Irish-speaking schoolmaster of Kerry origin, O'Sullivan came from a background utterly different to that of the Kickhams, but like them he discovered and successfully exploited the profitable business of shopkeeping in a district ready (despite the abject poverty of a large section of the population) for an advance into the world of modern commerce. Like O'Sullivan (and unlike his own father and brother who went in for general retailing), John Kickham's main interest was in the single lucrative line of drapery. All the indications are that he was a very successful businessman. He eventually became middle landlord of twenty holdings in the village and acquired a farm. Thus Charles J. Kickham grew up in financial security and comparative luxury.

John O'Leary, a close friend in later years, wrote of Kickham that:

> knowledge in the ordinary sense he had little, knowing, I think, science not at all, very little history, no ancient or modern language save that of the Saisenagh, and little of what those languages contained. What he did know he mostly knew well, and among the authors whom I remember as familiar to him were Shakespeare, Tennyson and Dickens.[11]

While we have no complete account of his education, we know enough about Kickham's early life to explain the main features mentioned here. His greatest strength, as O'Leary implied, was his mastery of the English classics; they were the basis of his command of language, his literary style and much of his sensibility. The foundation of this confident familiarity was laid in the Kickham home where the reading aloud of the best English literature was a regular practice. Near the end of his life Charles J. could recall having been introduced in this way at a young age to Shakespeare, Defoe, Goldsmith and Dickens.[12]

It has been said that John Kickham engaged a private tutor for his eldest son, but this is a rather doubtful claim which made a suspiciously late appearance and may have been based on an over-exact interpretation of a deliberately vague expression in an early biographical sketch to the effect that 'his father . . . engaged a competent teacher for him'.[13] The young Kickham went to school to one 'classical' master or more in the village. He probably at some stage attended the academy of a Mr. Jenkins who in 1824 was reported to be instructing seventy-seven pupils in Mullinahone and was still there in the 1840s. We have Kickham's own word for it that in 1844, at the age of sixteen, he was the pupil of a Mr. James Fox. Fox's establishment, located in a large upstairs room, seems to have been typical of its kind. The master occasionally relieved his feelings by 'violent and indiscriminate application of the rattan all round among the smaller fry at the far end of the room'. [14] 'A small group of embryo ecclesiastics' sat apart from the others around a table. Presumably they concentrated on the study of Latin, a language of which Kickham himself acquired a smattering.

An unverifiable tradition holds that Kickham was intended by his parents for the medical profession, but, if he was, that hope was blighted at the age of thirteen. Under circumstances which have not been clearly recorded, a flask of the gunpowder used in his father's hunting gun was ignited by a spark from the kitchen fire and exploded near the boy's face, knocking him senseless. He may have been attempting to dry out damp powder, or he may have been experimenting in boyish fashion by throwing grains into the fire.   At first his life was thought to be in jeopardy, and then for a much longer period there were fears that, owing to the severity of his facial injuries, he would never see again. In the belief that it would save the

sight, severe blistering was applied behind the ears. The outcome was that hearing and sight were seriously impaired and
both deteriorated gradually over the remainder of his life. In
addition, his face was noticeably and permanently disfigured.[17]

It would be futile to speculate about the psychological
effects on Kickham of this traumatic accident which involved
a near-miraculous escape from death and set him apart from his
fellows as well as maiming his senses; but there were some
obvious practical consequences which helped to determine the
course of his career. To take up medicine or any other profession was now impossible; to participate in the running of the
family business, if not impossible, would be difficult. The
result was that Kickham grew to manhood having a great deal
of leisure time which allowed him to read widely (despite his
impaired eyesight), get an intimate knowledge of the people
and places about him and reflect on all he saw. Here may lie at
least a partial explanation of a quality remarked upon by
O'Leary:

> But there was another kind of knowledge. . . possessed
> by Kickham, and in this I have never met with anyone who
> excelled him. He knew the Irish people thoroughly but
> especially the middle and so called lower classes.[18]

However, the most important consequence of the young
Kickham's peculiar circumstances may have been to make it
feasible for him to take up a mission in life, if he should find
one to inspire him.

As a well-to-do shopkeeper with a good command of English,
John Kickham belonged to a class which played a most
important part in the popular political campaigns of the first
half of the nineteenth century in Ireland. Consequently it is
no surprise to find that he was in frequent demand for the
formulation of resolutions for public meetings, and that he
addressed a number of anti-tithe gatherings during the 1830s. [19]
He was by no means an important public figure but clearly he
was sufficiently involved in contemporary politics to communicate to his son a keen awareness of public affairs.

The first popular movement to catch the young Kickham's
imagination was the temperance crusade launched by Father
Theobald Mathew in 1838. Father Mathew's campaign included
a great amount of public display, platform oratory and banner-

waving, which is to say that like most temperance movements it had a political dimension. Kickham caught the infectious enthusiasm of the movement at an early stage and was over-joyed when Mathew eventually visited Mullinahone on 6 March 1843. He took the pledge and bought the temperance badge, and felt enormously honoured when the great man picked him out of a group of boys, playfully pulled his ear and asked him a few commonplace questions. As well as honouring to the end of his life the pledge to abstain from alcohol (except on medical prescription) he never missed a suitable opportunity of praising the 'apostle of temperance' and declaring his own discipleship.[20] The same enthusiasm and perseverance were to be displayed in respect of more explicitly political causes.

In October 1842 James Kickham of the Square was per-suaded to become an agent for the newly-launched *Nation* newspaper.[21] From the beginning a copy was sent weekly to the house of his brother, John, where the leading articles, the repeal speeches and the literary items were read aloud. So it was that Kickham came under the influence of the romantic, ideological nationalism of Thomas Davis and the Young Irelanders. John O'Leary has described the sudden and dramatic change, com-parable only to religious 'conversion', that he himself underwent on reading the poems and essays of Davis,[22] There is no evi-dence that the effect on Kickham was so spontaneous, but it was equally complete. His life was to be dominated by devotion to the idealised concept of Irish nationality inculcated by the *Nation* during the days of his youth. Kickham became an enthusiastic admirer of Davis when the *Nation* introduced him posthumously to the wide readership which had hitherto known him only by his nom-de-plume 'The Celt'. Scribbling disjointedly in bed within a year of his own death Kickham recalled that:

> The ballads and songs of the 'Celt' were familiar to me; but I had not the least idea who or what the 'Celt' was, till I opened that number of the *Nation* with the funereal bordering, on Saturday 20 September 1845. Yet the words 'Death of Thomas Davis' filled me with a vague sense of loss. This sense of loss lost all its vagueness as I read about him, and was shared by the whole family circle, particularly by my mother, who actually shed tears for a man whose name she had probably never heard while he

lived.[23]

Davis, the son of a British army man, was an especially re-assuring hero for the budding Irish nationalist conscious of Cromwellian ancestry. The little detail about his mother (one of the few direct references to her that he ever put in print) deserves some speculative elaboration. If she wept over the obituary of a poet and patriot, may we not visualise her as a sensitive, sentimental idealist with romantic literary and political sensibilities, a model for her famous son? However, exceptional individuals like Davis apart, most people who adopt political ideals base them on more elemental, often atavistic, political emotions. From another reference we have a hint that Kickham's mother had emotive stories to tell of the sufferings of rebels and their families in 1798, when her own relations had come under suspicion. (Some, at least, of the Kickhams had been on the other side.)

By his own recollection, the youthful Kickham was the first in the parish to contribute to O'Connell's repeal rent when he ran to the parish priest, Father Flanagan, with a shilling 'to repeal the union'. In due course the movement was organised in Mullinahone, as in so many other parishes, and weekly sales of the *Nation* in the village reached approximately 100 copies.[24] For Kickham the high point of the campaign was the monster meeting addressed by O'Connell near Thurles on 25 September 1845. He retained vivid impressions of that day to the end of his life:

> I can recall the good-humoured face of more than one parish priest on horseback at the head of his parishioners as his battalion halted on reaching the main road, and anxious repeal wardens endeavoured to put the ranks into order, and tried to impress their men with the importance of marching steadily and keeping the step. My absorbing thought was that I would see O'Connell and hear his voice that day. And as I approached the town of Thurles I became nervous with excitement, and had a vague fear lest the immense crowds on foot and on horseback, and in vehicles of all kinds, might surround the Liberator like a sea and prevent me from catching even a glimpse of him.[25]

He need not have worried. He was sufficiently well connected to gain access to the best vantage points. For the meeting he was on the platform and within yards of great Dan himself as he addressed the multitude in 'the wonderful, deep mellow tones that were all, and more than all, I had imagined them.'[26] He was taken aback to discover that O'Connell was not physically the giant of a man he had been led to expect by newspaper rhetoric.

That evening the catholic middle classes of County Tipperary had O'Connell and his entourage to themselves at a banquet costing ten shillings a head, when the 'frieze-coated peasantry' and the lower orders generally, had scattered. Kickham paid his half-sovereign to join the banqueters and, by his own account, neglected the food to concentrate on the political personalities and the speeches. [27]   From the orations and exchanges the observant seventeen-year-old obtained clear intimations of incipient divisions within the ranks. Morgan John O'Connell was called upon to disavow federalism; Michael Doheny was heckled by a priest in the course of a fulsome tribute to the recently-deceased Davis. It was only a matter of days since the Kickhams, mother and son, had discovered Davis and even in the interval Charles J. had suffered the pain of hearing his parish priest refer to the deceased patriot as a 'dangerous man'. [28]

The three years that followed were confused and calamitous for Irish nationalist politics. We have no details of Kickham's response to such crucial developments as the split between Young Ireland and O'Connell, the formation of the Irish Confederation, the death of the Liberator and Mitchel's secession from the Confederation. But it is certain that in general his sympathies were with the Young Irelanders against the O'Connellites. Moreover, as surely as his political ideas and rhetoric had been given form by Davis, so also did they subsequently bear the indelible impress of the thought of John Mitchel as it appeared in the *Nation* in 1846-7 and in the *United Irishman* of 1848.

The Irish Confederation operated through largely middle-class clubs in the cities and large towns. The Young Irelanders in Mullinahone did not carry sufficient weight to form such an association and their 'Fag-an-bealac' club did not get off the ground until events at home and abroad induced Young Irelanders and 'Old Irelanders' to work together once again in the early months of 1848. Soon the Mullinahone club had among its members the non-radical Father Daniel Corcoran, parish priest since 1846. Inevitably, Charles J. Kickham was there but he was not, as later accounts would have it, the bright light and inspiration of the group. That position was held by a slightly younger man named Thomas Wright, son of a local protestant gentleman residing in the village, student of Trinity College, Dublin, and ardent Young Irelander.[29] Wright harangued the crowd and presented an address from the 'Fag-an-bealac' club to Michael Doheny and Thomas F. Meagher when they held a mustering of the clubs of south-east Tipperary on Slievenamon, four miles south of Mullinahone, on 16 July 1848.[30]

The calling of the Slievenamon meeting was an acknowledgement of the disaffection of the surrounding countryside and of its apparent preparedness for an uprising. The same considerations caused William Smith O'Brien and the other leaders of the Confederation, wandering in search of a rebellion, to gravitate before the month was out to this area — roughly a triangle linking Callan, Carrick-on-Suir and Killenaule. On 25 July Kickham heard the rumour that they were coming to Mullinahone. This was the rising and he was prepared for it, or at least he knew how to go about preparing — he had read all about rebellion in the *Nation* in the preceding months. The first thing was to procure weapons; there was no available supply of firearms but the *Nation* had written convincingly about the utility of pikes and had given instructions on how to manufacture them. Following this blueprint, Kickham had an ash tree cut down, and set a carpenter to work reducing it to pikehandles; then he engaged a blacksmith to turn out pike-heads. Meanwhile, about five o'clock in the evening, Smith O'Brien, John Blake Dillon and their company arrived in the village and were received in the house of either John or James Kickham. When Charles J. got word of their presence he rushed from the blacksmith's forge and met them on the street looking for himself and the other active members of the club. As a well-read young man, Kickham knew that no proper revolution could start without the sounding of the tocsin and accordingly he obtained O'Brien's permission to ring the chapel bell. The gates and doors were locked but Kickham and some friends scrambled over the wall and forced a window to gain entry. He began the ringing and then left others to continue at it while he returned to the street to rejoin the leaders. They had just been joined by Thomas Wright and they now accompanied him to his father's house where they set up headquarters.

The ringing bell brought excited people pouring into the village and Dillon sent messengers to more distant parts to summon all available hands. By evening there were thousands of men in the streets of Mullinahone. Some of them were armed — with fowling pieces, impromptu pikes and pitchforks — and the forge and carpenter's shop were over-run by eager crowds in search of the semblance of a weapon. Dillon discussed with Kickham the siting of barricades. An effort to impose rudimentary military discipline met with some success. O'Brien addressed the throng and articulated their grievances, as he understood them — famine and the government's failure to protect them from it, the denial of their rights and the imminent threat to his own liberty for demanding these rights. The people, Kickham declared later, were ready to face death beyond all question. However, the apparent revolutionary possibilities of the situation quickly disappeared.

The priests in Mullinahone as elsewhere during July 1848 used all their influence to oppose rebellion, and they put up the same convincing argument as elsewhere: that there was no hope of success, at least not until after the harvest. The curate, Father Cahill, had debated the matter with the leaders as soon as they arrived in Mullinahone. The following day Father Corcoran backed by five or six shopkeepers approached Smith O'Brien and urged upon him the wisdom of postponing action. By then the little army was gradually melting away; after waiting all night the people were hungry and they saw no prospect of getting breakfast anywhere except in their homes.

During the morning morale was weakened by a botched attempt on O'Brien's part to secure the surrender of their weapons by the constabulary in Mullinahone, who had apparently decided to remain calm and wait for the trouble to pass on to another village. O'Brien, accompanied by a few followers, entered the open door of the barracks and in gentlemanly terms requested the handing over of the firearms. The police replied that they would gladly comply as soon as they might do so with honour: perhaps if he were to come back with a really formidable contingent so as to outnumber them heavily they could then surrender without disgrace to their credit as courageous Irishmen. Beguiled by some such palaver, O'Brien withdrew; when he was safely out of the way the policemen left the barracks by the back door, carrying their weapons, and escaped from the village.

Some time afterwards the Young Ireland leaders decided that they, too, would leave and proceed towards Ballingarry and the colliery district in the Slievardagh hills where the employees of the mining company were reported to be ready for action. They left Mullinahone accompanied by a few hundred men whose homes were near enough for them to get food, or who could afford to buy it. Some distance outside the village they were met by a contingent from Ballingarry, and at Dillon's suggestion the Mullinahone men turned back. At the moment of parting Kickham contrived to shake hands with O'Brien, Dillon and a younger member of the group named James Stephens.[31]

Within a few days the futile attempt at rebellion had collapsed in the farce of 'the widow Cormack's cabbage garden' just north of Ballingarry, and a rather leisurely official retribution began. The principal sufferer in Mullinahone was Thomas Wright who was singled out by the local magistrate, William Despard of Killahy (a close relation of his), no doubt because he was felt to have betrayed his own. He went on the run and was featured in the *Hue and Cry*.[32] Eventually he escaped to America where he subsequently made a career for himself at the bar.

There is no evidence in official sources that Kickham was sought by the authorities at this time, but of course they would have had sufficient pretext to prosecute him if they had so desired. Kickham himself appears to have left no record of having been on the run in 1848 but from the statements of so many others on the subject it must be accepted that he went into hiding in anticipation of arrest, for an unknown length of time. [33]   After the events of 25-26 July many people in the Mullinahone area had reason to fear repercussions. Father Corcoran took up the matter directly with Dublin Castle and, after emphasising his own role in discouraging revolt, gave cogent reasons why none of his parishioners should be

molested. He stated plainly that the authorities would need to
be guided by himself if they wished to bring matters to a satisfactory conclusion in his area.[34]   The parish priest's initiative
must have hastened the development of a situation in which it
was possible for Kickham and others like him to return quietly
to their homes.

The political and quasi-military experiences of 1848 and the
immediately preceding years, though intensely exciting for
Kickham, paled by comparison with the economic and social
upheaval of the great famine. Years later he recalled the deep
impression made upon him by the severe distress he had seen in
his own area. This impression, he said, was made still deeper
by the fact that the suffering in his district attracted no
outside publicity, being overshadowed by even greater tragedies
in other places.[35] Mullinahone was in the Callan poor law union,
the records of which bear witness to serious distress during the
famine years. At one period during 1847 the number of people
in the union in receipt of relief reached almost 49 per cent of
the 1841 population.[36] This was the highest percentage for any
union in Leinster. The census of 1851 showed a decline of 21
per cent in the population of the union since 1841. However,
the decrease for the Mullinahone electoral division of the
union was considerably above that average, at 32 per cent.[37] The
village was down by almost 23 per cent to just over 1,000.

The social disruption involved is illustrated strikingly in the
catholic marriage register for Mullinahone. In the years from
1840 to 1846 inclusive, 35 weddings on average were registered
each year, the lowest in any year being 27. In 1847 the number
dropped to 13. In 1850 it was down to 9. Not surprisingly,
some wholesale clearances of tenants-at-will underlie these
figures, as, for example, on the estate of the magistrate, Despard
of Killahy. His property was heavily mortgaged and with
debts amounting to over twenty times his net annual rental he
could not afford to be very lenient with his pauperised small
tenants even if he was that way inclined.[38] As a result the townland which had 109 people living in 18 houses in 1841 was
reduced to 20 people in 3 houses by 1851. A commentator
(who was capable of exaggeration) later stated that John
Kickham 'gave unto hundreds who were evicted from their
little farms not only clothes from his store but also money to

The former Kickham shop in Fethard Street, Mullinahone as it looked in the mid-1970s. (Photograph in possession of Mrs Sheila Foley)

able them to emigrate to America'. [39] (Of course, it was understood that they would repay the debt when able to do so.) Concerning his descriptions of rural upheaval and suffering Charles J. Kickham was able to say truthfully: 'I have got none of my materials at second hand.'[40]

His youth provided a thorough introduction to political questions and to literary modes of handling them. In later life he came to some prominence in both politics and literature through a fortuitous series of developments, but above all because of the moral seriousness inherent in his character.

Centres of authority in pre-famine Mullinahone:
Below: Oakfield House, residence of the parish-priest
Bottom p.26 : Killahy Castle, residence of William Despard, J.P.
Top p.26: The Constabulary barracks.

Chapter Two

A YOUNG GENTLEMAN OF LEISURE

John O'Leary's sister Ellen has left an interesting sketch of
Kickham's physical appearance:

> In person Charles J. Kickham was tall and strongly built.
> He walked like a sailor, swaying from side to side. He had
> a fine picturesque head, on which the wavy brown hair . . .
> grew in soft curls, . . . a large forehead . . . and a rough
> skin, somewhat scarred by that terrible powder accident.[1]

Very little about this facial disfigurement has been put on
record by contemporaries. Writing with thinly-veiled hostility,
Richard Pigott hinted that he preferred not to dwell much on
Kickham's personal appearance, adding that the accident had
'seamed his face with ugly scars'.[2] No doubt, the beard which
Kickham wore for almost all his adult life served to cover
much. His death mask shows marks on the cheek that were not
concealed by the beard, but these do not appear on any of the
few surviving photographs, which were probably touched up.
There were marks on the side of his neck, also, caused by
recurring open sores associated with glandular infection, and
thought at the time to be a symptom of scrofula or consump-
tion. People seeing Kickham for the first time without actually
making his acquaintance were often put off. A correspondent
reporting on his trial, in the *Nation* on 13 January 1866,
found 'the general appearance of his face rather wild'. The wild-
ness of aspect may have been caused not only by disfigurement
but also by a tendency towards excessively nervous, fidgety
behaviour in tense situations. Appearing before a court for the
first time in November 1865 he was (according to the
Freeman's Journal of 13 November) restless in manner and 'he

did not by any means appear to possess decision or coolness'. The *Irishman* correspondent at his trial concluded that 'the soul that is within him has no representation in the person of Charles J. Kickham'.[3]

That 'soul' achieved its most enduring 'representation' in his writings but was manifested most strikingly in his affection for his friends. In their company he exuded a childlike warmth of feeling and a tender sympathy which (even allowing for inevitable exaggeration in laudatory reminiscences) must have been quite out of the ordinary. Along with that went a refinement of manner reminiscent of the Victorian ideal of the well-bred lady. Female company he found particularly congenial, and one acquaintance remarked on his 'womanlike gentleness'.[4] He was commonly referred to as 'the gentle Charles'.

There was another side to his character. 'His demeanour was simple and childlike until his sensitiveness would be stung by word or act discordant with his exalted and distinctive propensities.'[5] In other words, he could not bear to be crossed and reacted badly to contradiction, challenge or inconvenience. When provoked he could readily become angry and even rough-spoken. (No doubt the ladies were spared these outbursts.) As he grew older he came to acknowledge this propensity to lose his temper, especially with his relations. John Devoy, one of many who saw an irony in the phrase 'the gentle Charles', recalled that 'when his stomach was out of order the world was coming to an end'.[6] In his character one could discern the lineaments of an indulged eldest son, although that was only part of the picture.

Political friends were treated like personal friends. Almost anyone who made a convincing show of attachment to Kickham's own ideals was made a comrade and confidant, at least until he demonstrated indubitable unfitness for the honour. Conversely, those who held opposing views were assumed to lie beyond the reach of friendship and, worse still, Kickham had a tendency to equate wrong political policies with morally wrong motives. He was inflexible not merely regarding his long-term objectives but also in his day-to-day dealings with others. In other words, he lacked the ability to compromise, to dissemble or otherwise cope, in the manner of the successful public man, with the diversity and complexity of political life.

It was a weakness and it seriously delimited his field of
endeavour, but it proved in some ways to be an advantage. In
any case it was a feature of his entire personality, not just of
his intellect. He never acquired a *persona* and he never felt the
need for one, which must have added to his attractiveness as a
friend. Nowhere in his surviving correspondence or in his
published work is there any striving to make a personal
impression, and presumably his conversation was similarly free
of self-advertisement.

His character and personality scarcely fitted him to bear
misfortune, much less tragedy, but in the event his burden was
to be exceedingly heavy. The gunpowder accident, so serious
in itself, was the harbinger of a life-long series of catastrophes.
Job on his dunghill had little more to complain of than
Kickham in his last years, deaf and almost totally blind,
wretched in health, bereaved of most of his family, deprived of
his home and possessions, dependent on the charity of others
for shelter and support. His response to tragedy had a quality
better described as human rather than heroic: he maintained
dignity but not without lapses into petulance and self-pity. At
the same time, his disabilities and misfortunes increased the
impressiveness of his achievements.

Already, in his twenties, misfortune was rife. His mother died
in 1848 from a cause that has not been recorded and one of his
sisters died soon afterwards. John Kickham never recovered
from the loss of his wife: 'her death preyed sorely on his mind',
according to one account.[7] Some time in the early 1850s the
family was struck by a second firearms disaster when Thomas,
the youngest son, 'shot off his leg while fowling'.[8] Despite these
upsets Charles enjoyed an enviable existence at this period of
his life.

Because of his disabilities he was not expected to undertake
any work, and he lived comfortably as a member of a well-
off household, confident of inheriting at least a substantial
portion of his father's wealth. Even when the father withdrew
prematurely and in a state of depression from the management
of his business, Charles was not seriously discommoded:
Thomas took on responsibility for the shopkeeping and for the
family finances.[9] (The other surviving son, Alexander, was
sent to Dublin to be apprenticed to business in the city.) Mean-

while Charles occupied himself as he pleased, in essentially gentlemanly pursuits. In season, day after day was devoted to fishing, shooting (he was a notoriously poor shot) and horse-riding. His circumstances, way of life, character and demeanour earned him among the people of Mullinahone the title 'Master Charles', employed with both deference and affection. 'Master Charles is the grandest man in Ireland', T. P. O'Connor was informed by Denny Shea, a harness-maker in the village.

A life without external challenge or pressure might easily have degenerated into sloth and aimlessness, but Kickham escaped that fate because of his native enthusiasm and his sense of duty. He never diluted his commitment to the ideals acquired in his youth, even when prudence or experience suggested the need for a change. In his twenties he may have been free from more ordinary cares, but his life was filled with concern for political and social matters, involvement in such agrarian and political movements as he found congenial, the writing of poetry and non-remunerative newspaper articles, and eager reading of journals and fiction.

True to the stereotype of the young literary-inclined romantic, Kickham in his mid-twenties experienced heart-breaking disappointment through infatuation with a young and beautiful girl who was pushed by her parents into an arranged marriage with a widower — but not before the tragic lover had expressed his emotions in lyric verse. The girl in question was Bessy Blunden, eldest daughter of a local medical practitioner who belonged to a family of minor protestant gentry. At the age of five she was sent to live with a relation in Dublin and went to school there. Her formal education completed, she returned to Mullinahone in September 1853, a month before her sixteenth birthday.[10] Kickham may have met her before this during her holidays, but he was her senior by nine years and can scarcely have paid much attention to her previously. He always admired intensely the effects of formal schooling on young ladies, and in a provincial setting Miss Blunden with her Dublin finish must have appeared like a superior being. She had acquired a taste for poetry and she affected some literary romantic sentiment; and, apart from her educational accomplishments, there were her 'queenly eyes of blue' to attract an admirer.[11]

A mere six months after her return to Mullinahone she married Robert Bradshaw of Lismoynan, Drangan. In the interval Kickham sought her affections, but apparently without success. Even if she had reciprocated his love, that would not have mattered very much in a society which looked upon marriage as a business transaction and as far too serious to be governed by considerations of affection and romance. Bessy's family decided that she should marry Bradshaw, and she complied, accepting, unlike Kickham, that romantic love belonged only to the world of poetry. A tradition that the difference of religion prevented her from marrying Kickham implies that, in addition to his protestations of love, Kickham actually made an offer of marriage, but there appears to be no documentary evidence of that. In any case the obstacle would not be so much religious as a subtler one of caste. The Blundens lived by property, medicine and the church, and would have been unhappy about an alliance with a family that had made its money by shopkeeping. On her marriage Bessy received a present of over £400 from her paternal grandfather. That was the kind of inducement which could ensure compliance with parental criteria for the selection of a partner.

From her disappointed admirer Bessy received as a wedding present a poem, sadly sentimental in tone, entitled 'The last dream'.[12]   Because of Kickham's use of the conventional phraseology of romantic poetry this provides little factual information that can be relied upon — we can scarcely take literally the assertion that a girl of sixteen had already been ⌐ the light of his life 'through many a weary year'. Similarly, a protestation about 'the joy I feel that you are happy now' is not very convincing under the circumstances. The conclusion was a studied reproach from one

> Whose love was all your own
> And burned so true, while doomed to burn,
> Uncared for and unknown.

However, love, no more than the pastimes of the countryside, could not distract Kickham from public matters. As far as we know, he had no connection with the secret movements that sprang up in the wake of the failure of July 1848, movements that were especially strong in Counties Kilkenny, Tipperary and Waterford and reached a head in the attack on the con-

stabulary barracks in Cappoquin in September 1849. So, while
his future fenian colleagues, John O'Leary and Thomas Clarke
Luby, were being initiated into the ways of conspiracy, the
Mullinahone man was living within the law. It was not that he
was any less disaffected, but that the opportunity was lacking;
he was undoubtedly being watched by the constabulary and the
parish priest. In 1849 and the years immediately after he was
preoccupied with the problem of agrarian relations, which
were in turmoil in the aftermath of the famine. In the heat of
the famine crisis John Mitchel and Fintan Lalor had forged in
their minds an almost millenarian union of the national
question and the land question. So did Kickham, but it is
impossible to tell the extent to which he was influenced by the
writings of the others, or if he simply made a similar response to
the same conditions. Through most of his career he saw a just
settlement of the land question not merely as a sure consequence
of political freedom, but as the other side of the same coin; one
could not exist without the other. Nevertheless, he took an avid
interest in the tenant movement that began in Callan in October
1849 under the guidance of the curates, Fathers O'Shea and
Keeffe.

In the Callan district as in so many other places the post-
famine redistribution of land at the different levels of ownership and occupation gave rise to conflict between landlords and
tenants. Tillage farmers hurt by reduced yields and disastrously
low prices in this time of near-anarchy were unable or unwilling
to meet the rents demanded by landlords who needed every
available penny to regain or retain financial solvency. The late
summer and autumn of 1849 witnessed what the *Nation* called
'the scramble for the crops'[13] as landlords sought to seize the
harvest in lieu of unpaid rents. Numerous recalcitrant tenants
were threatened with eviction. The Callan Tenant Protection
Society was a combination of farmers and their closest
sympathisers — the clergy and the shopkeepers — to secure the
interests of the tenantry against the exercise by the landlords
of rights that were upheld by the law.

It was typical of Kickham that, on hearing about the new
movement in Callan, he went to see the curates to hear about
their ideas at first hand.[14]   Their plan was that the society
would consider each case of disputed rent and decide on a just

figure. If the landlord refused to accept this verdict and proceeded to attempt an eviction, moral force would be used to defeat him: anyone taking the farm in question would be ostracised. Both object and means appealed to Kickham so much that he set them out in a poem; it concluded as follows:

> But true men met together
> And full soon they did agree,
> To brand him as a traitor slave,
> Whoever he might be,
> Who, with the robber landlord,
> Would the plundered booty share;
> So no honest man would touch it
> And no grasping 'jobber' dare.
>
> His honour then discovered
> That his land a waste would stay,
> And *praiseach buidhe* and thistles
> But little rates would pay;
> So he left this honest farmer
> In peace at home to dwell;
> And may he long enjoy it,
> For he fought his battle well.[15]

Another poem composed by Kickham around this time was also directly inspired by 'the scramble for the crops'. Landlords distraining for rent were not allowed by law to seize growing crops, and so could take the initiative only after harvesting had begun. Besides, seizure could be made only between sunrise and sunset. Some legal-minded friend of the farmers hit upon the plan of cutting and removing the corn by moonlight when the landlord's hands would be tied by the law. The practicability of the idea must have been rather limited but it appealed to Kickham's imagination and moved him to write 'The harvest moon':

> The harvest moon is beaming now,
> And its silvery light is streaming now,
> Over hill and plain
> Of waving grain
> With the wealth of our island teeming now.

Slievenamon.

Carraigmoclear.

Village of Mullinahone

A map of Mullinahone showing the house property (numbers 1-12A) which Kickham inherited from his father. Number 10 was Kickham's own premises (note the laid-out garden). (J. F. X. O'Brien papers)

Then we'll to the fields away, my boy,
For should we till morning stay, my boy,
While sleeping in bed
The corn might shed!
So we'll cut it ere dawning of day, my boy!

Oh! if night be only for sleeping boy,
Say why is the fair moon keeping, boy,
Longest watch in the sky
When harvest is nigh?
'Tis to cheer us on with the reaping, boy.

Then let fools have the ripe sheaf strewn, my boy,
To scorch in the sultry noon, my boy,
Oh! *our* toil is more light
In the cool dewy night,
'Neath the smiles of the harvest moon, my boy.[16]

Mullinahone was one of the earliest among the many parishes in Leinster and Munster that followed the lead given by Callan and its Tenant Protection Society. In early November 1849 an inaugural meeting was attended by 'the clergy and respectable inhabitants of the town and parish of Mullinahone', with James Kickham in the chair. Following the Callan pattern,- a committee was selected; its members included the parish priest, the curate, James Kickham and John Kickham![7] The affairs of the society were directed by a weekly meeting held on Sunday. Charles J. Kickham used to travel on foot throughout the countryside collecting statements and other evidence for consideration by the Sunday meetings.

The tenant protection movement was less than a year old when its guiding lights, the Callan curates, were prevailed upon to lead it into the Tenant Right League![8] This was later represented by Kickham as the first step in the ruination of the movement,[19] but there is no evidence that either his principles or his foresight caused him to have doubts at the time. In fact he was an enthusiastic supporter of the league at its commencement and was one of the first to forward a contribution.[20] However, the Mullinahone delegate at the meetings of the league was almost invariably the curate, Father Cahill.[21] The fact that

Kickham had his first personal meeting with Charles Gavan Duffy as late as 1881 establishes that he was never in the higher ranks of the Tenant League: it was not the kind of organisation to give an opening to a man in his early twenties, whatever his talent and zeal.

In 1851 the league entered parliamentary politics when it established links with the 'Irish brigade' MPs on the basis of a policy of remaining 'independent of and in opposition to' any government that failed to legislate for tenant right. In the general election of 1852 almost fifty professed supporters of independent opposition were elected for Irish constituencies (out of a total of 105 Irish MPs). Before the year was out, however, a number of these had gone back on their promises and were supporting a new government under the premiership of Lord Aberdeen, although no concessions had been made to tenant demands. Two of them — William Keogh and John Sadleir [22] — accepted junior positions in the government. The defection of Sadleir and Keogh dispelled the hopes of tenant right legislation and precipitated a bitter split in Irish catholic politics. On one side were those who proclaimed continuing fidelity to independent opposition and heartily denounced Sadleir and Keogh as renegades; in this camp were most of the leading figures of the tenant campaign — Gavan Duffy, Frederick Lucas, and the Callan curates; they were supported enthusiastically by George Henry Moore, MP for Mayo, and Archbishop MacHale of Tuam. On the other side were those who refused to condemn Sadleir and Keogh, and who in effect were in favour of supporting a whig-dominated government (even if it refused to give legislative concessions) in order to keep the tories — the allies of the Irish ascendancy — out of office. This group included Archbishop Cullen of Dublin and most of the Irish catholic bishops.

In Kickham's view moral and political principle was patently on the side of independent opposition and he never forgave what he saw as the perfidy of those who took the other side. He blamed their political treachery for the decline of the tenant movement before it had achieved its full potential. The Tenant League did indeed run out of steam after 1852 (although it survived until 1858), but the main reason for its decline was economic rather than political. The return of agricultural prosperity in the 1850s made more income available for division between landlord and tenant and so facilitated compromise and agrarian peace.

The MPs elected for County Tipperary in 1852 were both pledged to independent opposition. Since both belonged to the family circle of John Sadleir, one being his brother (James) and the other his cousin (Francis Scully), they predictably abandoned their commitments and supported the Aberdeen government. The steadfast supporters of independent opposi tion in the county were chagrined by having two such faithless MPs, especially after working so enthusiastically to have them returned. Resentment against Scully and Sadleir acquired an organ of expression in January 1855 with the appearance of the *Tipperary Leader* (Thurles), a weekly newspaper dedicated to exposing and denouncing what it called 'Sadleirism'.[23] This was probably the first journal to publish a leading article by Kickham.[24] As far as parliamentary politics were concerned, writers in the *Tipperary Leader* were vociferously in favour of independent opposition. However, doubts about the useful ness of any form of parliamentary policy for attaining desirable national and social objectives were raised by a number of con tributors, including Kickham.

One lesson to be learned from the experience of the 1850s was, in Kickham's words, 'that "going against the priest" was not so very heinous a crime, seeing that priests could go against one another',[25] as they did with such gusto for as long as independent opposition and the behaviour of Sadleir and Keogh remained live issues. But Kickham himself did not need any such headline; he had much earlier shown that willingness to 'go against the priests' for which he was to receive much post- humous admiration — perhaps more than he deserved. In respect of the clergy as in respect of everyone else, Kickham never departed from his innocent youthful conviction that people should act in accordance with principle. The ideal to which he expected the clergy to conform included active political effort on behalf of their people. Far from deprecating political and social leadership by the clergy, he demanded it; but it had to be leadership in the direction which he himself believed to be right. Kickham could never understand when others — priests, politicians or landlords — failed to live up to his own principles which he was convinced were universally binding.

Before, during and after the great famine many public men concerned with the welfare of Ireland suggested that organised emigration to America or Australia would provide a safety-valve, and would be conducive to the prosperity of those going away and of those remaining. One who publicly advocated such a scheme was the influential parish priest of Graiguecullen, County Carlow, Father James Maher. Writing in the *Nation* of 8 December 1849, he urged the advantages of planned emigration in a time of comparative stability as opposed to the alternative — a panic-stricken rush to the ships at a time of crisis. Here was a pastor showing concern for the welfare of his flock. But Kickham was not favourably impressed: he was against emigration on principle. In the thinking of pragmatists it might be the road to a better life for the individuals concerned, but for Kickham and other romantic nationalists who viewed the nation as a living being it was the haemorrhage of a country's life-blood. So Father Maher had to be rebuked. This was done in an ironic adaptation of John Banim's sentimental eulogy of the faithful priest, 'Soggarth Aroon'.

A REMONSTRANCE

And will *you* leave us too, Soggarth Aroon,
You who were always true, Soggarth Aroon.
The thought made our cold hearts glow —
You'd be the last to go,
Whether come weal or woe, Soggarth Aroon.

Why do we hear you say, Soggarth Aroon,
'Haste from this land away', Soggarth Aroon?
Since as *all* cannot fly,
Tho' some might want defy,
Millions should stay and die! Soggarth Aroon.

Say, if you can, to them, Soggarth Aroon,
'Old scenes and home contemn', Soggarth Aroon,
But as you hope to find
Fortune, or Heaven, kind,
Leave not the poor behind, Soggarth Aroon.

Yet ev'n if *all* could flee, Soggarth Aroon,
Would we then happy be, Soggarth Aroon,
Could we the thought suppress —
However Fate might bless:
Erin, a wilderness, Soggarth Aroon.

Oh! this one thought of home, Soggarth Aroon,
Cloud-like would ever come, Soggarth Aroon.
Dimming enjoyment's ray,
Chasing Hope's smiles away,
Saddening each weary day, Soggarth Aroon.

Then, in the poor old land, Soggarth Aroon,
Let us still, hand in hand, Soggarth Aroon
Struggle to end her thrall,
And should the worst befall —
God is above us all! Soggarth Aroon.[26]

The logical force of this and many similar attacks (whatever about their emotional appeal) was much weakened by the fact that a well-intentioned individual was being denounced for failure to conform to another's principles. Kickham was on more solid ground when he rebuked clerics for failing to live up to their own principles, and especially for the abuse of their religious office. The clergy in Ireland in the mid-nineteenth century enjoyed extensive prestige and social influence in their parishes. The temptation to subordinate the role of minister of religion and charity to that of petty local tyrant was strong, and for many it was irresistible. The classical expression of this abuse was the altar denunciation.

The parish priest of Mullinahone from 1846 to 1862, Father Daniel Corcoran, was an able, domineering man. He had a reputation as local strongman even before coming to Mullinahone, and his correspondence with Dublin Castle in 1848 showed that in respect of the catholic population of his parish he had taken over many of the functions of a local magistrate. When in 1849 Kickham composed a poetic rebuke for a priest who had indulged in non-religious oratory in the sanctuary, the culprit was almost certainly Corcoran. It is perhaps Kickham's most undeservedly neglected verse work.

THE ALTAR

The altar! oh, profane it not
    It is a sacred place,
Wherein flows to heal the wounded heart,
    The balm of hope and grace.
There weary wanderers find repose,
    And mourners' tears are dried,
For there descends to soothe our woes,
    The Lamb, the Crucified.

Yes, there — as once on Calvary —
    To prove his boundless love,
He makes himself a sacrifice
    For man to God above.
Oh, then — as when upon the Cross,
    His life he freely gave —
He gives his blood to erring man
    To nourish and to save.

Then let no words but words of love —
    Of hope — of bliss to come —
Or sweet persuasive eloquence
    To win the wanderer home —
Be ever heard to desecrate
    A spot so sanctified,
As that which represents the Mount
    Where man's Redeemer died.

And man, frail man, when you ascend
    The Altar of the Lord,
Beware lest you degrade it
    By foul or bitter word.
'Tis not within the temple where
    Religion bends the knee,
That sneering jest should e'er be heard,
    Or mean scurrility.

> Behold those lowly penitents
>   Approach the sacred shrine,
> To seek for consolation
>   In the mystery divine.
> They're hungry for the Bread of Life,
>   You offer them 'a stone',
> They ask for Christ's heart's blood — you give
>   The venom of your own!
>
> Oh, man, frail man, pollute not this
>   The Altar of the Lord,
> With low vindictive ribaldry,
>   Or foul or angry word.
> For nought within the Sanctuary,
>   Where true faith bends the knee,
> Should e'er be heard but words of hope,
>   Or God-like charity.[27]

As denunciation of a clerical vice by a sincere catholic 'The altar' had few betters in nineteenth-century Irish verse, but it does not appear to have got into print until long after its composition. The intensity and sincerity of righteous outrage at the abuse of clerical power that it reveals should be remembered when assessing Kickham's criticisms of the political actions (or inactions) of bishops and priests. So, too, should his readiness to praise churchmen who met with his approval, such as Archbishop MacHale and Father John Kenyon, the Young Ireland priest. Kenyon was eulogised in a Kickham poem published in 1861 which began as follows:

> Your dome-like brow is resting on your hand,
>   Father John
> Deep sadness marks your features meek and bland,
>   Father John,
>   And the blinding tear-drops rise
>   To your mild and dreamy eyes:
> You are mourning o'er the sorrows of your land,
>   Father John.[28]

It continues thus unctuously through thirteen further stanzas.

An individual who influenced Kickham considerably in his late twenties was Dr. Robert Cane of Kilkenny, a powerful orator and a man of imposing physical stature who enjoyed considerable wealth derived from an extensive practice among the gentry of Kilkenny and neighbouring counties. He had been mayor of Kilkenny city on a few occasions in the 1840s and an active participant in the repeal campaign. He had been a confidant of Thomas Davis and Charles Gavan Duffy and had presided over the confederate organisation in his city in 1848. [29] During the 1850s Cane, prosperous and secure, was a fixed point in the shifting network of mostly impoverished former leaders of Young Ireland. Gavan Duffy before setting out for self-imposed exile in Australia in 1855 entrusted to his care the records of the Irish Confederation. By 1857 Cane felt that he was in contact with a sufficient number of literary-minded people to justify the launching of a journal of 'national literature'. He called it the *Celt* and its avowed purpose was the education of the people to love of country and an assortment of virtues besides. There was an obvious harking back to the spirit of the early *Nation*. The contributors included Cane himself, another Kilkenny doctor called John Campion, who had written for the *Nation,* and a number of writers who subsequently attracted some attention for their literary or journalistic efforts elsewhere: William Kenealy, Michael J. Heffernan, John Walsh (of Cappoquin), Robert Dwyer Joyce, Christopher M. O'Keeffe, Charles Beggs and Kickham. Following the example of the *Nation* circle in the mid-1840s (of which he had been a member), the proprietor and editor of the *Celt* held occasional social gatherings for contributors. These took place in Kilkenny, probably at Cane's house and certainly at his expense.[31] Living at a distance of fifteen miles from Kilkenny, Kickham had a shorter journey to travel than most of the participants.

Beginning on 1 August 1857, the *Celt* was published weekly until the end of the same year. It re-appeared as a monthly in March 1858 and continued until Cane's sudden death in August 1858. Four numbers appeared from August to November 1859 and that was the end.[32]

Although poems and ballads by Kickham had been appearing in print since 1849, and continued to appear up to, and indeed after, his death, most of his best-remembered verse was published from 1857 to 1859, much of it in the *Celt*. 'Patrick Sheehan' appeared in the *Kilkenny Journal* of 7 October 1857. On 28 November 1857 the *Celt* carried 'Rory of the hill'. The same journal in August 1859 carried 'The peasant girl' which has passed into popular balladry as 'She lived beside the Anner'. The following issue contained 'Home longings', which is still popular as 'Slievenamon'. The *Celt* published four prose items by Kickham which are best described as 'tales'. They could scarcely be called fiction since they involve merely the retelling of traditional stories and the recounting of near-contemporary local happenings; but they were the first steps on the road to *Knocknagow*.

The *Celt* of December 1857 carried a biographical sketch and appreciation of the poet Edward Walsh (1805-50) written by Kickham. Apparently Walsh's widow made letters and papers available for the project which was intended to elicit financial assistance for herself and her children. The memoir exploited to the full the pathos of Walsh's impecunious life and early death, and in a number of respects it was a most unhappy essay.

Edward Walsh was an Irish speaker and an Irish scholar.[33] It was obvious, however, that this held comparatively little interest for his biographer in the *Celt*. There is no evidence that Kickham knew any Irish apart from some words and phrases such as anybody in contact with the English speech of rural Ireland would have picked up. Yet he must have encountered a great many Irish speakers in his own locality in his youth. A contemporary and fellow-parishioner of his, John Dunne of Poulacapple, was composing in Irish at least as late as 1855,[34] and even though Dunne realised that the old language was dying around him, 25 per cent of the population of the barony were returned as Irish-speaking in the 1851 census.[35] Kickham certainly had ample opportunity to make contact with the language if he so wished. His case is probably similar to that of the Sullivan brothers of Bantry who, according to John Devoy, knew not a word of Irish, though brought up in the midst of an area where it was widely spoken.[36] However, whereas the Sullivans took an active interest in the preservation of the language, Kickham did not. In his writings there is only one extended reference to the fate of Irish: in a tale set early in the nineteenth century he has a character say:

> I trust . . . that our language shall be preserved and culti-
> vated to the end of time. But the Saxon tongue has taken
> root in the country, and must ere long be the language of
> the majority of the people.[37]

Kickham obviously did not consider that the Irish language was essential to the life of the nation. The character quoted above was reflecting Kickham's own convictions when he added:

> It is my opinion that Ireland may yet have a ballad litera-
> ture which, though in the language of the stranger, may be
> as thoroughly Irish as if written in the [Irish] language.[38]

Significantly, none of Kickham's tales has any connection with the great mass of Gaelic tradition. Here again is a contrast with John Dunne, who garnered much folklore in the hills near Slievenamon.[39] In fact, antiquarianism of any kind, if it lacked political significance for the Ireland of his day, held no interest for Kickham. What intrigued him most about the old ruined castle in his native village was its link with the troubles of 1798. His persistent lack of interest in Irish antiquities is all the more surprising since during the 1850s Kilkenny city was an important centre of activity in such matters, being the head-quarters of the pioneering Kilkenny Archaeological Society. Kickham was not a member. The society was dominated by people whose political opinions were strongly pro-establishment, but Dr. Cane was a member, and so was Jeremiah O'Donovan Rossa, who at the time lived well over 100 miles from Kilkenny. lived well over 100 miles from Kilkenny.

Chapter Three

THE MAKING OF A FENIAN

The one consistent element in the Young Ireland propaganda of the 1840s was romantic nationalist feeling. The various talented contributors to the *Nation* ignored practical political policy, wrote about it in vague and general terms, or else contradicted one another. As a consequence there was no agreed programme to fall back on in the 1850s and the inheritors of the Young Ireland tradition had to decide individually what political action, if any, was consistent with their aspirations. By the middle of the decade Kickham had formed the immovable conviction that parliamentary politics was a harmful waste of time. He was speaking for himself when he claimed subsequently that one of the lessons of the early 1850s had been that 'parliamentary action, "independent" or otherwise, was, and always must of necessity be, a demoralising sham'.[1] Somebody with Kickham's impatient idealism could scarcely ever have found full satisfaction in parliamentary politics and whatever enthusiasm he may have had for it had been dissipated by 1855. Disillusionment with the conduct of Sadleir and Keogh, and even more so with the failure of the independent party's supporters to unite in condemnation of them, drove Kickham to adopt an extreme attitude which happened to accord perfectly with the inclinations of his personality. Until the introduction of the secret ballot, in 1872, he could denounce parliamentary politics on the ground that elections were the occasion of great suffering, with the conflicting parties bringing cruel pressures to bear on unfortunate voters, who might be evicted from their holdings or denounced from the pulpit for following their consciences on polling day. This, however, was merely a supple-

mentary argument: his real reasons were more fundamental.
Both his enthusiasm and his high sense of moral purpose were
affronted by the compromise and delay inevitable in electoral
and parliamentary politics: he could not bring himself to
participate, and it was a short step from that to denouncing the
participation of others. A touch of naivety is evident here, a
refusal to accept the imperfection of life. But there was no
intellectual weakness involved: he was a perspicacious analyst
of the manoeuvres of the parliamentarians and would-be parliamentarians, and like every good political commentator he
could see what the politicians were up to before they were
aware of it themselves.

In the early 1850s a well-led parliamentary movement
with a strong nationalistic tone might have had some slight
chance of satisfying his passionate, patriotic enthusiasm
sufficiently to obtain his support, however grudging. Instead of
that, what he saw sent him hurrying along the path indicated
both by his instincts and by the implacable rhetoric of John
Mitchel. As early as 1848 Kickham was by inclination a physical
force separatist; he was consciously and unalterably that by
1855.

During that year a group of Irish-American militants in New
York mooted the idea of sending a force of armed exiles back
across the Atlantic to spearhead an insurrection in Ireland, now
that Britain was involved in a difficult war in the Crimea.
Rumours of this pleased Kickham enormously and prompted
him to compose for the *Tipperary Leader* an up-dated version
of the 'Shan Van Vocht' in which the Irish-Americans rather
than the French were 'on the sea':

> There are ships upon the sea,
>   Says the Shan Van Vocht,
> There are ships upon the sea,
>   Says the Shan Van Vocht
> Oh, they're sailing o'er the sea,
> From a land where all are free
> With a freight that's dear to me
>   Says the Shan Van Vocht
> They are coming from the West,
>   Says the Shan Van Vocht[2] ....

Here then is evidence of enthusiasm for armed rebellion, but also of an impractical, even reckless, approach to the issue: announcement in advance in the public press was scarcely appropriate preparation for an armed invasion. A passion for open defiance characterised Kickham's statements of policy at this time and for some years afterwards. In February 1856, again in the *Tipperary Leader,* he openly advocated the acquisition of arms by the populace.[3] He had an almost mystical belief — surely derived from Mitchel — in the beneficial results to be expected from arming the population. He was not thinking simply of establishing numerical superiority to the arms of the garrison: the acquisition of arms was to be an essential part of the process of revitalising the national spirit.

The rejection of parliamentary politics had as its corollary a loss of confidence in that section of society which dominated such politics in Tipperary — farmers, members of the professions, shopkeepers and above all the clergy. Looking back near the end of his life he was convinced that he had experienced disillusionment with them all at an early age. In their midst at the O'Connell banquet in Thurles, in September 1845, he had recoiled:

I felt the most sovereign contempt for the patriots whom I saw gobbling up soup on every side — two patriots to one plate — each seeming in mortal terror lest his competitor should get a single spoonful in advance of him.[4]

From the middle class he turned to the workers: once again the rhetoric had been laid on by John Mitchel who in 1847 had revived Tone's supposed policy of appealing to 'the men of no property', *faute de mieux.* In retrospect Kickham claimed to have had an intimation of the superior spirit of the 'sons of toil' at the age of fourteen when he attended a 'rustic merrymaking' near Cashel:

It seemed to me that the better class of unmarried day-labourers were more manly and intelligent and far more full of fun and humour than the sons of the small and middling farmers.[5]

His earliest extant eulogy of the working class was an article entitled 'The labouring man' in the *Tipperary Leader* of 25 August 1855:

Only poor labouring men! And when was Ireland ever formidable to her oppressor without them? Could emancipa-

tion have been won without them? Did not their example
shame the 'respectable' classes, and even the priests themselves, into doing their duty? Was it not the labouring men
who made the O'Connell meetings monster meetings, and
their shillings that swelled the O'Connell treasury?. . . .
For if ever a successful blow is to be struck for the poor
old country, it is the hand of the toiler that will strike it.
James Stephens, the founder of the fenian organisation —
Irish Republican, or Revolutionary, Brotherhood (IRB) — was
expressing similar sentiments three years later. This secret society
was launched in Dublin in March 1858 and within a short time
Stephens — making in his turn a virtue of necessity — was proclaiming his preference for 'the men of no property'. On other
issues also his views coincided with those of Kickham who
could be expected to give an enthusiastic welcome to the new
revolutionary movement. (He had been excited about far less
promising projects.) On a visit to Kilkenny city about the
middle of 1858 Kickham was approached in his hotel by
Stephens, who obviously saw the Mullinahone man as a potentially valuable recruit.[6] Little is known about the meeting
except that it ended without Kickham becoming a fenian.
Despite having much ground in common the two men differed
on a fundamental point of policy: while Kickham longed for
public — even defiant — displays of national sentiment, secrecy
and circumspection were essential to Stephens's strategy. That
difference alone would have been enough to prevent Kickham's
adhesion to the IRB in 1858. Just like Kickham, numerous
other Young Ireland enthusiasts turned down approaches from
Stephens at this time, usually because of the fenian leader's
dictatorial attitude. Stephens demanded from all his followers a
measure of obedience that his social standing was unable to
sustain when he was dealing with educated middle class
gentlemen. Only a few such people overcame the barrier.
Kickham was one who did, but not until some years after 1858.
    The quick early growth of fenianism was blighted at the end
of 1858 by police moves against the organisation. Key members
were arrested in Kerry and West Cork in December. In the early
days of 1859 the authorities struck in Callan, County Kilkenny,
putting half a dozen young men in prison to await trial. For the
next two years fenianism in the country at large was moribund.

Other quasi-political movements flourished briefly during the period, and one of them moved Kickham to new heights of excitement. This was the Irish Papal Brigade.

With the forces of Italian nationalism about to burst upon the Papal States and dispossess the pope, the government of Pius IX moved belatedly in the Spring of 1860 to summon volunteers from catholic Europe. Over 1,000 Irishmen answered the call and set out for the Papal States where they were formed into a battalion. Before the end of the year they were back in Ireland, defeated but not disgraced. They had gone quietly and as individuals, but they returned (after a brief incarceration as prisoners of war) as a group, a battalion of Irish soldiers, capable of exciting popular admiration. While the London *Times* jibed, Irish nationalist newspapers portrayed them as valiant heroes. Welcome-home demonstrations were the order of the day.[7]

The few dozen men forming the Mullinahone contingent received a particularly warm reception which continued for more than one day and delighted the heart of Charles J. Kickham. His first cousin James J. Kickham (son of James) was the non-commissioned officer of the company. Another first cousin, Rody Kickham (son of Thomas of Clonagoose), who had just returned from a visit to America, was prominent in the organisation of the celebrations, which included public exhibitions of military drill by the 'papal brigadiers' and a night of entertainment conducted 'after the manner of the Irish-American military balls'. Charles J. Kickham provided the rhetoric. He composed an address 'to the friends of Ireland' in the name of the Tipperary members of the brigade and got the Mullinahone men to sign it. The sentiments were undiluted Kickham:

> We, the undersigned Tipperary men of the Irish brigade take this opportunity — the first that has been afforded us — of giving public expression to our heartfelt gratitude to the hierarchy, clergy and people of Ireland for the prompt and successful manner in which we were conducted from the prisons of the Sardinian government to our native land and to our homes.
>
> No words could convey the feelings of happiness and pride enkindled within our breasts by the more than

enthusiastic welcome which has everywhere greeted us
since our arrival in Ireland . . . .

We are satisfied that we have done our duty; and believe
we can point in proof of that to the despatches . . . of the
foe, to whose overwhelming numbers we were forced to
succumb.

The memory of the kindness shown us by the glorious
people of France, while passing through their magnificent
country, shall never be effaced from our hearts. We wish to
let them know that in this country we are slaves — but not
contented slaves.

The right to have arms or to practise any sort of military
discipline is forbidden us. And we feel this galling humilia-
tion all the more keenly since we have learned the real
value of arms and of discipline. To say 'halt' or 'march'
is an offence against English law in Ireland . . . . We protest
against this intolerable tyranny, and denounce to the
world the hypocrisy of England in pretending to be the
friend of freedom and of struggling nationalities.

An invitation to address the returned soldiers and their
assembled admirers gave Kickham a further opportunity. Never
one to use symbolism lightly, he was moved to invoke it now:

I heard people say that the brigade men should be asked
to scatter the seed during the spring, as in that case the
harvest would surely be good. I hope they will scatter
another kind of seed broadcast too, and it will grow and
ripen.[8]

The fact of young Irishmen finding self-assurance in military
combination was what delighted Kickham about the brigade.
He had very little concern with the issues of the Italian wars.
There was manifest illogicality (of which many others as well
as Kickham were guilty) in lauding defenders of the *ancien
régime* in Italy while seeking to apply the principle of national
self-determination in Ireland. He was not unaware of the contradiction and he ignored it rather than attempting to deny it.
Indeed, Kickham never displayed any great concern for the
maintenance of the temporal power of the papacy. There is no
evidence that he originally supported the formation of the papal
brigade: his approval is documented only for the months
following the failure of the Italian mission. The almost

James Stephens

54

John O'Leary (left) with Thomas Luby (centre) and Denis Mulcahy

John O'Mahony

inevitable Kickham poem on the brigade did not appear until late November 1860.[9] An unwary reader might get the impression that the heroes of these verses had returned from victory at the Yellow Ford, Benburb or Fontenoy, rather than defeat at Perugia, Spoleto and Castelfidardo. An oblique reference to the business that brought them to Italy is significantly apologetic:

> To guard a despot's throne and laws,
>   Our ranks have no aspirants;
> But even if 'twere a tyrant's law —
>   Thank God, 'tis not *our* tyrant's!

Fenianism in Ireland began to revive early in 1861 following a visit of some months' duration by the leader of the American branch of the organisation, John O'Mahony. He contacted leading fenians in Dublin and shamed James Stephens into returning from a lengthy sojourn in the safety of Paris. But he did not involve himself in organisational work and he made only one recruit — Kickham.[10] Many biographical notices of Kickham assert that he was related to John O'Mahony through his mother who was, of course, a Mahony by birth. But there is no convincing evidence of such a relationship, and it need not be postulated to explain their meeting in late 1860 or early 1861 during O'Mahony's visit. O'Mahony had private as well as conspiratorial business on hands and spent weeks in the Carrick-on-Suir area where his sister, Mrs. Jane Mandeville, was in possession of the property that would have been his but for his exile. This gave Kickham an opportunity to meet the local hero of 1848. The introduction was probably effected by Denis Dowling Mulcahy of Redmondstown, Clonmel, a fenian since 1858 who was acquainted with Kickham through the *Tipperary Leader,* and whose father was an old friend of O'Mahony's from Irish Confederation days.

Kickham and O'Mahony at once struck up an enduring friendship based on mutual admiration and dedication to common interests. The American fenians wished for a far more comprehensive movement in Ireland than Stephens was willing to tolerate and no doubt O'Mahony was dismayed that a man of Kickham's qualities had been excluded. Kickham's initiation did not involve the taking of the fenian oath; the process may have amounted to nothing more formal than an invitation from O'Mahony to join in the work of the organisation and exhortation not to be put off by the arrogant pretensions or dogmatism of James Stephens. Kickham and Stephens met shortly afterwards at a fenian gathering in Carrick-on-Suir to which Kickham was introduced by Denis Dowling Mulcahy. The 'chief' was not pleased to see the new member, but they came to a *modus vivendi* and to outward appearances they were on good terms for a number of years.[11]

The occasion of their meeting in Carrick-on-Suir was a St Patrick's Day banquet organised by the fenians of that town and attended by several hundred supporters from neighbouring parts of Counties Tipperary, Kilkenny and Waterford. The town hall was decked out for the occasion with representations of sunbursts, harps and round towers, of Davis, Emmet and Wolfe Tone. There was live oratory and singing of patriotic songs organised around the formal procedure of toasts and replies. At least one of the speechmakers was eloquent on the futility of speechmaking — a recognition of the fundamental contradiction in a public celebration organised by a secret society.[12] John O'Mahony had politely declined an invitation and James Stephens did not make himself conspicuous. The event was symptomatic of a change in the nature of fenianism. Stephens's organisation had developed a momentum of its own and was moving in a direction neither envisaged nor approved by him. It was becoming a social movement addicted to public display at the expense of secrecy and revolutionary preparedness. Stephens devoted much of his efforts during the period 1861-6 to curbing the tendency of his followers to reveal themselves in open demonstrations. When he could not prevent public displays he tried to reduce the likely damage to a minimum by getting control of them himself: that was what happened in the case of the funeral of Terence Bellew McManus in November 1861. Kickham was in Dublin for the McManus demonstration and made the acquaintance of Michael Doheny the veteran Repealer and Young Irelander who had returned from his American exile for the occasion.[13]

The change in the character of fenianism suited Kickham admirably. He had a powerful emotional need to belong to a militant nationalist movement, but he also took ecstatic delight in popular social functions and in the convivialities of the ordinary people. (Tradition has preserved record of his attendance at house dances in the countryside.) As the fenians took to banquets, picnics, sports meetings and open-air drill in 1861 and the years immediately following, he was closer to the spirit and feelings of the rank-and-file than any other important figure in the organisation except Rossa. Under these conditions he quickly assumed the leadership of the movement in Mullinahone; he was the natural leader of a band of young men who combined some drill with much conviviality. Most of them probably joined with as little formality as Kickham himself.

Far from attempting to conceal the activities of his group, Kickham actually sent a report of a particularly interesting function to the newspapers. It was a Sunday outing in July 1863:

> A little bridge a few hundred yards from the town was the place of rendezvous. The men took their places without noise or confusion, and set off, two deep, marching as well, or nearly as well, as disciplined soldiers . . . . Their destination was the hill of Carraigmoclear, some four miles from Mullinahone, and memorable in connection with the history of '98 . . . .
>
> The day was bright and warm, and the little party of a hundred active young fellows winding up the steep acclivity in regular array, with their coats off, was something worth looking at. They were greeted heartily by a large number of the boys and girls of the mountain foot; the music was ready, and on went the dancing upon a patch of velvety green sward among the rocks on the summit of the hill. Leaping and stonethrowing went on in other places; some took to 'Davis's Poems' and 'The Last Conquest' while many, stretched at full length, gazed over the rich green plains spread out before them . . . .
>
> I wish you could see those graceful girls, with their shining hair waving in the breeze. They dance all the dances I know of, except waltzing and the 'polka', which exceptions are not to be regretted . . . . Before separating, some national songs were sung and chorused. . . . Our party

returned by the village of Ninemilehouse — every man
keeping his place and the step till we reached the bridge of
Mullinahone, where we all separated quietly and silently.[14]
Kickham included in his account praise of the benefits to be
derived from teaching young men how to march. Among
other things it would discourage drinking, as a man under the
influence of alcohol would 'put the whole procession into
disorder' and so would incur the censure of his fellows.
Kickham never relented in his war against alcohol, and in this
respect alone he was out of sympathy with the social fenianism
of the early and middle 1860s. A significant proportion of the
conviviality of the brotherhood was generated in public houses,
and Kickham's preoccupation with temperance appeared more
and more like an antiquated survival from the days of Father
Mathew.

From gatherings like that on Carraigmoclear it would be only
a short step to formal political demonstrations. James Stephens
might tolerate marching, picnics and banquets, however un-
willingly, but he could not allow his followers to indulge in
explicitly political public meetings. Kickham was quite slow in
coming to appreciate that. As late as October 1862 in an
emotional moment he had countenanced the idea of public
demonstrations. [15] A series of them was being planned at the
time by a group of Tipperary men with fenian connections.
When, at length, the project bore fruit Kickham found himself
in a predicament. The planned location of the first meeting
was the summit of Slievenamon and the date was 15 August
1863. The place was evocative: Thomas Francis Meagher and
Michael Doheny had convened a crowd there in 1848. Another
feature of the gathering calculated to make it appeal to rank-
and-file fenians was the news that Kickham would speak. By
then he had come to see the inadvisability of such ventures
(probably following instruction from Stephens), but he knew
that if he did not make a speech on Slievenamon, somebody
else would. Either on his own initiative or at Stephens's suggestion, he resolved to use the opportunity to ensure that as well as
being the first it would also be the last of the planned series.

Doubts about the advisability of the Slievenamon meeting
had been spread sufficiently well through local fenian circles
to keep the attendance small and less than 1,000 climbed the

mountain. At the summit they waited for Kickham to arrive. He was late, and when he did come he damped the proceedings by referring to the uneasiness about the business that was abroad. His speech included the recital of grievances expected by the audience but it also was a lecture on the uselessness of words in the struggle for freedom:

> My friends, I do not believe the cause of Irish nationality can ever be served much by speech making . . . . If you crowded every mountain top and proclaimed your wrongs in language the most eloquent and pathetic that ever fell from human lips — if you proved the justice of your claims and the holiness of your cause by reasons and arguments the most convincing — and if you hurled defiance at the Saxon in words the most vehement, tell me, for how much would your wail of defiance count in the minds of English statesmen, rulers or people ?[16]

Some of the organisers spoke later; but Kickham had made his point, and the planned series petered out with just one further meeting being called. It attracted very little support.

Official reaction to the Slievenamon meeting bears out the wisdom of Stephens's fear that such events would attract unwelcome attention. Alerted by the advance publicity in the newspapers, Dublin Castle instructed the resident magistrates at both Carrick-on-Suir and Cashel to investigate the meeting. The constabulary concentrated men from surrounding districts in the Ninemilehouse barracks. One of the magistrates actually climbed Slievenamon to attend the meeting and sent a detailed eye-witness account to Dublin Castle next day.[17] The matter was considered serious enough to merit the attention of the Lord Lieutenant, Lord Carlisle. The possibility of bringing charges was investigated by a law officer. His advice was that a criminal prosecution could be sustained but that it would not be warranted under the circumstances. Nevertheless Carlisle felt obliged to send a personal report and copies of the relevant documents to his prime minister, Lord Palmerston.[18] So for the first time, a file containing Kickham's name arrived on the desk of a British premier.

Visiting the Kilkenny Agricultural Society's show on 25 August, the lord lieutenant felt that the time and place of the Slievenamon meeting were both sufficiently near to make

reference to it topical. In a speech frequently quoted and
referred to in subsequent weeks and months, he expressed his
confidence in the country's prospects, and continued as
follows:

> There are now two sets of principles and influences at
> work for mastery over its future destinies. On that
> mountain-top which overlooks so great a portion of the
> county, on the majestic Slievenamon, one set of those
> principles and influences finds its vent in shrill and ill-
> omened shrieks for strife, for discord, and for the blood-
> shed of those who possess and those who till the soil.
> The other or counter set of principles breathes through
> such organs as this and other kindred societies, of which
> it is the humanising and healing purpose to spread the
> knowledge of useful improvements, encourage the
> proprietors of land to reside upon their estates and to take
> an interest in the land they live on and the men they live
> with, and to unite all classes and all grades, landlords and
> tenants, farmers and labourers, in a blessed reciprocity of
> good will and good deeds.[19]

But the few bloodthirsty remarks concerning landlords that
were made on the mountain-top did not come from Kickham.
Indeed, the lord lieutenant would have been surprised if he had
known how closely the second 'set of principles' approximated
to the agrarian ideals of the principal speaker on Slievenamon.

These years during which Kickham came to find fulfilment
as a local fenian leader were marked, like every other period
of his career, by misfortune and suffering in his private life. He
lost his father on 2 August 1861 by sudden violent death.
Local tradition has not preserved a whisper about the passing
of John Kickham but the following contemporary newspaper
account shows that it created quite a stir:

> With deep regret we have to announce the melancholy
> and lamented death, on last Friday, by the accidental
> explosion of firearms, of John Kickham, Esq., at his
> residence, Mullinahone, Co. Tipperary. Mr. Kickham, who
> had for some time past been an invalid, was in the habit
> of amusing himself by shooting rats, and on Friday evening
> last had incautiously left the loaded gun near the foot of
> the bedstead in such a position that it was almost

impossible to remove it without striking some part of it against either the bed or the door. As far as can be ascertained, the hammer caught in some manner against the bedstead on Mr. Kickham opening the door on the fatal evening, and when the report brought his family hurriedly to the spot, the unfortunate gentleman was found a corpse on the floor . . . . An inquest on the body of Mr. Kickham was held on Saturday evening by Mr. Shee, coroner, and an intelligent jury, when a verdict was returned of 'accidental death'.[20]

Another report on the tragedy in the same paper indicated that the deceased had been 'suffering from nervous affection for some time past'. Notwithstanding the findings of the 'intelligent jury', it is difficult to avoid the suspicion that John Kickham had been mentally unwell for some years, that in this condition he took his life and that — as so frequently happened in rural Ireland in such cases — a pretence was made by all that the death had been accidental. The evidence does not verify such suspicions absolutely but it provides very considerable grounds for them. The silence of tradition on the subject proves nothing, but it is suggestive. However the bizarre death came about, it must have caused shock and extreme anguish to the immediate family.

A less traumatic misfortune struck the family within two years. Charles's sister Maria was married to a Clonmel businessman named James Cleary who got into financial difficulties in 1863 and had to emigrate to America to make a new start. Because she was pregnant his wife was unable to accompany him and she came to live in Mullinahone with her two young daughters.[21] Her third daughter was born there on 9 August 1863. It was decided that she should take the new-born infant with her to America and that the others, aged one and two years, would remain on in the Kickham home for the time being. This particular family problem had the result of bringing Kickham to America and into contact with internal fenian politics at the highest level.

As his sister made preparations to cross the Atlantic with her daughter, Kickham resolved to accompany them, largely out of a sense of family responsibility. He decided to keep a diary for the duration of his trip and it was subsequently

published (with a few names suppressed).[22] Entries were made
spasmodically and they consisted of Kickham's reflections
rather than a complete account of his itinerary or an accurate
description of what he saw. He sailed with his sister and niece
from Queenstown on 16 September 1863. Once he had
recovered from an inevitable bout of sea-sickness, Kickham
found his romantic soul responding to the wonders of the
ocean:

> In spite of wind and weather I remain up on deck from
> morning till late at night, sometimes drenched with salt
> water, which ever and anon dashed on the deck and high
> up, in spray, among the rigging.
>
>   Surely the ocean in its fury is the grandest object in
> creation! I have seen it in all its moods — now sleeping,
> and like an infant, smiling in its sleep back at the placid
> moon, dancing and sparkling and quivering, as if in ecstasy
> 'in the pride of sunny morn', and anon leaping up and
> rolling and tumbling in obstreperous sportiveness. Then it
> has its black, portentous, subtle mood, which, to look
> upon, is awe-inspiring. But, above all and before all, give
> me the ocean lashed into anger by the mad winds. To feel
> its full power, though, you must be in its midst and at its
> mercy. At such a moment the soul is elevated and
> expanded to the utmost.

But it was human phenomena that inspired most of his reflections. The theme of emigration always moved him deeply and
travelling from Ireland to America in 1863 he was shoulder to
shoulder with the subject. He was moved to tears at the thought
of the heartbreaks and miseries lying behind most decisions to
leave the old country. Simultaneously, his nationalist feelings
were harrowed by the thought — and much more the sight —
of Ireland losing people. Even the evidence of many formerly
impoverished Irish people happily and prosperously settled into
American society did not persuade him to take a more balanced
view of emigration.

  He had a deep sense of veneration for the United States of
America as the model of independent democratic nationhood:

> As we approach the shores of the republic — when I think
> that in a few hours I shall stand, for the first time in my
> life, upon free soil — my pulse begins to beat quick . . . .

This young giant, with hot blood in his veins, is an object more worthy of reverence, more provocative of high and holy aspirations, than all the crumbling relics of nations that have withered, put together . . . . Magnificent Democracy! I kiss the hem of your garment. Bunker Hill! I worship you.

In New York he was forcibly struck by the manifestations of democracy in the manners of the population:

They are a polite people, too, but altogether deficient in the outward semblances of politeness. Your free and enlightened citizen, flung back in his armchair, with his legs thrown over another armchair, will hand you the newspaper in which he is buried, if you ask for it; but he will do so precisely as if you were a vendor of the article, and he did not want it . . . . A bow or a smile are not in your free and enlightened citizen's line, by any means.

Kickham realised that there was a conflict within himself between 'democracy' and the yearning for a more deferential kind of society in which the formalities of social intercourse counted for something.

His delight in 'the great American achievement' was dimmed by a shadow like that of 'a sin that must be atoned for'. It was 'the shadow of the red man'. His reaction to blacks was outrageously patronising by later standards and reflected the unsympathetic attitude of most of his Irish-American friends, but he acknowledged, however indirectly, the iniquity of slavery. On the rights and wrongs of the Civil War, then over two years in progress, Kickham was unable to make up his mind, and his feelings were of no help in solving the dilemma as they pulled in both directions. There is a hint of indefensible indifference to one of the bloodiest wars in history in his remark (inspired by seeing a few soldiers mingling with the New York multitude as it went about 'business as usual') that 'this war, I fancy, if it does nothing else, will infuse a dash of chivalry into this dollar-hunting people; which will be an improvement'. By his own admission Kickham's only deep concern about the war was that it should end quickly and thus set free the thousands of Irish soldiers on both sides for a fenian rising in Ireland. The Fenian Brotherhood (as the American wing called itself) was poised to take advantage. Nothing else in America interested Kickham as

much as the brotherhood. He had corresponded regularly with
the Head Centre John O'Mahony since their meeting in 1861
and while Kickham was in New York they met almost every
day. The visitor met numerous other fenians and sympathisers
in New York including General Michael Corcoran of the famous
sixty-ninth regiment of the New York militia.

As it happened, O'Mahony was just then making preparations for the first ever convention of the Fenian Brotherhood,
to be held in Chicago on 3, 4 and 5 November. Kickham waited
on in America to witness this assembly of fenians, and made his
way in good time by train to Chicago. On the proposal of
O'Mahony, he was formally admitted to the convention and
given a seat on the platform,[23] from where he witnessed three
days of deliberation and oratory. The impression made on him
by this hall-full of loud talkers was immense, and he came away
convinced that an invasion of Ireland by the Fenian Brotherhood was not an empty promise but a moral certainty — once
the Civil War ended. Understandably he assumed that the dele-
gates had grounds for their confident and reiterated assurances
about the preparedness of the Irish-born soldiers — Federal
and Confederate — to re-traverse the Atlantic once the
American war would have been concluded.

Kickham was prevailed upon to make a number of visits to
the homes of Irish people — fenians and others — in Chicago
and its vicinity and was given a particularly warm welcome by
a prosperous fenian named Michael Scanlan who like his guest
had some talent for verse. On the return journey to New York
Kickham, accompanied by O'Mahony, made a detour to 'do'
Niagara Falls. Back in New York, he made a round of visits to
Irish people including the family of Michael Doheny. Before
sailing for home he had his photograph taken and gave copies
to a few friends; and he received the present of an ear-trumpet
from a fenian admirer.

Returning to Ireland in late November 1863 he was in a
rather delicate situation in terms of fenian politics. Throughout
his visit he had been listening to angry complaints from
O'Mahony about Stephens's pretensions to leadership of the
fenian organisations on both sides of the Atlantic. O'Mahony
intended the Chicago convention to provide a re-assertion of his
own position. Stephens knew this, and, far from approving of

Kickham's trip to Chicago, he had written to him on 14 October with orders to return home as soon as possible. The entire proceedings of the convention were published by the brotherhood with the exception of three secret resolutions. [24] The first of these concerned the proclamation of the Irish republic. The second declared James Stephens to be the chief organiser of the Irish people, and, while superficially appearing to honour him, it in effect endeavoured to cut him down to size by confining his authority to Ireland and implying that he was subordinate to O'Mahony. The third resolution commissioned Kickham to convey the other two to Stephens.[25] Kickham delegated that particular task to someone who would find it less embarrassing. He was returning himself to work for Stephens and the I.R.B. in a new role, that of full-time newspaper propagandist.

Chapter Four

WITH THE *IRISH PEOPLE*

During John O'Mahony's Irish visit in 1860-61 Kickham and himself had discussed the need for a forum for regular exposition of fenian policy but nothing was done about it just then, although the opposition of A. M. Sullivan's *Nation* to the brotherhood made the problem urgent.[1] In April and May 1862 the *Nation* carried a comprehensive and extended denunciation of the activities of the American fenians and of the policies promulgated in John O'Mahony's paper, the *Phoenix,* published in New York. A number of fenians and fenian sympathisers in Ireland replied in the pages of the *Irishman,* not itself a fenian-controlled organ. The most remarkable of these *ripostes* came from Kickham.[2] It was a blistering personal attack on the unnamed A. M. Sullivan, gaining intensity from the esteem in which Kickham held O'Mahony. The brilliance of the invective drew attention to Kickham's ability as a political propagandist, and within a few months he became a frequent contributor of leading articles to the *Irishman.*[3] For much of 1862 these provided the nearest thing to regular public expression of fenian views on current and general topics.[4]

Stephens decided in the summer of 1863 to launch a wholly-controlled IRB newspaper, to be called the *Irish People.* He went on a tour to promote the project and arrived in Clonmel in September to enlist the support of the local fenians.[5] He remained for a few days and held at least two meetings. Three of those who attended the Clonmel meetings eventually worked on the paper in one capacity or another: Denis Dowling Mulcahy, in whose father's house one of the meetings was held; a teacher in Powerstown national school named Pierce Nagle;

and Charles J. Kickham.[6] With his not inconsiderable experience of writing for periodicals and in view of his recent excellent work in the *Irishman,* Kickham had invaluable potential as a member of the projected paper's team of writers. Stephens told him as much and went with him to Mullinahone to continue discussions.[7] Kickham was not being asked simply to submit pieces for publication: Stephens wished him to be involved with a few others in the day-to-day running of the new paper. That would entail living in Dublin. Much as he must have relished the prospect of conducting a newspaper together with men of compatible political views, the decision to leave home cannot have been an easy one. His deep attachment to Mullinahone and to the people and places round about was one of the fixed points in his life. Nevertheless he accepted Stephens's proposition.

He was already set to go on his family errand to America. Stephens saw no problem in that, as a few months were likely to elapse before the preparatory work on the new paper could be completed.[8] Stephens was so well-disposed towards Kickham at this time — outwardly at least — that he assisted with the arrangements for the American trip.[9] Kickham promised to return within a reasonable time and he undertook to send a letter from America to be published in the first issue. He estimated that this would be in very good time if posted before the year's end. He was agreeably surprised to learn in New York on 20 November that he had been pessimistic in his calculations and that the first issue was due on 28 November.[10] His first contribution appeared in the third number, on 12 December 1863, by which date he had taken up his duties on the staff of the paper in Dublin.

Stephens had commissioned him to act as editor jointly with two others, Thomas Clarke Luby and John O'Leary.[11] Kickham had known Luby as a travelling IRB organiser since 1861.[12] O'Leary was a new acquaintance.[13] He shared with Kickham the Tipperary shopkeeper-cum-rentier background and the youthful conversion to romantic nationalism. The differences were striking too. O'Leary was a cold-mannered, widely-travelled, formally-educated *savant,* apparently without any of Kickham's sense of devotion to people and place. The mixture of common interests and differences was correctly balanced and the two quickly developed a lasting — though not uncritical — mutual admiration. Temperamentally, Kickham had more in common with the business manager of the paper, Jeremiah O'Donovan Rossa, but they never became quite such close friends.

The three-fold division of the editorial function proved unworkable in practice, and by agreement John O'Leary soon assumed overall responsibility. [14]   As a general rule O'Leary, Luby and Kickham seem to have contributed one leading article each per week.[15]   These articles were unsigned, but by various means the authorship of many of them can be established. (See bibliography below, pp.241, where articles attributable to Kickham are listed.) Owing to the quality of the leading articles and to O'Leary's judicious editorial policy, the *Irish People* has acquired a high reputation in the history of Irish political journalism.

The fenian newspaper gave Kickham the opportunity to develop to the full his talents as a controversialist and propagandist. He dealt with many topics in its pages but his treatment of one question in particular has earned him lasting fame. Kickham's *Irish People* campaign against clerical attacks on fenianism has assumed a permanent place in Irish republican tradition and in Irish historiography.

From the beginning clergymen had opposed fenianism wherever they found it. With the revival in 1861 clerical opposition was renewed and formal episcopal denunciations began to appear, particularly from the pen of Archbishop Cullen of Dublin.[16]   Before the *Irish People* was many months old the priests in many parishes were campaigning vigorously against the local fenian presence. Bishops and priests were gravely concerned about the spiritual and moral welfare of young men caught up in an oath-bound society. That does not invalidate the argument of fenian supporters that churchmen were using their spiritual authority to oppose a political policy of which they happened to disapprove.

Little has ever been said about the impact of the social aspect of fenianism on clerical thinking, though it must have been very important. Even eighty or ninety years later the clergy of an Irish rural parish would have objected strenuously to the organisation, without their approval or involvement, of a social function like the Sunday outing to Carraigmoclear in July 1863 already described. Social control is much more tangible and immediate than the theoretical rights or wrongs of revolutionary conspiracy, and a parish priest who might react quite nonchalantly to an episcopal exposition of the theological and canonical objections to secret societies, would feel his personal position threatened by the sight of someone other than himself organising the pastimes of the local youth. This social dimension gave a particular seriousness and determination to the clerical onslaught on fenianism in the mid-1860s. That in turn made it necessary for the fenian leadership to embark on a life-or-death propaganda struggle. Local circles needed to be fortified against vigorous local assaults, which could take the form of admonitions from the pulpit or in the confessional, and direct approaches by clergymen to suspected fenians (including anyone buying or selling the *Irish People*), to their parents or even to their employers. There was very good cause for the urgency of the counter-offensive in the *Irish People* with which Kickham has become permanently identified.

A quarter of a century later, when revealing Kickham's authorship of the bulk of the anti-clerical articles, John O'Leary explained that he had been chosen because, unlike O'Leary himself (a non-believer) and Luby (a nominal protestant), he was a practising catholic.[17] Of course, at the time of publication scarcely anybody outside the *Irish People* office knew the identity of the author, so O'Leary's statement really means that Kickham was given the task because he was best fitted for it as a catholic who had wrestled with the problem of being loyal to his church while disagreeing violently with the policies of its ministers. At the height of his propaganda war against the clergy Kickham informed John O'Mahony of his gladness that Ireland was 'as catholic as ever', and added that he himself would not 'give up the old faith even for liberty'.[18] The next sentence was an assertion of the unthinkability of such a choice having to be made.

To Kickham's way of thinking nationalism and his religion were both orthodoxies that demanded unquestioning allegiance and conflict between them was impossible. He never had the slightest doubt about the correctness of his own interpretation of what the true nationalist faith demanded in any particular set of circumstances. Hence anyone who disagreed with him, churchman or politician, was in error. His certainty of the correctness of his own views was such that no allowance was made for the status of opponents. After his initial Young Ireland indoctrination Kickham was never inclined to judge political ideas on the basis of who held them. Instead he 'looked into his heart', a procedure that left him open to the charge of dogmatism: Archbishop Cullen denouncing fenianism did not sound any more dogmatic than Kickham denouncing Archbishop Cullen.

There was, however, more to Kickham's rejection of the clerical lead in politics than simple self-opinionation. His attitude to ecclesiastical authority when it did not cross his political opinions was quite sophisticated. Neat illustration is provided by an entry made in his diary while he was crossing the Atlantic in 1863.

> Friday. Now here's a difficulty. No fish for dinner; and the steward gives me politely to understand that I cannot have any. A general dispensation to us papists, in the matter of abstaining from flesh meat on Friday aboard ship would be a disderatum. However, I go in for obedience in all matters of a purely religious nature. But in matters temporal I am prepared to beard the College of Cardinals without the slightest compunction when convinced that I have the truth on my side. [19]

This balanced intellectual position co-existed throughout his adult life with a most intense feeling of disillusionment (almost amounting to an obsession) with the majority of the clergy as he actually found them.

The growth in the intensity of this disillusionment during Kickham's early adult years is well demonstrated by a comparison of a second version of 'Soggarth Aroon', published in 1863, with the 1850 version. Measured disappointment with the attitudes of an individual priest in 1850 had given way by 1863 to unmeasured disgust with the clergy in general. He accused them as a body of reneging in traitorous fashion on a compact between faith and fatherland from which they had benefited in penal times:

680 THE IRISH PEOPLE. SEPTEMBER 16, 1865.

TERMS OF SUBSCRIPTION:

STAMPED EDITION.				UNSTAMPED EDITION.			
Yearly	£0	13	0	Yearly	£0	8	8
Half-Yearly......	0	6	6	Half-Yearly......	0	4	4
Quarterly.........	0	3	3	Quarterly.........	0	2	2

A Single (Unstamped) Copy, 2d.

We here give notice to our readers that we cannot hold ourselves responsible for anything that may appear in our columns of original correspondence.

Persons favouring us with occasional contributions must send in their communications by Tuesday at latest. It will be utterly impossible to make any exceptions to this rule.

Persons who don't get their papers punctually should at onc complain to the Manager.

Literary communications must be addressed to "the Editor," anp left in the letter-box. Communications on business are to be addressed, and money-orders made payable to "the Manager," O'DONOVAN ROSSA.

Country agents are requested to send in their orders as early as possible in the week.

☞ News agents wanted for all parts of Ireland, England, and Scotland.

ANSWERS TO CORRESPONDENTS

HENRY O. C. M'CARTHY.—Ireland has lost one of the most earnest men that laboured in her cause. Henry O. C. M'Carthy is dead. He was a man of great force of character. He did an amount of work which would be enough to crush a dozen ordinary men. Mr M'Carthy possessed extraordinary business talents, but he devoted them to a higher end than the pursuits of wealth—the regeneration of the suffering land of his fathers. The following is the only account that has reached us of Mr. M'Carthy's death; but we are sure the Fenian Brotherhood will pay all fitting honour to his memory:—

"DEATH OF H. O. C. M'CARTHY.—A despatch received from St. Paul announces the death at the lakes near Minneapolis, Minnesota, at 2 p.m. on the 24th of August, of Henry O. Clarence M'Carthy, for many years engaged on the periodical press of New York, and latterly prominent among Irish revolutionary leaders as Deputy Head Centre of the Fenian Brotherhood, and President of the Fenian Central Council. He had repaired to Minnesota, hoping the climate and scenery would relieve him of a hemorrhage and pulmonary disease contracted during a lecturing tour for the Fenians, and which eventually terminated in his death. He was born in America, and was a man of intellectuality and marked republican progressiveness. His loss will be felt by the Fenian fraternity, both in this country and in Ireland. The remains are in charge of his brother, and will be conveyed to St. Louis, for interment near his mother's grave."—*Pilot.*

We give elsewhere, from the *Pall Mall Gazette*, a specimen of the astounding articles with which the English have been favouring us of late. Perhaps the queerest part of this article is the talk about Saxons and Celts. We need scarcely tell our readers that we know no difference between Saxons and Celts in Ireland. Many of us do not know whether we are Saxons or Celts, and most of us do not know how much Saxon or Celtic blood may be in our veins. In fact, we care nothing from what part of the world, or at what period of its history a man's ancestors came to Ireland. The *Pall Mall Gazette* is, however, right in one point, and that is, that the people care very little for the abolition of the Church Establishment. By-the-bye, it is strangely suggestive that papers like the *Times* and *Pall Mall Gazette*, and papers like the *Nation* and *Universal News* should be of one mind about the Fenians.

"KATHLEEN."—Try a more simple style, and you may do better. We don't like too much thunder and lightning in poetry. By the bye, "thunder" does not rhyme with "slumber." "Kathleen," like many of our correspondents, mistakes high-sounding rhetoric for vigorous song.

"A CARRICK BOY."—Your letter is too vague and too rambling, and is not equal to the subject with which it deals. Could'nt you find some local topic to deal with?

"CON CREGAN" (Quarryhole Bridge, Clonmel), writes complaining that his name had been used by a correspondent in the IRISH PEOPLE of last week. "This correspondent," he says, "must, if he be a constant reader of the IRISH PEOPLE, have seen that "Con Cregan" was the signature of another writer in that paper, and, therefore, should not have adopted it." We quite agree with "Con Cregan," that correspondents should not adopt the signatures of other writers in the IRISH PEOPLE.

"A DUNGANNON YOUTH."—You'll probably get the information you want in another way. You should not have looked to the source you did for it.

"SHAMROCK."—We don't think the publication of your letter could serve any good purpose. Parts of it 'twould be impossible to give.

"AN APPRENTICE BOY."—You ought to have sent your name. The facts may be as you state them, but it is not for us to give them publicity.

"TOM OWENS."—In the letter, which appeared in our last issue, acknowledging 10s for the Lambert fund, the Victoria Hotel, Kilkenny, was printed for the Royal Victoria Hotel, Lakes of Killarney.

"J. B." (CORK)—We got your letter, and might have given the part about the "Sergeant," but that 'twas mixed up with a good deal about his family, which we felt was no concern of ours.

"STEEL."—We are sorry we cannot insert your letter, but we are glad you have so sensible a parish priest.

"J. M."—We could not print the song you send us. It is a mere street ballad of no poetical merit, and of little merit of any kind.

"CORKONIAN."—Your "Soggarth Aroon" is in bad taste.

"VOX HIBERNIAE."—Your war song belongs to a class which we do not care to encourage. Choose some better model, and we think you will do better.

"NOT A FENIAN" is, if we are to judge from his letter, fit for a lunatic asylum.

"A LISTENER" (Cork).—If you give us your name in confidence, we may publish your letter next week.

"[illegible]"—[illegible] can serve his country better by doing a man's work than by writing rhetorical letters on general subjects. When he has any fact worth publishing to communicate, we shall be glad to hear from him.

"A QUEEN'S COUNTY BOY."—Your letter came too late for publication. It is, however, scarcely worth while correcting the mistakes of the *Morning Post.* Of course everybody (in Ireland) knows that 'twas at Killala, and not at Castlebar, the French landed, and that there were not several thousands of them, but about eleven hundred. Some time ago we gave a long account of Humbert's expedition in this journal.

"SPRIG OF THE SHANNON."—We quite agree with you that there are ways to serve Ireland besides writing letters to the newspapers. But there is no reason for concluding that men who write letters do nothing else.

"SHOP-BOY" (Strokestown).—We are glad to hear that the IRISH PEOPLE is so much read in your town. You say the mechanics and working classes are good Irishmen; but "shopkeepers, with their elbows on their counters," are no better than slaves. Strokestown, we fear, is not singular in this respect.

"HACKLEIR BOCHT AN T-SEANNA H-AIMSHAIRA" (Lisronagh, Clonmel) writes to say that Father John Power, P.P., of Powerstown and Lisronagh, has threatened to call from the altar the names of all the so-called Fenians in his parishes within a fortnight, if they don't come forward to him and give up their connexion with that organisation. Perhaps it would be as well if Father Power did. Father M'Ginn, C.C., Dundalk, has also threatened to "put the officers of justice upon the track of a party who had dared to administer the oath of disloyalty."

SONG.

Air—"Over the Hills and Far Away."

Oh, wirrasthrue, my heart is lone,
For Willie dear from me has flown;
He sailed across the stormy sea,
Unto the land of liberty.
His locks were like the raven's wing,
'Twould cheer your heart to hear him sing,
For him I sigh, the live-long day,
He's over the seas and far away.

'Tis sweet to hear the wild bird's lay,
'Tis sweet to see the flowers so gay;
But what on earth could yield me joy
When absent is my darling boy?
His locks were like the raven's wing,
'Twould cheer your heart to hear him sing;
For him I sigh the live-long day—
He's over the seas and far away.

Methinks full oft his voice I hear
When roving by yon river clear;
But the sighing breeze it seems to say,
He's over the seas and far away.
His locks were like the raven's wing;
'Twould cheer your heart to hear him sing.
For him I sigh the live-long day—
He's over the seas and far away.

Last night he stood before my face,
The vision bright I well can trace,
These words he spoke with voice so bland,
"I come to strike for fatherland."
His locks were like the raven's wing,
'Twould cheer your heart to hear him sing.
I know he'll come to join the fray
From over the seas and far away.

CROM ABOO.

"A FREEMOUNT BOY" writes to say that the only mistake he made in his letter concerning the Rev. Mr. Cosgrave's sermon was in stating that the reverend gentleman "*named* the lads of the village." He merely expressed a hope that "the boys of this village who might have had the misfortune to join the condemned society, would withdraw from it." Our correspondent asserts that this was the only mistake in his letter. He uses hard words against "A Milford Boy"—but we see no use in scolding. The "Freemount Boy" is probably in the right, and that is enough.

We are sorry to be compelled to hold over "Hugo del Monte," "The Liverpool Lounger," and "Square Toe."

"O'LOUGHNAN."—You are rather sensitive. We are not bound to answer all correspondents, though we generally do so. We answered you, but under a different name. We think the verses spirited, but rather rugged.

"NATIONAL CHORUS"—If the air be "first rate for marching," you ought to write more spirited words to it.

THE IRISH PEOPLE.

SATURDAY, SEPTEMBER 16, 1865.

PRIESTS IN POLITICS.

Nothing would please us better than to keep clear of the vexed question of "priests in politics," if we could do so without injury to the cause which we are endeavouring to serve. But the question was forced upon us. We saw clearly that the people should be taught to distinguish between the priest as a minister of religion and the priest as a politician before they could be got to advance one step on the road to independence. The people for whom God created it must get this island into their own hands. If they do not the Irish nation must disappear from the face of the earth. Our beautiful and fruitful land will become a grazing farm for the foreigner's cattle, and the remnant of our race wanderers and outcasts all over the world if English rule in Ireland be not struck down. Our only hope is in revolution. But most of the bishops and many of the clergy are opposed to revolution. Is it not then the duty of the Irish patriot be he priest or layman to teach the people that they have a right to judge for themselves in temporal matters? This is what we have done. We have over and over declared it was our wish that the people should respect and be guided by their clergy in spiritual matters. But when priests turn the altar into a platform; when it is pronounced a "mortal sin" to read the IRISH PEOPLE, a "mortal "sin" even to *wish* that Ireland should be free: when priests actually call upon the people to turn informers, and openly threaten to set the police upon the track of men who are labouring in the cause for which our fathers so often bled; when true men are reviled and slandered; when the uprooting of the people is called a "merciful dispensation of Providence"—when, in a word, bishops and priests are doing the work of the enemy, we believe it is our duty to tell the people that bishops and priests may be bad politicians and worse Irishmen.

Long before the establishment of this journal the bishops solemnly condemned "dangerous brotherhoods," whether oath-bound or not, and altar-denunciations were the order of the day. The Brotherhood of St. PATRICK, an open and legal association, was denounced in precisely the same language as has since been applied to the so-called Fenians; and, though it had a priest for vice-president, its members were denied the sacraments of the Church. In fact, the cry raised against oaths and secrecy was a mere pretence. The Fenian Brotherhood in America, with the hope of steering clear of ecclesiastical censure, substituted a word of honour for the oath; but they gained nothing by the change. They were told a pledge was just as bad as an oath. In fact it is nonsense to talk of conciliating priests and bishops, who think it a crime to attempt to gain our liberty "by force "and the aid of foreign armies." They would be opposed to any movement that might lead to the desired end. Liberty must be won by force or not at all. It is criminal in the eyes of certain ecclesiastics to attempt to save our country by force. Therefore we must either give up our country in despair, or teach the people to disregard politico-ecclesiastical dictation. The course we have pursued in reference to priests in politics was the only course open to us. We have never written a word calculated to injure religion in the slightest degree. We challenge our assailants to point to a single sentence in the IRISH PEOPLE, from its first number to the present, which could be construed into an attack upon religion. The charge that we are enemies of the Catholic Church is a vile calumny invented by trading politicians, and perhaps believed by weak men who are ready to believe any thing of any one who would dare to question their right to dictate to the people, or to disturb the peaceful contentment of their lives.

Some persons find fault with the letters of our correspondents, and we have published the letters of the fault-finders as willingly as we have those to which they object. But for the life of us we can't see why well-meaning men should object to those letters. When an Archdeacon O'BRIEN tears down the placards of the IRISH PEOPLE, and denounces the man who sells it as Antichrist, we see no reason why such conduct should not be publicly condemned.

We would call the attention of our readers to a letter which we reprint from the *Irish American.* The writer, it will be seen, is as hard upon anti-Irish priests as any correspondent of the IRISH PEOPLE could be. Yet the *Irish American* is a Catholic journal, and greatly admired by some of our assailants. This fact ought to convince honest men that the cry raised against us on the score of attacking priests is mere clap-trap.

But after all the war we have been forced to wage against ecclesiastical dictation in politics has done some good. The people are now so used to denunciation there is no reason to fear they will be frightened by it when the time has come for the final struggle. This is something to be thankful for.

THE FENIANS AND THE FAIRIES.

From the legendary lore of old Ireland we have learned something of the Fenians and Fairies of old. If our recollection serve us rightly the Fenians were, before the coming of St. PATRICK, the military defenders of the island. Their leader was FIONN MAC CUMHAIL, and the legions were, after his name FIONN, called Fiann-h-Erionn. To gain the honour of becoming a private in the ranks, a man should be able to go over anything the height of himself, or under anything the height of his knee, without his

The leader page from the final number of the original *Irish People,* with a typical Kickham article on 'priests in politics'. (See also p.72)

THE IRISH PEOPLE.

SATURDAY, SEPTEMBER 16, 1865.

PRIESTS IN POLITICS.

Nothing would please us better than to keep clear of the vexed question of " priests in politics," if we could do so without injury to the cause which we are endeavouring to serve. But the question was forced upon us. We saw clearly that the people should be taught to distinguish between the priest as a minister of religion and the priest as a politician before they could be got to advance one step on the road to independence. The people for whom God created it must get this island into their own hands. If they do not the Irish nation must disappear from the face of the earth. Our beautiful and fruitful land will become a grazing farm for the foreigner's cattle, and the remnant of our race wanderers and outcasts all over the world if English rule in Ireland be not struck down. Our only hope is in revolution. But most of the bishops and many of the clergy are opposed to revolution. Is it not then the duty of the Irish patriot be he priest or layman to teach the people that they have a right to judge for themselves in temporal matters? This is what we have done. We have over and over declared it was our wish that the people should respect and be guided by their clergy in spiritual matters. But when priests turn the altar into a platform ; when it is pronounced a " mortal sin" to read the Irish People, a " mortal " sin" even to *wish* that Ireland should be free ; when priests actually call upon the people to turn informers, and openly threaten to set the police upon the track of men who are labouring in the cause for which our fathers so often bled ; when true men are reviled and slandered ; when the uprooting of the people is called a " merciful dispensation of Providence"—when, in a word, bishops and priests are doing the work of the enemy, we believe it is our duty to tell the people that bishops and priests may be bad politicians and worse Irishmen.

Long before the establishment of this journal the bishops solemnly condemned " dangerous brotherhoods," whether oath-bound or not, and altar-denunciations were the order of the day. The Brotherhood of St. Patrick, an open and legal association, was denounced in precisely the same language as has since been applied to the so-called Fenians ; and, though it had a priest for vice-president, its members were denied the sacraments of the Church. In fact, the cry raised against oaths and secrecy was a mere pretence. The Fenian Brotherhood in America, with the hope of steering clear of ecclesiastical censure, substituted a word of honour for the oath ; but they gained nothing by the change. They were told a pledge was just as bad as an oath. In fact it is nonsense to talk of conciliating priests and bishops, who think it a crime to attempt to gain our liberty "by force" "and the aid of foreign armies." They would be opposed to any movement that might lead to the desired end. Liberty must be won by force or not at all. is criminal in the eyes of certain ecclesiastics to attempt to save our country by force. Therefore we must either give up our country in despair, or teach the people to disregard politico-ecclesiastical dictation. The course we have pursued in reference to priests in politics was the only course open to us. We have never written a word calculated to injure religion in the slightest degree. We challenge our assailants to point to a single sentence in the Irish People, from its first number to the present, which could be construed into an attack upon religion. The charge that we are enemies of the Catholic Church is a vile calumny invented by trading politicians, and perhaps believed by weak men who are ready to believe any thing of any one who would dare to question their right to dictate to the people, or to disturb the peaceful contentment of their lives.

Some persons find fault with the letters of our correspondents, and we have published the letters of the fault-finders as willingly as we have those to which they object. But for the life of us we can't see why well-meaning men should object to those letters. When an Archdeacon O'Brien tears down the placards of the Irish People, and denounces the man who sells it as Antichrist, we see no reason why such conduct should not be publicly condemned.

We would call the attention of our readers to a letter which we reprint from the *Irish American*. The writer, it will be seen, is as hard upon anti-Irish priests as any correspondent of the Irish People could be. Yet the *Irish American* is a Catholic journal, and greatly admired by some of our assailants. This fact ought to convince honest men that the cry raised against us on the score of attacking priests is mere clap-trap.

But after all the war we have been forced to wage against ecclesiastical dictation in politics has done some good. The people are now so used to denunciation there is no reason to fear they will be frightened by it when the time has come for the final struggle. This is something to be thankful for.

A typical Kickham article on 'priests in politics' from the *Irish People* (see also p.71)

And 'stags' you would make us now,
           Soggarth Aroon
You'd stamp on the bondsman's brow,
           Soggarth Aroon,
Foul treason's red burning brand —
Oh! doomed and woe stricken land,
Where honour and truth are banned,
           Soggarth Aroon.

On those dark days we now look back,
           Soggarth Aroon,
When the bloodhound was on your track,
           Soggarth Aroon,
Then we spurned the tyrant's gold,
The pass then we never sold,
We are still what we were of old,
           Soggarth Aroon.[20]

The passage of years had greatly heightened the irony that Kickham saw in the traditional phrase of loving veneration.

The second 'Soggarth Aroon' was one of the very few pieces of verse by Kickham to appear in the *Irish People*. By comparison with it, his numerous leading articles on the clergy were restrained and moderate in tone — whatever about content. But a more fundamental contrast has to be investigated. Far from postulating an alliance of 'faith and fatherland' the editorials of the *Irish People* are generally understood to have denied the existence of any such conjunction of interests. James Stephens, T. C. Luby and John O'Leary were all, to a greater or lesser extent, anti-clericals in the French sense who would have looked on with equanimity at the dissolution of the catholic church. The idea that the *Irish People* preached a nationalist doctrine that was thoroughly secular and that it cut the ground from under the clergy in ideological terms was propagated in later decades by Stephens and O'Leary.[21] That is what they would have liked the paper to do if it were tactically feasible. But the great majority of the fenian rank and file were instinctively loyal catholics who felt no conflict between their catholicism and their nationalism and had no appreciation of continental anti-clericalism. Kickham was their spokesman at

the editorial desk. The vigorous and apparently straightforward
'No priests in politics' line of the *Irish People* masked considerable differences of attitude. 'No priests in politics — ever'
would be a fair summary of Stephens's sentiments, while
Kickham's own view was: 'No priests in politics just now,
because in our generation the majority of the clergy have gone
seriously astray in political matters'. But Kickham would have
loved to see priests involved in political affairs, provided that
they were on his side. In the 1850s he had been among those
who denounced Cullen for forcing 'patriotic' priests out of
politics.

Kickham's *Irish People* articles made the distinction over
and over again between spiritual and temporal affairs and,
while challenging church authority in respect of the latter, he
exhorted his readers to be guided by the priests in spiritual
matters. O'Leary would never have given such an exhortation
and in later years he dissociated himself from it. He would not
presume to tell people to go to the clergy even for spiritual
advice.[22]   But in the devising of an agreed editorial line
Kickham, too, suppressed or modified some of his own views
(but without undergoing any fundamental change of heart).
Thus, regret at the political defection of the clergy was replaced
by the assertion that on historical precedent nothing else could
be expected.[23]   And the alliance of clergy and people in penal
days, which he had formerly idealised, he now represented as an
unhealthy development by which the priests acquired an
'abnormal and illegitimate authority which was the necessary
consequence of the ignorance inflicted by an unscrupulous foe
upon the Irish people'.[24]

Some of Kickham's articles on the clergy and politics are
masterpieces of leader-page polemics. Being a good propagandist
he conducted the argument in the pages of the *Irish People* on
his own terms. He purported to see the ecclesiastical offensive
as an attack on nationality itself and dismissed episcopal
concern about fenian oath-taking and secrecy as a diversion. He
never attempted to defend his position in terms of theology or
canon law: that would have involved hazarding his case on
abstruse points of interpretation and definition, and would have
utterly confused the question for his readers. Besides, it would
have meant challenging the clergy on their home ground.

Pointing out apparent contradictions between the church's preaching on Irish politics and its own actions from time to time was an obvious mode of attack and one used frequently by Kickham in the *Irish People* as, for instance, in the following comments on the Irish papal brigade which appeared on 16 January 1864:

The no-drop-of-blood doctrine — which well nigh converted a nation of men into a nation of helots — was promulgated [by O'Connell] in order to convert bishops and priests into agitators. Strange to say, it was reserved for the bishops and priests to sweep the last vestige of the abomination from the face of the land. The temporal authority of the pope was encroached upon and the Holy Father wanted men and money. He wanted soldiers to fight — that's what he wanted. We wonder had His Holiness any notion of what a precious thing a drop of blood was in Ireland. Well, our bishops and priests, forgetting (when it suited them) the pricelessness of the commodity, actually appealed to the young men of Ireland to gird up their loins, and, leaving fathers and mothers and country and friends, to go forth to the battle field and pour out their drops of blood under a foreign sky, and leave their bones to bleach far away from poor old Ireland, where to fight would be a sin and a shame. For the pope said there was no use '*reasoning* with a robber', which, indeed, is very true.

Fenianism stood up remarkably well to the clerical assault.[25] The contribution of the *Irish People* — and so of Kickham — to this resistance was significant. But the effort was in vain, as failure on other fronts ensured the defeat of the movement.

The clergy did not monopolise Kickham's attention in the editorial columns of the *Irish People*. He also took notice of non-clerical advocates of constitutional politics. For some years A. M. Sullivan, John Martin, The O'Donoghue MP, P. J. Smyth and others had been endeavouring to start an open political movement. Such a movement would be an alternative, and so a serious threat, to fenianism. Accordingly the *Irish People* maintained a constant barrage of invective against the concept and against its advocates. Not just one but two such organisations were founded in 1864 — John Martin's National League in January and the National Association, with Archbishop Cullen's support, in December. The leader-writers of the *Irish People,* including Kickham, contributed all they could to the early decline of both societies.

James Stephens did not depend solely on leading articles to counter his political rivals. On a number of crucial occasions from 1861 to 1865 he utilised strong-arm tactics to nip conventional political efforts in the bud. On 22 February 1863 a public meeting called by A. M. Sullivan and others was held in the round room of the Rotunda in Dublin, to protest against the re-allocation for a statue of Prince Albert of a site in College Green previously marked out for an effigy of Henry Grattan. The cause was calculated to appeal to the emotions of all nationalists, fenians included. If successful the meeting might have provided the basis for a movement with broader objectives and this Stephens could not tolerate. Fenians went in their hundreds to the meeting and by arrangement they raised a riot at the first mention by the chairman of the name of A. M. Sullivan, who was on the platform. Sullivan and his supporters fled in confusion leaving the hall in the possession of rampaging fenians. [26] Shaken but not demoralised, Sullivan determined to hold another meeting a week later for which he would be better prepared. During the interval attempts were made to bring about some kind of amicable arrangement between the two nationalist factions. A parley was arranged at which Kickham and O'Leary represented the IRB, but no agreement was reached. [27] At the second Rotunda meeting entry was restricted to those holding tickets, which had been carefully distributed beforehand. On this occasion the violence occurred outside the hall as ticketless fenians sought unsuccessfully to force a way in, while Stephens directed tactics from a nearby public-house. [28] Like O'Leary and Luby, Kickham had his better judgement over-ruled at this time by the forceful personality of the fenian chief, then at the height of his influence and achievement. Endorsement, however tacit, of Stephens' policy of intimidation (and denial of free speech) was contrary to Kickham's better principles, and indeed to his practice at other times.

The editorial staff of the *Irish People* appear to have attended at the office during business hours from Monday morning until

Thursday evening, or even Friday evening when the paper was despatched to the newsagents. Certainly Kickham's comings and goings were sufficiently normal and regular to give his landlady in Rathgar the impression that he was engaged in some proper business. She was a widow who took good class lodgers to support herself and her household. Like many others who got close to Kickham — but not too close — she was charmed by his kindness and gentleness of manner. Being strongly loyalist in attitude she was shocked when eventually her lodger was revealed as a fenian: she had always thought him a gentleman.[29]

His bill for board and lodging was just over sixteen shillings per week — not very high for a gentleman, but he was never extravagant. He almost certainly supported himself out of his inherited wealth. Stephens had promised appropriate remuneration for his editorial staff, but pay-day at the *Irish People* office was a movable feast, and whenever money for wages was available those in greatest need or those who shouted loudest appear to have received preference.[30] Kickham's main reward, apart from the work itself, was the company which he now enjoyed. After days at the office with O'Leary and the others there were frequent social evenings, mostly at O'Leary's lodgings. There was usually drink for those who wished to partake (whiskey punch for O'Leary and Luby, bottles of Guinness for Stephens, lemonade or tea for Kickham and the ladies), but the emphasis was on literary and political conversation. Despite increasing difficulty with his hearing, Kickham participated fully. O'Leary recalled later that 'especially did Kickham talk, and provoke talk, about books and their writers'.[31] These occasions were usually crowned in Kickham's eyes by the presence of one or two women with literary taste, especially O'Leary's sister, Ellen, who contributed poetry to the *Irish People*. She took a sisterly interest in Kickham's welfare and became a lifelong friend.

Another Dublin friend was his cousin, Michael J. Crean from Knockelly, barrister-at-law and veteran of the papal brigade. Crean and his brother Thomas, a medical doctor with a practice in Clonmel, occasionally called to see Kickham at the *Irish People* office. As their political opinions were decidedly moderate, Luby and other fenians did not trust them and they were not involved in the *Irish People* 'soirées'. Michael J. Crean certainly would have qualified on the basis of an interest in literature, since by 1864 he was editor and proprietor of a serial publication, the *Hibernian Magazine* (previously *Duffy's Hibernian Magazine*). From July to December 1864 this carried a story entitled 'The untenanted graves'. Kickham was the author, though his name was not given. 'The untenanted graves' was a new departure for him. It was his first major serial work and his first attempt to use Irish rural life as he knew it as material for a fictional work. While there is no absolute certainty about when it was written, we can reasonably assume that composition as well as publication took place in 1864. Living away from his native area for the first time, he was able to view it in perspective and to see in it the makings of a novel. In a number of ways his decision to leave home and work on the *Irish People* was the major turning point in Kickham's career.

Chapter Five

IN PRISON (1865-9)

Late on the evening of 15 September 1865 the Dublin police, directed by the Castle, took possession of the *Irish People* headquarters at 12 Parliament Street and seized the entire contents of the office. The few members of the staff still on the premises were arrested; others were picked up in the streets or at their homes.[1] Thus, the authorities suppressed the mouthpiece of the fenian movement after it had been publishing for less than twenty-two months.

The most wanted man, James Stephens, escaped the net; so did Kickham. Whatever about Stephens, Kickham's escape was accidental rather than the result of precaution. In fact no arrest warrant was issued for Kickham and he may have been in some doubt for a week or two as to whether or not he was on the wanted list. He subsequently claimed to have moved around the city in normal fashion for an unspecified period following on the first arrests.[2] Meanwhile he was becoming an object of interest at Dublin Castle. Documents taken by the police from the *Irish People* office and from the homes of arrested fenians revealed his importance in the affairs of the suppressed paper; they also created a strong, perhaps exaggerated, impression of his importance in the fenian conspiracy. Just how deeply he was implicated, in the opinion of the authorities, became evident on 30 September when O'Leary, Luby, O'Donovan Rossa and other arrested associates appeared before a police magistrate for preliminary investigations.[3] In Luby's house there had been found a document signed by James Stephens and dated 9 March 1864 which empowered O'Leary, Luby and Kickham to exercise executive authority over the IRB while the chief absented himself on business in America.[4] This 'executive document' as it came to be called was a characteristic piece of Stephens eyewash and Luby had attached so little importance to it that he had not even bothered to inform Kickham of its existence. Now Kickham could read all about it in the papers and see himself characterised as a ringleader, already apparently convicted by a most damning piece of evidence.

Other parts of the proceedings of 30 September were even more disturbing. Because of expressions of disquiet, in England as well as in Ireland, about the suppression of a newspaper at the whim of the authorities, and because of the large number of arrests made subsequently in Dublin and the provinces, Dublin Castle felt the need for a convincing — even hair-raising — *exposé* of the fenian menace. That was provided by counsel for the crown on 30 September. Charles R. Barry QC, putting the most disturbing possible interpretation on the evidence, represented fenianism as being not simply a political conspiracy aimed at rebellion, separation from Britain and the setting up of an Irish republic, but also as having concerted plans for wholesale expropriation of land and private wealth, and for a thoroughgoing massacre of all the higher and middle ranks of society, not excluding the catholic clergy.[5] When the opportunity eventually came Kickham revealed the anger that he felt about this misrepresentation. The hurt was particularly bad because his name was mentioned in the context of the alleged conspiracy against property. Some months after the Slievenamon meeting of 15 August 1863 he had received from an obscure Irish exile in Paris a letter of congratulations which, however, showed total misunderstanding of the intent of Kickham's mountain-top oratory by going on to advocate a policy of crop-burning and cattle-houghing to discourage evictions.[6] Kickham retained the letter as a curiosity, only to have it seized with other papers that he had kept in the *Irish People* offices. Now it was used to instance the kind of thing that he and the other fenians allegedly had on their minds. The association of his name with the advocacy of such outrages was one of the most painful humiliations of his career.

Yet another part of the proceedings of 30 September 1865 provided a shock for Kickham: the chief witness for the crown was an acquaintance of his and a fellow-fenian from south

Tipperary, Pierce Nagle. Kickham had never shown any particular liking for him and had only known him since the summer of 1863, but he had been responsible at that time for bringing Nagle back into the IRB after he had been barred for some months owing to a disagreement with Denis Dowling Mulcahy.[7] Nagle left, or lost, his position as national teacher in Powerstown in September 1863 and he moved to Dublin later in the year. There he supported himself, his wife and his family by small clerical and teaching jobs, including a few hours per week folding papers in the *Irish People* office. From early 1864 his income was supplemented by irregular payments from Dublin Castle for information about the fenian organisation which he had persuaded the police to buy, with some difficulty at first.[8] In due course his material proved extremely useful, but as the identity of the informer was known only to a few detectives, he was arrested on 15 September along with other frequenters of 12 Parliament Street. The crown sorely needed a witness from within the fenian organisation, and although Nagle had not bargained for that particular role earlier, it was one of a small number of unpleasant alternatives now open to him and he undertook it with a show of willingness.

Although even yet no warrant for his arrest was issued, Kickham knew beyond doubt from 30 September that he was a wanted man, and it was probably at this stage that he went into hiding. He took refuge with James Stephens at Fairfield House, a gentleman's secluded residence in Sandymount, rented some months earlier in anticipation of an emergency.[9] From Fairfield House Stephens continued to direct the IRB which seemed to have actually increased its support as a consequence of the arrests. Comings and goings were kept as circumspect as possible, but Kickham made a point of attending church on Sundays as usual.[10]

From Sandymount Kickham wrote to John O'Mahony assuring him that the organisation was thriving. As for himself, he said, being in Stephens's company and 'trusting to his star' he felt 'tolerably safe'.[11] This sense of security was proved false in the early morning of 11 November 1865 when Fairfield House was surrounded by dozens of armed detectives. For over two months the police had been straining every nerve to apprehend Stephens; now they had him and as a welcome bonus they found Kickham and two other important fenians, Edward Duffy and Hugh Brophy. Kickham had in his possession £40 in gold coins, £33 in notes and a cheque for £40.[12] Although there were revolvers in the house, no resistance was offered and within hours the four prisoners were appearing before the chief police magistrate in Dublin Castle. They were charged with high treason and after completion of the formalities they were remanded until the following Tuesday, 14 November 1865.[13]

On the Tuesday the crown had an array of sworn informations and witnesses (including Nagle) available for the magisterial examination. Kickham's poor hearing posed an obstacle to the proper conduct of proceedings, and the magistrate decided to pass on to him copies of all the informations as they were sworn, and give him time to read them. Stephens, who was affecting amused indifference, exploited the opportunity to introduce an air of levity. He undertook to provide Kickham with a commentary on the proceedings by means of an ear trumpet, and this allowed him to repeat very loudly and with humorous effect many of the statements of the magistrate and the witnesses.

At the first opportunity Kickham protested vehemently against the way in which his name had been blackened on 30 September, especially by the misuse of the letter from Paris. Counsel for the crown assured him that the letter was not being used as evidence against him, but that was not sufficient satisfaction for Kickham who pointed out that what mattered was that it had been used against him with the public. Stephens was making no attempt to defend himself in court and had not engaged any legal assistance, unlike O'Leary and the others arrested earlier. Their solicitor, John Lawless, was in court as an observer on 14 November and during the day it was arranged that he would act on Kickham's behalf. Meanwhile the presentation of evidence continued until the late afternoon when the court adjourned until the following morning. The purpose of the magistrate's investigation was simply to establish if there was enough evidence against the prisoners to send them for trial in a higher court. The outcome was a foregone conclusion and on Wednesday 15 November, Stephens, Kickham and the others were committed for trial by an already arranged special commission.[14]   Stephens never stood trial. On the night of 24-25

November he staged a spectacular escape from Richmond Jail where he and the others were being held.[15] Kickham was in a cell next to that from which Stephens was let out by an accomplice within the prison. Next day the fenian prisoners were moved to the more secure jail at Kilmainham.

The government had decided to set up a special commission to deal with the fenian cases rather than hold them over to the Spring assizes of 1866 when they would obviously clog up the calendar. The special commission was not a special court but an extraordinary session of the normal assize court with the normal procedures: the fenians were to be tried by juries of Dublin citizens and with all the protection afforded to the accused in a normal court. However, the choice of the judges was not re-assuring. One of them was the blackest of all Kickham's *bêtes noires,* William Keogh, collaborator with John Sadleir at Westminster in the early 1850s, and for Kickham and others the personification of treachery. His appointment to the bench in 1856 had been depicted by independent oppositionists as a reward for perfidy. In the editorial columns of the *Irish People* he had been attacked by name not just for the conduct of his political career [16] but also for the severity of some of the sentences he had imposed as a judge.[17]

Justice Keogh and his fellow commissioner, Justice J. D. Fitzgerald, began the fenian trials in Green Street courthouse on 27 November. At the outset Keogh announced that although the prisoners had been committed on charges of high treason they would be tried under 'a very lenient and merciful statute passed in 1848 reducing in certain cases what was before high treason to the rank of felony'. [18] In other words, the charge was now one of treason-felony, which, unlike high treason, did not carry the death penalty. The grand jury quickly got through the formality of finding a true bill against the accused and the trial proper began, the first prisoner into the dock being T. C. Luby. The indictment against him (which was substantially the same in the cases of all the other prisoners) alleged felonious intention on 1 January 1863 and other dates, and conspiracy with other named prisoners to encompass the intended felony. The treason-felony act of 1848 required that in order to be indictable the felonious intention should be manifested by some overt deed or act or by publishing some printing or writing.

Consequently the indictment named and quoted articles which had appeared in the *Irish People* and presented them as manifestation of intention. At least five of these were by Kickham, but their authorship was irrelevant to the prosecution's case. Luby was tried, convicted and sentenced to a long period of penal servitude; so in turn were John O'Leary, Michael Moore and John Haltigan. Kickham was brought forward next, on 9 December. [19]

At once, delaying tactics came into operation. From subsequent events it is evident that Isaac Butt, leading counsel for the defence was determined to put off Kickham's trial for as long as possible. In this he had the support of Kickham's fellow-prisoners. They had apparently agreed, in consideration of his infirmities, to give him the advantage, whatever it might be, of a later trial. It is not clear just how they expected a later trial to be more favourable, except perhaps that they anticipated more lenient juries later on. (As a new jury was sworn for each individual trial there was a considerable turnover.) Kickham was possibly unaware of the delaying tactics used at this stage, and he subsequently accused the prosecution of having purposely brought about the delay — a totally unfounded accusation. [20]

Just as Kickham's trial was about to commence on 9 December, Butt suddenly raised the question of his own licence to act for the defence. As a queen's counsel he needed a licence from the attorney-general to act in a second interest. He had received such a licence at the opening of the commission and on foot of it he had acted in four trials; nobody was questioning its continuing validity, yet he now began to express qualms himself. The court had no choice but to join in the charade. Judge Keogh intervened, ostensibly on Butt's behalf, to ask the attorney-general for an assurance that all the necessary licences would be forthcoming. Otherwise, he explained, he would be forced to put back the prisoner. With a show of reluctance the attorney-general gave the required assurance and the court addressed itself to the trial of C. J. Kickham. He was arraigned on the same indictment, *mutatis mutandis,* as the earlier prisoners; yet Butt raised an objection on the grounds of a technical fault in the phraseology. A lengthy session of legal argument followed before Judge Keogh over-ruled the objection. The question was then put to the prisoner, who pleaded not guilty. When asked if he was ready for his trial he replied in the affirmative.

However, Butt was still not beaten. What happened next does not appear in the published record of the day's proceedings,[21] but an informal discussion took place involving Butt, the attorney-general and Keogh.[22] As a consequence Butt got his way: Kickham was put back and Jeremiah O'Donovan Rossa was brought forward for trial. As well as being offensive to Keogh, Rossa's conduct during his trial was obstreperous in the extreme.[23] John Devoy later said that Rossa prolonged his own trial for the sake of delaying Kickham's.[24] In any event Rossa's trial dragged on until 13 December which was the commission's last day in Dublin before it was due to move to Cork for a few weeks to attend to similar business there. So Kickham's trial was put off until January.

On 2 January the attorney-general sent word that Kickham would be called first when the commission resumed in Dublin on 5 January. No advantage had been taken of the previous three weeks for preparing a defence, and Butt had not yet returned from Cork. On 4 January Kickham's solicitor, Lawless, received a letter from Butt advising that on resumption an application for habeas corpus should be sought in respect of T. C. Luby and a fenian just convicted in Cork, Charles Underwood O'Connell. This was done and the grounds for the application were set out in an affidavit by Kickham: he believed that the so-called 'executive document' used in evidence against Luby and O'Leary would be used in his trial also and he wanted Luby in court to prove that he (Kickham) had no knowledge of this document; O'Connell could testify that the secret resolutions of the Chicago convention of November 1863 had not, despite internal indications, been transmitted by or forwarded through Kickham.

The application was received badly by bench and prosecution. Keogh felt that it was a poorly-disguised attempt to have the trial postponed once again. The attorney-general pointed out that Kickham could have been tried without notice at any time since 9 December; as reported in the public press, Luby had been removed to Pentonville on 23 December and bringing him back would take some time, even if in fact the commission had the power to order his return. William J. Sidney, counsel for the accused, speaking in the continuing absence of Butt, offered, as a proof of good faith, to let the trial proceed and take a chance that the convict witnesses would have arrived by the time they were required. This was clearly a bluff as the judges could not grant the application without ensuring that the witnesses would be in court on time and to be sure of that they would have to be prepared to grant a further postponement. After much legal argument and an adjournment for consultation Keogh dismissed the application. There was one further delay: defence counsel claimed that the use of the 1865 book of jurors was improper as the new year had begun. After some discussion this objection was over-ruled. The jury was then sworn in, and all seemed set at last for the trial. But further diversion was in store.

As the case was about to open Kickham interrupted to protest against the dismissal of the application for habeas corpus, which, he declared, was proof that his trial was but a mockery. That being the position, he said, he was dismissing his counsel. The bench and counsel admonished him on the inadvisability of such a course — as they were bound to do. Was this move secretly approved by his legal advisers or simply made on his own initiative? In either case, it was calculated. The prisoner's indignant outburst did not take place, and counsel was not dismissed, immediately after the judicial decision that was cited as the pretext, not indeed until after another objection had been heard and the jury selected. The effect (and probably the intention) of Kickham's dismissal of counsel was to place a new obstacle in the way of a speedy trial — the quite rare problem of trying a deaf man without counsel to act as his 'ears'. Keogh's notes show that he (or somebody else) looked up a number of legal casebooks to find precedents for the trial of an unrepresented defendant 'mute by act of God', which was Kickham's technical condition as he could not answer an address from the bench. Keogh solved the problem by undertaking to make full notes of the evidence and to hand them page by page to Kickham for perusal. In addition, somebody could sit beside the defendant with the ear trumpet and communicate at appropriate times. In the event his brother Thomas, his solicitor, and an unoccupied crown lawyer took turns at this.

Nothing now remained to delay the judicial process, unless the prisoner would break his spectacles, and he did not do that. Hope, however, had not been lost: though left to his own devices, Kickham set about trying to win the case. His problem was to obtain a 'not guilty' verdict from a middle-class Dublin jury, a difficult task under the circumstances but not impossible. Unlike Rossa, who had baited Keogh, Kickham was sweetly reasonable throughout his trial.

The attorney-general in his opening address outlined the evidence that would be used to establish Kickham's involvement in the fenian conspiracy: the sworn statements of Pierce Nagle; numerous letters and documents referring to Kickham; and articles by him in the *Irish People*. Nagle was called to the witness box. Under examination he stated that he had acted as a member of the fenian organisation and was well acquainted with its workings; from conversation and from seeing him at meetings in the Clonmel district in 1863 he knew Kickham to be a fenian; and he had seen him repeatedly at the *Irish People* office. Nagle identified the manuscript originals (seized in the *Irish People* office) of four articles published in that paper, as being in Kickham's hand. At the conclusion of Nagle's examination the accused asked for, and was granted, an adjournment until the following morning to give him an opportunity to examine the copies of the documents presented in evidence prior to cross-examining the witness. The jury retired to the Gresham Hotel while Kickham was taken back to his cell in Kilmainham where he was to have the gaslight on for as long as he wished into the night.

At 10.30 next morning, Saturday 6 January 1866, Justices Keogh and Fitzgerald resumed their places on the bench and Kickham began his cross-examination. He questioned Nagle closely about the meetings and conversations in 1863 which convinced him that he (Kickham) was in the fenian organisation. With the witness's replies being conveyed to him through the ear trumpet, he operated quite effectively and showed up some haziness on Nagle's part. He next questioned Nagle's knowledge of his handwriting and his competence to verify manuscripts. Nagle claimed to have had a letter from Kickham in 1863 and also to have seen him write on other occasions.

Kickham forced from Nagle the significant admission that he had not selected the manuscripts he identified for the court as Kickham's from any larger collection. The inference came across clearly that Nagle was prepared to identify as Kickham's whatever was presented to him by the crown as Kickham's. After Nagle had committed himself about his ability to identify the prisoner's handwriting, Kickham passed him a small scrap of manuscript and asked if it was in his (Kickham's) hand. Nagle said he thought so. On being handed another document the witness said that he could not be sure whether it was in the prisoner's hand or not.

The prosecution introduced a number of police witnesses to give evidence of arrest and to establish the sources of the various seized documents. Kickham did not cross-examine any of them. The crown had concluded its case by 12.45 p.m. and the prisoner was given a short break to complete the preparation of his defence.

At 2 p.m. the court resumed. Kickham's address in his own defence was the work of a man hoping to achieve acquittal without disowning his past or his principles. He argued cogently against the evidence for the prosecution, and he endeavoured to establish that if he was convicted it would have to be for his writings in the *Irish People*. What then, he asked, about freedom of speech? He admitted that he had written for the controversial paper; he even admitted that it had been the organ of conspiracy; but, he argued, being connected with the paper did not prove that he was part of the conspiracy. Then he played his trump. He established that the first manuscript he had passed to Nagle during the cross-examination was not in his own hand (though Nagle said he thought it was); the second was in Kickham's hand — Nagle had not been able to say whether it was or not. By a brilliant ploy he had undermined the evidence linking him to the *Irish People* articles which were adduced as evidence against him.

Next Kickham called three witnesses: his brother, Thomas, and two neighbours from Mullinahone, Catherine Mulcahy and John O'Brien. They established that Kickham had been at home from 2 to 12 March 1864 and that accordingly he was not at hand when Stephens signed the 'executive document' in Dublin on 9 March 1864. The witnesses for the defence also established

accompanied them from Kilkenny station to the town centre. While Kickham rested for some hours in a hotel, numerous well-wishers waited to see him off.[62]   He timed his arrival in Mullinahone for late at night in the hope of avoiding a demonstration, 'but', an eyewitness later recalled, 'the townspeople were on the alert and crowded after the car shouting " 'Tis Master Charles" '.[63]

Chapter Six

MUTED FAME

What permanent effects did his period of almost three years and four months in prison have on Kickham? Certainly his hearing and eyesight deteriorated; the awareness that time was running out for his faculties must have greatly aggravated in Kickham's case that anguish over the loss of life's opportunities which affects all long-term prisoners. It was probably in Woking that he learned the 'finger' (or 'manual') alphabet, designed for those afflicted with loss of both hearing and sight. However, there is no reason to think that the imprisonment itself did any damage to his senses: they had been getting progressively weaker for years beforehand. Again, there is no conclusive evidence that his general health was permanently damaged by his frequent illnesses in prison. Although he was over forty, he was physically fit and exuberant enough some time after his release to challenge and defeat a younger friend in a 'hop and leap' contest.[1]

His political attachments were unchanged by prison, and their intensity was undiminished. The desire for an active part in his own kind of politics remained as keen as ever. Kickham's essential enthusiasm survived intact to the end of his life. Nonetheless, a change in tactics can be discerned in the years after his imprisonment by comparison with what went before, a greater appreciation of patience and circumspection being evident. This capacity for forebearance had been first displayed at his trial.

In 1869 he no longer enjoyed the financial security that had been his before his arrest. On 5 December 1865 while he was awaiting trial and — it seemed likely — long years of penal servitude, he had granted by indenture to his brother Alexander the landlord's interest in houses in Mullinahone inherited from his father.[2] Presumably there was an unwritten understanding that the property, which produced an income of about £50 per year, would be returned to Charles on his release. In 1868 Alexander used the Mullinahone property as security to raise a loan of £750.[3] This he put into a merchant warehousing business in which he was joined by two partners. The loan had not been repaid at the time of Charles's release, so there was no possibility of the property being restored to him just then. He was still the nominal owner of the drapery shop but he had left that totally in Thomas's hands and knew nothing of the business. It supported the attached family home where the young Cleary girls resided with a cousin as governess, and here Charles too could live in comfort. However, he was now a gentleman without a gentleman's income.

Kickham's imprisonment influenced his subsequent career principally by making him famous. Before the autumn of 1865 he was virtually unknown outside his own locality and the *Irish People* coterie in Dublin. At the time of his arrest one Dublin newspaper, realising that his name would mean nothing to most people, introduced him to the public as a relation of Rody Kickham.[4] (Rody was likely to be known to the readers, if at all, only for a few inconclusive court appearances in Carrick-on-Suir and Clonmel following his arrest as he left a public house in Mullinahone late on St. Patrick's Eve, 1864, with copies of the IRB oath in his pocket.)[5] The arrest, the trial, the controversies about his imprisonment and the publicity surrounding his release combined to give Charles J. Kickham a nation-wide reputation by March 1869. Fame gave him opportunities. It brought him the offers of publication that induced him to write *Knocknagow*. Michael Davitt was a much less celebrated character on his release in 1877 than Kickham had been in 1869; he nevertheless built on the opportunities for publicity and *entrée* to make himself into a major national figure. By contrast, Kickham deliberately rejected the chance of becoming a public personage. To do so would have been incompatible with the principles of fenianism as he understood them; more importantly, perhaps, it would have been incompatible with his personality.

Very shortly after Kickham's arrest the *Irishman* began to re-publish excerpts from his writings, thus exploiting public interest in the author.[6] In Kilmainham Jail awaiting his trial, Kickham spent much of his time revising some of his prose and verse works with a view to publication. After his conviction his belongings (including manuscripts) were sent from Kilmainham to Mullinahone, and Thomas assumed the role of literary agent.[7] He entrusted some 'literary friend', probably Michael J. Crean, with the task of preparing an anthology of his brother's writings.[8] The *Irishman* of 19 May 1866 carried a paid notice to advertise the forthcoming appearance of Kickham's *Ballads, songs and stories, with memoir and portrait of the author.* The author approved, and he included a dedication for the proposed volume in one of his letters from prison. However, the project never materialised. On a visit to Woking in autumn 1868 Thomas told Charles that his friends had decided to abandon the anthology lest its publication might injure him.[9] He was angered and disappointed by this news, and with some justification, for the project had been mismanaged by Thomas and a too large collection of advisers.

Spurred on by Charles's disappointment they now set about the easier task of bringing out in book form, with the minimum of editorial work, his most substantial piece of fiction to date, 'The untenanted graves'. It was already half-way through the printing press when the author reached Dublin on his way home from prison in March 1869.[10] He was obviously gratified and his first piece of writing for publication after his return to Mullinahone was a lengthy preface; the book was published in May 1869 as *Sally Cavanagh, or the untenanted graves*. It was well received in Ireland,[11] in Britain,[12] and in America where it was published in January 1870.[13] By the spring of 1870 an advertiser could presume to refer to Kickham as 'the greatest living Irish novelist'. [14] (William Carleton had died the previous year.)

Meanwhile, publications on both sides of the Atlantic catering for an Irish nationalist readership were avidly seeking material with the Kickham signature. Starting on 24 April 1869 the *Irishman* began reprinting a long series of articles which Kickham had published anonymously at various times and in different journals in the ten years before his arrest.[15] The New York *Emerald* was given some previously published material, as was the Dublin *Shamrock*.[16] The New York *Irish People* (which had been launched under John O'Mahony's auspices after the disappearance of the Dublin paper of the same name) was promised an occasional letter.[17] The editor of the Boston *Pilot* was also in the queue.[18]

The demand for his work, and especially the critical acclaim accorded to *Sally Cavanagh*, encouraged Kickham to undertake a more ambitious project than anything he had attempted hitherto — a full-length story of Irish life. The pleading of John O'Mahony (who was acting as an intermediary between Kickham and the publishers of the *Emerald*) eventually persuaded him to begin.[19] O'Mahony witnessed and forwarded to Kickham an undertaking by the proprietors of the *Emerald* to pay a substantial monthly fee for the story. O'Mahony promised to attend to Kickham's interests in the matter.[20] On 24 January 1870 the author despatched the first instalment to O'Mahony and on 12 March chapters one and two of *Knocknagow, or the homes of Tipperary* appeared in the *Emerald.*[21] The story continued in subsequent weeks and by arrangement each instalment was published in the Dublin *Shamrock* a week after its appearance in New York.[22]

Despite all the promises and guarantees, the *Emerald* sent only one remittance to Kickham who, on account of his friendship for O'Mahony, hesitated to press his demands and continued the regular despatch of instalments.[23] Eventually he wrote to O'Mahony threatening that he would have to wind up the story; in reply O'Mahony assured him that remittances would be on the way soon, and implored him to continue. [24] But no money came and soon he heard that the *Emerald* had ceased publication.[25]

Kickham's disappointment was great. He was mid-way through writing *Knocknagow* and only about one third of the full work he planned had been published.[26] He completed it without any certainty of publication. When it eventually did disappear, in June 1873, the credit was due to A. M. Sullivan who, despite the author's unconcealed hostility towards himself and his politics, had offered as early as 1868 to publish some of Kickham's writings at his own expense. [27] Hearing that Kickham was unable to dispose of the completed *Knocknagow*, Sullivan approached a number of London publishers on his behalf and when these efforts proved fruitless he had the book printed and published at the office of the *Nation*. [28]

The re-publication of old articles (including some from the *Irish People*) in the *Irishman* was the only aspect of Kickham's literary activity in the months after his release to which overt political significance could be attached. The *Irishman* under the proprietorship of Richard Pigott had carried out a profitable business *coup* by establishing itself as the mouthpiece of advanced nationalism following the suppression of the *Irish People* in 1865. Pigott subsequently let slip no opportunity of strengthening his paper's appeal to fenian sympathisers, especially by publicising the grievances of the fenian prisoners. Kickham at the time of his release was conscious of owing a debt of gratitude to Pigott [29] to whom he referred later in the year as 'an honest and conscientious journalist and patriot'.[30] Allowing the *Irishman* in 1869 to reprint a selection of his previously anonymous articles was a gesture calculated to benefit the paper commercially. However, after these reprints had been appearing for about eight months a rumour spread that the *Irishman* was about to be suppressed and prosecuted for publishing such inflammatory material.[31]   Kickham responded in the correspondence columns in the issue of 11 December 1869. He insisted that he rather than the editor of the paper bore responsibility for the publication of the articles. But the letter was written in a conciliatory tone reminiscent of his defence before the special commission. He argued cogently that a prosecution would be unjustified. The most seditious of the articles, he pointed out, had been included in the preface to *Sally Cavanagh*; the Gladstonian *Daily News* had praised this book and its author in extravagant terms. Would Gladstone, he asked, now bring this same author before the courts to answer for his writings? No prosecution was brought and the series continued for a further three months.

A small number of those pardoned in March 1869 made inflammatory speeches on returning home, but Kickham, who had reservations about speech-making at the best of times, was not one of them. He realised that provocative oratory would have been quite inappropriate coming from the released prisoners, especially as so many of their colleagues were still incarcerated. While Kickham was living in semi-seclusion in Mullinahone in the autumn of 1869, absorbed in writing, there was a series of mass meetings demanding an amnesty for all fenian prisoners. The amnesty campaign was actively supported by most fenian sympathisers, but Kickham took no part. He was invited at least once to attend a meeting; in his reply, while declining the invitation, he assured the organisers that he would be present in spirit.[32] On 15 August Kickham was in Waterford city while an amnesty meeting was being held. It had been poorly advertised, which probably explains how Kickham allowed himself to be found near it. A report on the proceedings stated that 'Mr. Charles J. Kickham was in town during the day, but took no active part in the proceedings, and seemed studiously to avoid observation'.[33]

In the autumn of 1869 a by-election became necessary in the constituency of Tipperary County owing to the death of one of the sitting MPs, Charles Moore. He and another supporter of Gladstone had been returned unopposed for the county in the general election in 1968. The catholic middle classes and farmers who dominated the constituency's electorate had as much reason in late 1869 as a year earlier to support the Liberal government for, true to his word, Gladstone had disestablished the Anglican church in Ireland, and a land act to give farmers greater security in their holdings was on the way. An excellent candidate to carry the Gladstonian banner in the by-election was found in the person of Denis Caulfield Heron, a catholic barrister with a record of support for tenant-right. He was formally invited by the Tipperary town branch of the Tenant League to stand for election and his candidature was endorsed unanimously by the county Liberal club and supported in a public statement by the archbishop and clergy of Cashel arch-diocese.[34]

Like virtually every Irish Liberal at the time, Heron declared himself in favour of amnesty (if not of the strategy employed in the amnesty campaign). That, however, did not endear him to the fenians, who saw Liberal placation of Irish opinion as a menace to Irish nationalism. (The ultimate objective of many amnesty campaigners was not to obtain the release of the prisoners but to embarrass Gladstone's government and the Irish Liberals.) In an imaginative bid to deprive Gladstone of an unchallenged vote of confidence from Tipperary County some younger fenians led by James F. X. O'Brien hit upon the idea of putting up one of the unpardoned convicts as a candidate in the by-election. O'Donovan Rossa was selected; he was the most demonstrative, the best known to the public, and the one who appeared to have suffered most.

Under the old electoral procedures still in operation in 1869 the formal nomination of candidates took place at a public meeting in the county town. If there were more candidates than seats a vote was taken there and then by show of hands. Only if a loser in this vote refused to accept the verdict was a poll arranged. Here, too, the voting was open.

At the Tipperary County nomination meeting in Clonmel on 22 November 1869 a large contingent of fenian sympathisers was present and two of them duly nominated O'Donovan Rossa. The others were sufficiently numerous (or sufficiently intimidating) to secure Heron's defeat on the show of hands. [35] In calling, as he then did, for a poll Heron could feel confident that the full electorate of the county would reverse the decision of an unrepresentative and manipulated gathering. The fenians who organised the nomination-day *coup* initially intended not to contest the poll, but the momentum generated carried them on to do that.

The majority of Tipperary voters faced a difficult choice. They were eager for the Gladstonian reforms represented by Heron. At the same time they sympathised with the sufferings of the fenian prisoners highlighted by the amnesty campaign and represented in the election by O'Donovan Rossa. Both sides brought all available pressure to bear on the unfortunate electors. Heron had all the advantages of social influence (including the support of a number of landlords), something that the opposition lacked. Rossa's candidature was advanced originally by pressure from people who did not have enough property to qualify for votes themselves, and who were the most enthusiastic supporters of amnesty and all that it represented. For the most part their pressure was less sophisticated than that used by the other side.

Mullinahone provides an interesting example of the 1869 by-election conflict. The parish priest, Father Thomas Hickey, canvassed the electors of the parish for Heron but less than a dozen seemed to have responded positively. They gathered at his residence on election morning so as to travel together, as

Kickham with Annie and Josie Cleary, probably 1869. (From photograph in the *Tipperary Annual* 1912).

Yours faithfully

Charles J. Kickham

An etching for the frontispiece of *Sally Cavanagh*.

830

The place took her hands in his, &, continuing to look
earnestly into his face, said:

" But you will come back & see my father again ?"

" Well, maybe I would" replied with a sorrowful smile, as he
clasped her hands tenderly between his. "An' whenever you think
uv old times, an' the old neighbours, I hope you'll remember
that Mat Donovan uv Knocknagow was your friend, an'
an' always, Bessy. Ay, "he added, gulphing down his emotion,
' a friend that'ud shed the last dhrop uv his blood for you."

He rushed out of the house, leaving Bessy standing in the
middle of the room, as if she were spellbound.

" Call him back, Fanny," she said hurriedly to her little sister.
" Tell him I want to speak one word to him."
The child overtook Mat Donovan before he had gone many yards
from the house, & brought him back, and discovered

"Mat," said Bessy Morris, speaking calmly and thoughtfully, "was
it you put the advertisement in the paper? I thought it might
be a girl I knew in Dublin, who came out last summer."

" Well, it was," he answered.

"And you came to America for nothing else but to find me?"

VOL. 5.   NEW YORK, APRIL 16, 1870.   NO. 115.

Knocknagow;

OR,

The Homes of Tipperary.

BY CHARLES J. KICKHAM.

[Entered according to Act of Congress, in the year 1870, by the Emerald Publishing Co., in the Clerk's Office of the District Court of the United States for the Southern District of New York.]

PART I.—CHAPTER XI.

It is right that we should follow the two gentlemen with whom we parted some hours ago on their way back from the old castle.

Mass was nearly over when they arrived at the cottage; and Richard quieted his conscience for losing it, by persuading himself that his absence was a case of necessity.

A table in the hall, raised to a sufficient height by means of two chairs upon the back of which it rested, served the purpose of an altar.

Mr. Lowe was again struck by the fervor of the people who filled the hall and kitchen, while not a few knelt on the frozen ground outside the hall door. He was not a little surprised to see Hugh Kearney, officiously assisted by Phil Lahy, "serving Mass."

Piloted by Richard he got into the hall, the people making way for them as they went on, into the parlor where Father O'Neill was still hearing confessions.

Mr. Lowe sat in the window seat next the door, where he could see the altar and the officiating clergyman. He saw that he was too late for the sermon he was so anxious to hear, as Father Hannigan was in the act of taking off his vestments.

But though Father Hannigan had delivered his regular discourse after the first gospel, it was his habit to address a few homely words to the people, at the conclusion of the Mass, upon what we may call local and individual topics. He now turned round and began, in his deep, *big* voice with:

"Now what's this I was going to say to ye?"

He pressed the fore-finger of his left hand against his temple, as if trying to recall something that had escaped his memory. Mr. Lowe thought he was about giving up the attempt in despair, when he suddenly jerked up his head, exclaiming—

KNOCKNAGOW.—"THE PRIEST EXHORTING HIS PARISHIONERS."

The first appearance of *Knocknagow* in print.

VOL. 5.   NEW YORK, MARCH 12, 1870.   NO. 110.

Knocknagow;
THE HOMES OF TIPPERARY.

BY CHARLES J. KICKHAM.

[Entered according to Act of Congress, in the year 1870, by the Emerald Publishing Co., in the Clerk's office of the District Court of the United States for the Southern District of New York.]

FIRST PART.—CHAPTER I.

IT is Christmas Day. Mr. Henry Lowe has just opened his eyes, and is debating with himself whether it is the gray dawn, or only the light of the young moon he sees struggling through the two round holes in the window shutters of his room. He has slept soundly, as well he might, after a journey the day before of some eighty miles on the outside of the mail coach, from the metropolis to the town of ——; supplemented by an additional drive of a dozen miles in his host's gig to his present not uncomfortable quarters.

The young gentleman knows little of Ireland from personal experience, having spent most of his life in what is sometimes oddly enough called "the sister country."

Mr. Henry Lowe is at present the guest of his uncle's principal tenant, Mr. Maurice Kearney. The visit was partly the result of accident and partly a stroke of policy on the part of the young man's mother. Her brother, Sir Garret Butler, owned—at least nominally—extensive landed property in the South of Ireland; and the prudent mother was trying to induce him to give her son the agency. And Mr. Kearney having gone to Dublin to see the landlord about the renewal of his lease, it was agreed that the young gentleman—whom we intend to introduce to the reader when he gets out of bed—should accompany him on his return home, and spend some weeks among his uncle's Tipperary tenantry.

And so we find Mr. Henry Lowe half buried in down, this clear Christmas morning, in the best bedroom of Ballinaclash cottage—for so Maurice Kearney's commodious, if not handsome, residence is called.

He had just settled the question with which the moon, and was relapsing into slumber, when it suddenly occurred to him:

KNOCKNAGOW.—" THE FAR-FAMED KNOCKNAGOWAN DRUMS SHOOK THE WINDOWS OF THE OLD TOWN OF KILTHUBBER."

Knocknagow with American illustrations.

was the custom, to the polling station at Cashel. Some distance
from Father Hickey's residence their cars were halted by a large
contingent of parishioners who were not themselves qualified
to vote but who were ardent supporters of Rossa. In place of
proceeding to Cashel the would-be voters were induced to retire
to a public house and to remain there until evening with the
'Rossa-ites' in close attendance. During the day the parish
priest, enraged by news of what had happened, arrived outside
armed with a pistol, but he failed to release the captive voters
and retired after a disedifying encounter with some of the
'kidnappers'.[36]   Perhaps the day-long detention was possible
because the voters concerned were happy enough with the
arrangement. Faced with a painful choice between two causes
both of which they supported, most of the county's electors
remained at home on polling day. Over 6,000 had voted in a
by-election in Tipperary in 1866, but on 25 November 1869
only just over 2,000 exercised the franchise. Of these
O'Donovan Rossa secured a majority of just over 100 votes.
Despite the low poll, Rossa's election was a substantial propaganda victory for extreme and anti-Gladstonian nationalism.

   On 10 February 1870 the House of Commons declared
O'Donovan Rossa unfit, as an unpardoned felon, to sit in
parliament, and another by-election was called.[37]   Heron was
again a candidate, but the backers of O'Donovan Rossa were
at odds about how they should act. Some favoured nominating
him again.[38] However, there was little to be gained by a repetition of the earlier victory, and with the voting so close a defeat
was quite possible next time around. Besides, participation in
the by-election could be construed as acknowledgement of the
validity of the action of the commons in rejecting Rossa, and
in any case, many fenians were basically unhappy about involvement in parliamentary elections. Placards were posted in mid-
February calling on nationalists to ignore the by-election. At
this juncture Thomas P. O'Connor of Laffana, Cashel, suggested
the nomination of Charles J. Kickham.[39]

   O'Connor had become friendly with Kickham in the 1850s
when they were both connected with the *Tipperary Leader*.
O'Connor had been an active fenian in the early 1860s, but he
had become disillusioned with James Stephens at an early
stage and sided with A. M. Sullivan against the IRB in the years

1864-5.[40] Quite exceptionally, he continued to enjoy a close friendship with Kickham despite this. The putting up of a radical candidate for election to parliament was the kind of move that appealed to his flamboyant and restless character; he had none of the orthodox fenian's qualms about parliamentary elections, and his closeness to Kickham enabled him to take liberties with the Mullinahone man that others would not dare to assume. In Clonmel courthouse on 19 February O'Connor and Thomas Mackey of Templemore formally nominated Kickham, who was supported by a large majority on the show of hands. Once again, Heron called for a poll; it was fixed for 26 February.[41] O'Connor subsequently claimed to have obtained Kickham's consent before the nomination meeting, though on the understanding that he would take no more part in the contest than the imprisoned Rossa had done.[42] Other sources insisted that Kickham was nominated without his consent.[43] The truth would appear to be that Kickham was entreated by O'Connor to accept a nomination and that he decided to remain passive, neither objecting nor giving formal approval.

In the week between nomination and polling Kickham was under pressure from various sources to withdraw formally from the contest. Some of his own relations were among Heron's strongest supporters, [44] belonging as they did to the interest groups most closely attached to the Liberal alliance — the clergy, large tenant farmers and the professions. The latter were represented by the Crean brothers. As a young catholic barrister anticipating much enhanced prospects of preferment under Gladstone's regime, Michael Crean had much in common with D. C. Heron. Indeed, he had quite recently presented himself as a candidate in a by-election in Waterford, but had withdrawn in favour of the veteran nationalist P. J. Smyth.[45] This could be seen as having set an example of disinterestedness for Kickham. Thomas Crean, the doctor, travelled from Clonmel to Mullinahone on a number of occasions to persuade his cousin to withdraw and give Heron a clear run. Eventually he was shown the door and subjected to some of Kickham's invective.[46] There was talk subsequently of an offer from Heron to subscribe six or seven hundred pounds to the fenian prisoners' relief fund if Kickham would withdraw. T. P. O'Connor claimed that this sum was to have been paid over to Richard Pigott (who was alleged to have a way of retaining portions of such monies for himself).[47]   Whatever the explanation, Pigott and some of the *bona fide* fenians then associated with him on the *Irishman* did encourage Kickham to withdraw in the days immediately after nomination. They were able to argue that as late as the previous week the fenians had been calling on the people to have nothing to do with the election.[48] But there was a popular groundswell — transcending fenianism — in favour of Kickham's candidature. It was an enthusiastic popular movement with a strong nationalistic content, and so was a source of joy to Kickham, and not at all because he himself was its hero. He hesitated to call a halt, even at the behest of the leading fenian strategists. But neither did he compromise himself as he felt he would have done by active participation in the campaign.

By contrast with what happened in the first contest, Heron and his followers were well prepared for the second by-election. In addition, the police, with large-scale military backing, were all set on this occasion to protect his supporters on their way to the polls. The Liberal candidate had carefully avoided giving any offence to popular feeling. His election address pointed out that he had refrained from lodging a petition against Rossa's return in November, though he could have done so with confidence of success and of being awarded the seat himself. Instead he had accepted the popular verdict given in November; it was parliament that had rejected Rossa.[49]   Heron stood to gain by taking this conciliatory approach, but on the other hand his cause was damaged by dissatisfaction with Gladstone's long-awaited land bill, which had been published on 15 February but did not contain as large a measure of tenant-right as had been expected.

The other side again lacked influential supporters and money, but its most striking handicap was the want of any positive indication from the candidate. When he did eventually break his public silence, his words were not of much assistance to those campaigning on his behalf. The *Freeman's Journal* of 26 February 1870, polling day, carried the text of a letter from Kickham to Pigott dated 24 February, and obviously intended for publication. It revealed enduring doubts about the advisability of his candidature and concluded with this assertion: 'I'm not going to leave the seclusion in which I choose to live, even for an hour.' In other words, he would not take his seat if elected. He subsequently told T. P. O'Connor that he wrote the letter because he was sure he would be defeated and he wished to provide his followers with a good face-saving excuse. [50]

Just over 3,300 voters came out on 26 February, which was about 35 per cent of the electorate. The campaign on Kickham's behalf was very successful in the centre and south of the county. From the polling stations at Tipperary, Cashel and Thurles he obtained a total majority of almost 800 votes. This was slightly reduced by defeat in Clonmel by a margin of just sixty votes. However, Kickham's supporters were poorly organised in the north of the county, and at Nenagh barely 100 of more than 900 votes cast were for him. The overall result gave Heron a majority of four, later revised to thirteen.[51]

The small margin of defeat allowed those who were so inclined to hail the result as another moral victory for advanced nationalism,[52] but it also made Kickham's refusal to co-operate all the more galling for his campaigners. A small effort on the candidate's part would surely have secured the few extra votes needed for victory. In February 1870 Kickham passed up a glorious opportunity of becoming a pioneer of abstentionism and a figure in public life.

The latter was something Kickham was incapable of rising to (stooping to, he might have said himself). He did, however, take delight in the success of the popular movement in his own part of the county. Although Father Hickey canvassed for Heron from the altar on Sunday 20 February, his tone was apparently quite moderate, reflecting awareness of strong contrary feelings in the congregation. A contingent of soldiers arrived in Mullinahone on polling day to conduct Heron's supporters to Cashel, but their journey was in vain: not one voter from the parish was willing to go against the tide. Earlier, dozens of Kickham supporters had set out from the village in convoy. That evening bonfires blazed on Slievenamon and in the streets of Mullinahone. One of them was opposite the parish priest's gate but 'Father Hickey passed through the crowd showing no sign of displeasure, and the people took no notice whatever of him', according to an observer. [53] Spirits were high because the full result was not known and the majority achieved in Cashel was assumed to be an indication of countywide success. Locally at least, it had been a famous victory for democracy — even if only in one of its more limited senses. 'The people are growing in independence', Kickham wrote to John O'Mahony: 'Think of what it would have been like in the old days with the priests and the landlords in the same camp.' [54]

After the declaration of the result O'Connor and Mackey (without Kickham's consent) lodged a petition against the election of Heron on the grounds that the clergy had used intimidation on his behalf and that Government agents had delayed telegraphic messages sent by Kickham's supporters on election day. They may have had the makings of a reasonably good case, but they lacked the money and the legal support to put it forward effectively. The petition was tried in Nenagh on 27 and 28 May before Baron Hughes. The petitioners' case was obviously poorly prepared: many necessary witnesses had not been summoned, or did not attend, and most of those who did were poorly briefed. Summing up, counsel for the petitioners conceded that most of the charges in the petition had not been proved.[55] After that the verdict could not be in doubt.

The most troublesome feature of losing was that the unsuccessful petitioners were responsible for the costs. Questions had been asked about the financial security of the petitioners before the trial and to remove these doubts a protestant gentleman of nationalist tendencies, George Roe, had lodged £500 as security on their behalf.[56] After the trial Roe had to be repaid and the balance of the costs, another £400 plus, had to be met. In addition O'Connor and Mackey were responsible for the debts outstanding on both Rossa's and Kickham's by-election campaigns. These had been very inexpensive campaigns by contemporary standards. The election agents on the 'national' side had provided their services free of charge (such people customarily received large payments from the candidate). Those who voted for Kickham and Rossa travelled to the polls at their own expense and received none of the customary refreshments at the expense of their favoured candidate. However, there were hefty election fees to be met and unavoidable expenses for printing of placards and the like.

Richard Pigott at the *Irishman* office had been receiving

subscriptions for a Tipperary election fund since November 1869,[57] but even if he did pass on all that he received, it made little enough impression on the aggregate debts. After the popular enthusiasm had died down the bills remained to be paid. The section of society best at lighting bonfires was the least well equipped for subscribing to election funds. Although he had no legal responsibility in the matter, Kickham took it upon himself to help in the effort to pay off the debt. This involved him in a long and difficult fund-raising campaign for which he acted as treasurer. Appeals, raffles and bazaars reduced the debt but only very slowly.[58]   In 1873 T. P. O'Connor left his business and his family and went to America where, by giving lectures and by otherwise reaching Irish-Americans who could be persuaded to contribute, he eventually succeeded in collecting the amount required to pay off the debts arising out of the Tipperary by-elections.[59]

After his release in 1869 Kickham was determined to settle in Mullinahone in the family home and to breathe his native air, as he put it,

> in the midst of scenes from which nothing could have tempted me to stray but a call the neglect of which would have made life insupportable. I am AT HOME. Opposite my window is an old ruin . . . and it has from my infancy possessed a strange fascination for me. Beyond I have a glimpse of the hills, every foot of which is as familiar to me as the streets below. I move my chair and the chapel cross looks in upon me . . . .[60]

Lack of income did not immediately disturb this idyll which (insofar as it had a basis outside Kickham's idyll-inclined mind) was founded more on human than on material surroundings. 'Wherever I turn', he wrote, acknowledging the immense good-will and affection of the people, 'I am greeted with something more deep and touching than mere popularity'.[61] Above all, the happiness of his little world came very soon to depend on his two young nieces, Annie and Josie Cleary – 'my sister's children, whom I see at play in the garden among the budding shrubs and the spring flowers'.[62] He would, according to T. P. O'Connor, 'bestow the fondest endearments' on them when they returned in the evening from school at the Convent of Mercy in Drangan.[63] When he went walking, one would cling to each of his arms. They learned the manual alphabet so as to over-come the barrier of his deafness and in due course they were called upon to act as interpreters between their 'Uncle Cha' and visitors who found communication with him impossible. [64] Above all, they eagerly read and responded to his literary work as it came from his pen. They entered so intimately into the making of *Knocknagow* that their efforts to influence the development of the plot are recorded in the author's dedication. It reads as follows: 'I dedicate this book about the homes of Tipperary to my little nieces, Annie and Josie, with many regrets and apologies that in spite of all their entreaties I was obliged to "let poor Norah Lahy die".'

However, even if he shunned public life and was apparently engrossed in writing, [65] Kickham was as attached as ever to revolutionary politics, and as the years passed he became more and more deeply involved in the new fenianism of the 1870s.

SALLY CAVANAGH;

OR,

THE UNTENANTED GRAVES.

A TALE OF TIPPERARY.

BY CHARLES J. KICKHAM.

"The pride of a peasant; yet England's proud queen
Has less rank in her heart and less grace in her mien".
DAVIS.

DUBLIN:
W. B. KELLY, 8 GRAFTON STREET.
LONDON: SIMPKIN, MARSHALL, & CO.
1869.

All Rights reserved.

The title-page of Kickham's first book

Chapter Seven

GUIDING THE NEW FENIANISM

The fenian organisation underwent major upheavals during Kickham's imprisonment. Stephens, after his escape from Richmond Jail in November 1865, kept up the strength and the hopes of the movement for another thirteen months by promising that he was about to launch the long-threatened rebellion before the end of 1866. When he admitted to the American fenians in December 1866 that he could not meet his pledges his credibility was demolished. Others moved in a confused and un-coordinated way to fulfil Stephens's promises and led the fenian movement in Ireland not so much into disaster as into fiasco in the rising of March 1867. Morale was shattered, and for a great many of the rank and file the organisation simply ceased to exist. But there were many eager to build anew.

Stephens had ruled the IRB in a dictatorial and arbitrary manner that could have been justified only by success. When he fell fenians on both sides of the Atlantic, who had long felt the need for a more representative form of government within the home organisation, resolved to end one-man rule. February 1868 witnessed the formation, following months of preparatory work, of a body calling itself the supreme council which purported to be the representative government of the Irish Republican Brotherhood.[1] The prisoners pardoned in March 1869 had the choice of supporting the supreme council or renewing their allegiance to Stephens (then resident in Paris), who insisted that he was still the one and only fenian chief. They threw their weight behind the supreme council, which in the summer of 1869 was remodelled and given a new constitution. This course was advocated strongly by younger members of the group, notably James F. X. O'Brien and James O'Connor, who resented the manner in which James Stephens had kept them down in the old days.

Kickham found the choice more difficult. Even before his release his views had been canvassed and at that stage he was non-committal. He had always known Stephens to have faults, he said, and he had not been silent about them; but good done should not be forgotten.[2] He was persuaded later that nothing would satisfy Stephens but 'the old thing'. 'That decided me', he told John O'Mahony: 'He has been wronged, but I will never consent to his playing *that* role again'.[3] For many long years Stephens harboured resentment against those who abandoned him, and he was particularly hostile towards Kickham after 1869 – as, of course, he had been up to 1861 or even 1863. In 1877 friendly approaches from Kickham, in a private capacity, provoked scathing comment from Stephens:

> The gentle soul!, . . . the double dealer, . . . my most effective enemy, . . . the gentle Pishogue . . . . I have been thinking over Mr. Kickham's message and everything considered, I decidedly decline seeing him under the circumstances. If he knew how to think, feel and act like a gentleman he would never have dreamed of sending me so boorishly insulting a message; but the Creighton of Mullinahone is only a half-cultured villager![4]

Kickham was closely associated in 1869 with the *Irishman,* as were also almost all of the young men involved in consolidating the supreme council. They were in contact with him and had the benefit of his advice and support, but we cannot be certain how much influence he exerted over their work. Years after Kickham's death John O'Leary made an important reference to this part of his colleague's career. In his published recollections, he said, he had treated of Kickham's part in the old fenianism that collapsed in 1867. There had subsequently been a new fenianism and although the time was not yet ripe to write its history he could lift the veil sufficiently to say that from his release to his death Kickham was its guiding spirit. 'Nearly all that was good in that came from his inspiration and nothing that was bad in it ever found favour in his eyes.'[5] Considerable weight must be given to this statement by a man who had a notorious aversion to hyperbole. But O'Leary was still in prison in 1869, and his testimony does not prove that Kickham was a leader or even a member of the supreme council in that year. He did become a member during the 1870s, and then president and leading light of the council for years before his death.

The 1869 constitution prescribed that the supreme council should have eleven members, one chosen by each of the IRB's seven organisational divisions (the four provinces of Ireland, the north of England, the south of England and Scotland) and four co-opted honorary members.[6] Three officials elected by the council — the president, the secretary and the treasurer — constituted an executive. As this executive was empowered to act by majority decision, no individual exercised untrammelled power. However, the president was clearly pre-eminent. When the constitution was amended in 1873 the majority rule remained but the president was given the duty of directing 'the workings of the Irish Republican Brotherhood in all its departments, subject to the control of the supreme council'.[7] And he was declared to be 'in fact as well as by right, president of the Irish Republic'. A veteran IRB man, John Daly of Limerick, in his scattered and truncated recollections written about forty years later, indicated that when he attended his first supreme council meeting (as representative of Ulster) Charles Kickham was also a member.[8] He gives no date for this, but his haphazard chronological references elsewhere suggest 1872 or 1873.[9]

However, our knowledge of the personnel of the supreme council before 1875 is very scanty and there appears to be no incontrovertible evidence available for Kickham's membership before 1874. At a meeting of the council in that year he was either appointed or reappointed to the presidency,[10] an office which he held to the end of his life (and one occupied a generation later by Thomas Ashe and — most effectively of all — by Michael Collins). Kickham was a member of the council by virtue of co-option[11] Not being a provincial representative, he did not have any local organisational duties to perform. A reading of the fragmentary extant records of supreme council proceedings in the mid-1870s[12] suggests that his presidential responsibilities caused him little trouble: he was present only at one of the four meetings for which we have the attendance. However, it is evident from other sources that Kickham attended most diligently to IRB business, though his deafness undoubtedly discouraged attendance at meetings. The indications are that at this time Kickham's participation in council meetings was limited even when he was present: another member was appointed to the chair, and the president sat through debates unable to hear them. Before a decision was made, the substance of the discussion was communicated to him by the finger alphabet.[13] His reaction could wield great influence over the meeting, but one can easily see why he may have skipped meetings if they were not crucial.

How did a revolutionary organisation, sworn to perpetual preparedness for military revolution come to choose a deaf, almost blind, literary man as its president? Undoubtedly it was an indication of the exceptionally high regard in which Kickham was held. John Daly's reminiscences[14] bear witness to this as do John Devoy's. In his *Recollections,* Devoy (who admittedly has a superlative for most of the fenian leaders) described Kickham as 'the finest intellect in the fenian movement either in Ireland or America, although his defective sight and hearing prevented the demonstration of that fact in public'.[15]   A fortuitous factor favouring Kickham's advancement was the unconditional nature of his release in 1869. When the next batch of fenians (including Luby, O'Leary and O'Donovan Rossa) was set free in 1871, there were conditions in the patents of pardon: the prisoners concerned were required to leave the country and not to return to the United Kingdom until the expiry of the term of their original sentences under pain of re-imprisonment.[16]   So Kickham was the only leading fenian of the mid-1860s still living in Ireland in the 1870s. The new IRB could see advantages in having a man of that vintage at the head of their affairs, all the more so if he had qualities of character and intellect that commanded general respect.

The most striking development in Irish politics in the early 1870s was the emergence of Isaac Butt's home rule movement. It campaigned for an Irish parliament to look after purely Irish affairs, but with Ireland continuing as an integral part of the United Kingdom and with the London government retaining control of defence, foreign relations and other 'imperial' matters. This formula (and the commitment to realising it by constitutional means) was rejected outright by doctrinaire fenians, but within a short time it was shown to be acceptable to the Irish nationalist community generally. Nor were all fenians intransigent doctrinaires; if the new movement gave serious promise of achievement, it would surely draw away a large section of the IRB's support. Not surprisingly, some fenians were strongly tempted to nip home rule in the bud, just as James Stephens had done with rival nationalist movements in the early 1860s. However, it was difficult to attack Isaac Butt in the name of fenianism. He had made himself virtually the tribune of the movement by his defence of the leaders before the courts from 1865 to 1867, and by his well-advertised headship of the amnesty campaign. He was now challenging the dominance over Irish political life established in 1868 by Gladstonian Liberalism (the great enemy of nationality in fenian eyes because it might conciliate the Irish people to the point of contentment). And, although home rule fell far short of the separatist ideal, it did at least put a national objective before any sectional or sectarian demand and to that extent it ministered to the susceptibilities of 'advanced' nationalists.

Butt assiduously cultivated the goodwill of the extremists. Prior to the meeting of 19 May 1870 in the Bilton Hotel, Dublin, at which he launched the home rule movement (with the formation of the Home Government Association), he had a conference with two members of the supreme council. They promised 'benevolent neutrality' towards his project on the part of the IRB.[17] As a consequence he was able to give his hearers in the Bilton Hotel the following assurance: 'As for the men whom misgovernment has driven into revolt, I say for them that, if they cannot aid you, they will not thwart your experiment.'[18]

Three years later when Butt took his movement a crucial step forward by the formation of the Home Rule League he again made sure of fenian tolerance. It was especially important on this occasion as the new league was to be launched at a large and widely-representative conference to which disgruntled elements could readily gain access. Whatever the deficiencies of the IRB in the early 1870s, Butt knew that it was still well equipped for the disruption of public meetings, either physically or by means of resolutions embarrassing to the platform. Butt purchased freedom from extremist disturbance by entering into an agreement with some members of the supreme council.[19]   They undertook to give his movement three years in which to prove itself. On the third day of the conference, 20 November 1873, a pair of senior IRB men (C. G. Doran and John O'Connor Power) brought forward a resolution (which was supported by Butt and carried by the meeting) that sought to commit home rule MPs returned at the next general election to be ready 'in any emergency that may arise . . . to take counsel with a great national conference to be called in such a manner as to represent the opinions and feelings of the Irish nation'.[20]   The prospect of a future assembly of the same kind at which they would again have an effective veto, and perhaps enhanced tactical advantages also, induced the fenians to look benignly on the conference of November 1873.

The understanding with Butt gave rise to much dissension within the fenian ranks. Some, such as O'Connor Power, interpreted the arrangement as giving them permission to become fully involved in the Home Rule League while remaining in good standing with the IRB. Justification for this course could be found in the revised constitution of 1873 which pledged the brotherhood — while awaiting patiently the perhaps distant day of battle — to support 'every movement calculated to advance the cause of Irish independence, consistently with the preservation of its own integrity'. [21]   O'Connor Power stood successfully for home rule in a by-election in Mayo in 1874. A home ruler returned for Cavan in the general election of that year, Joe Biggar, was admitted to the IRB after his election and was subsequently co-opted to the supreme council. [22]

There must have been majority support in the council at this time for the mixing of parliamentary and underground politics. The idea of an open and constitutional campaign being complemented by some kind of military organisation in one all-embracing national movement had been advocated over and over again in the 1860s by a range of Irish nationalists from John O'Mahony by way of P. J. Smyth to G. H. Moore. James Stephens would have none of it, because it would have meant interference with his despotic authority over the IRB. In the

1870s this determination to have no truck with public movements was kept alive and was elevated to the level of a principle
by a section of the fenian leadership in apparent contradiction
of the constitution of 1873. These people certainly had a point
as far as actual membership of parliament was concerned: as
MPs and IRB men, Biggar and O'Connor Power were in the
ludicrous position of owing sworn fealty to both Queen
Victoria and the Irish Republic.

While Kickham was clearly inside the 'intransigent' camp, his
precise attitude needs further definition. He was not positively
hostile to the home rule movement as some were, for example
Denis Dowling Mulcahy and John Daly. Kickham was well-
disposed towards Butt and regarded his movement as an honest
effort in the national interest.[23]   He himself did not expect it
to achieve anything, and he deplored the idea of thoroughgoing nationalists wasting time on it, but he felt that home
rulers should be left to discover for themselves the futility of
their efforts.

While other fenians were identifying themselves with the
campaign of the home rulers in the 1874 general election,
Kickham made a gesture that was calculated to demonstrate his
fundamental lack of confidence in the movement. As the campaign got under way an invitation to stand for election was sent
by telegraph from some nationalists in Cork to John Mitchel,
exiled since 1848 and then living in New York; in reply he stated
that he would not object to being nominated for election and
that if elected he would return to Ireland.[24] No man had ever
denounced more passionately or more loudly than Mitchel the
sending of members to Westminster; he had fathered in 1847-8,
and had nurtured during his exile, a fanatical tradition of total
rejection of any compromise with British institutions. (Kickham
was profoundly influenced by this, but he had not hesitated
to remonstrate publicly with Mitchel for his attacks on
fenianism.)[25]   Mitchel's rhetoric of more than quarter of a
century constituted implicit and total denunciation of the
policy of home rule. There was no possibility that he would
take his seat in parliament if elected.

When news of Mitchel's willingness to stand in the elections
became known moves were made by extreme nationalists
(though not necessarily fenians) in Tipperary to nominate him

for the county. Kickham publicly supported his candidature. The by-election candidate of 1870 who had refused to ask votes for himself could justify encouraging people to go to the polls in 1874 on the pretext that, as the old form of election had given way since 1872 to voting by secret ballot, a man could now vote as he pleased without fear of victimisation.[26]   Of course, he was not advocating parliamentary politics, but rather the use of parliamentary elections to undermine parliamentarianism.

The campaigns on Mitchel's behalf in both Cork and Tipperary were poorly organised and in each county he was defeated by home rulers.[27]   Nevertheless, Mitchel broke his long exile in the summer of 1874, despite the risk — which did not materialise — of arrest as a felon who had not served his full sentence or obtained a pardon. He returned to America again after some weeks, but not before he had made arrangements to stand for any suitable by-election that might occur: he even left the text of an election address in the hands of his brother-in-law, John Martin. When a seat became vacant in Tipperary County in January 1875, Kickham took the lead in putting forward Mitchel's name. He did so with the full co-operation of C. G. Doran, who was by then secretary of the supreme council. [28] While Mitchel made haste to return from America, a vigorous campaign was conducted on his behalf. Home rulers with pretensions to the status of thoroughgoing nationalists were embarrassed (which pleased Kickham and Doran). Thus, John Martin, home rule MP for Meath since 1871, felt obliged to support his brother-in-law's candidature even though he recognised that Mitchel despised home rule.[29]   (Mitchel's election address proclaimed mockingly that, of course, he was in favour of 'home rule', by which he understood the sovereign independence of Ireland.)[30]   And John O'Connor Power, MP found it advisable to publicly advocate Mitchel's election, for the sake of the gesture it would be, but went on to say that he disagreed with Mitchel's policies. [31]

The campaign was so successful that no sustained opposition was forthcoming and Mitchel was the one candidate nominated. He was declared elected on 16 February while still crossing the Atlantic. [32] Next day he reached Queenstown, and during the week that followed he was the centre of enthusiastic popular demonstrations in Cork, Tipperary and Clonmel. In the latter town Kickham was alongside him when he appeared on the balcony of Hearn's hotel to acknowledge the plaudits of a large assembly of well-wishers.[33]   When Mitchel was declared ineligible, as an undischarged felon, to sit in parliament. Kickham favoured leaving the matter to rest and ignoring the subsequent by-election.[34] Mitchel himself declared that he would stand as often as he was disqualified.[35] On the second occasion he was opposed by a conservative candidate, Stephen Moore, who was badly defeated in the voting on 11 March but was subsequently awarded the seat by the house of commons.

That, however, did not happen until 25 May and in the interval the possibility of yet another by-election kept up a lively interest in the constituency. Events took another turn when Mitchel died on 20 March. Who would take his place as the agreed popular candidate? Within a week County Tipperary parish priests, including Father Hickey of Mullinahone, were being circularised by the parish priest of Rathdrum, County Wicklow, Father Richard Galvin, in advocacy of his local protestant squire, a comparatively unknown young man named Charles Stewart Parnell. Father Galvin laid great stress on the Parnell family's anti-Tory record and mentioned that Charles had been a candidate for Dublin County in the 1874 general election on a platform of 'home rule, denominational education and fixity of tenure'.[36]   In other words, here was a man of property (and one who could therefore meet his own election expenses) prepared to represent the moderate-nationalist, catholic and tenant-right aspirations which the clergy shared with the majority of the county's voters. But anything like popular unanimity would be impossible if the advanced nationalist element in the county objected. Recognising this, Father Hickey canvassed the opinion of Kickham.[37] Parnell's name was not new to Kickham; a few weeks previously he had subscribed £20 to the Mitchel election fund (of which Kickham was treasurer) and he had ostentatiously advertised the fact in the *Freeman's Journal,* while at the same time dissociating himself from Mitchel's policies.[38]   A decade before, his sister Fanny had contributed patriotic verses to the columns of the *Irish People,* at a time when Charles Stewart was unconcerned with either politics or poetry.[39] Kickham's justification for his

John and James O'Connor

advocacy of Mitchel was that the old intransigent would never take his seat in parliament. If Kickham was going to support anyone in the next by-election, he would have to be another intransigent; but young Mr. Parnell obviously could not get to Westminster quickly enough. However, Kickham was patronisingly tolerant towards him, being gratified that somebody of his background should espouse even a milk-and-water version of nationality In his reply to Father Hickey the fenian leader spoke well of Parnell, while declining to support him.[40] Before the end of the month John Martin was dead leaving a vacancy in the representation of Meath, to which constituency Parnell immediately turned his attention. He was MP for Meath before the end of April.

He had passed out of Kickham's area of interest, but only to return with greatly enhanced stature. The remainder of Kickham's career was to witness a complicated and bewildering series of interactions and manoeuvres involving parliamentarians and fenians that culminated in Parnell 'striding like a colossus' at the head of the Irish nation while a (metaphorically) bloody but unbowed Kickham led the tiny rump of die-hards bereft of influence that was the IRB of 1882. In the unfolding of these events the Irish in America played a crucial role.

By the mid-1870s the Fenian Brotherhood in America was in irreversible decline and was already reduced to a shadow of its former self. The one American organisation devoted to fenian principles that showed signs of life was Clan na Gael, also known as the United Brotherhood. Not many of the exiled fenian convicts supported the Clan but the most dynamic single individual of them all did. He was John Devoy. After remaining neutral for a number of years in the conflicts between rival Irish revolutionary organisations in the USA, the supreme council of the IRB in 1875, overlooking the question of legitimacy, ratified a 'compact of agreement' with Clan na Gael.[41] This undoubtedly caused Kickham some regret, as it amounted to the abandonment by the IRB of the Fenian Brotherhood, still espoused by John O'Mahony and other friends of his. Soon the leaders of the Clan, particularly Devoy and Dr. William Carroll, were displaying concern about the apparent abandonment of fenian principles by some of their new-found allies on the supreme council.[42] They had in mind particularly O'Connor

Power who visited the USA in 1875 and 1876 as an IRB envoy. In March 1876 O'Connor Power and Devoy became involved in a public altercation.[43] Clan na Gael had already decided to take practical steps to bring a more revolutionary group into control of the supreme council.[44] As part of this project Devoy sent Denis Dowling Mulcahy to Europe; he carried a message for John O'Leary in Paris and another for Kickham.[45] We have no details of the letter to Kickham but from the reply we can deduce that it suggested that something be done to get the IRB back on the path of revolution.[46]

The reply also gives the impression that the two men had not previously been acquainted, and that Devoy had opened the exchange with some justified trepidation. While being courteous and civil, Kickham's letter contained a series of rebukes. Devoy, who had raised the topic himself, was ticked off severely for his pragmatic plea of guilt at his trial in Dublin all of ten years before:

> If you were the greatest general that Ireland ever saw, and if you could with certainty effect your escape after having pleaded guilty, I'd tell you not to do it if I were consulted . . . . I wish to heaven ye would all agree to pitch Machiavelli to the devil. In fact if you ever allude to this matter publicly you will be doing more good for Ireland by acknowledging your error and saying you are sorry for it than if you were able to organize an Irish legion of 50,000 strong.

Next there was a swipe at the self-righteousness of the Irish-American organisations:

> Ye seem inclined to absolutely ignore the existence of a patriot of the right sort anywhere in the wide world outside the island of Manhattan.

The Clan na Gael was cut down to size:

> If I saw fifty or a hundred regiments armed and disciplined in the U.S., I'd believe in the affair with the Gaelic name; and having done so much themselves, I'd admit their right to look after other people. To tell the honest truth, I don't believe there is much reality in it.

On the issue of the moment Kickham was equally scathing:

> This senseless attack upon H.R. [Home Rule] is a blunder both as regards time and manner — to say nothing of other

considerations. It was always intended that a second conference should be called, and pressure put upon the MPs to
take the first fitting opportunity to withdraw from the
London parliament. If the thing must be blown up it
should be done from within. Those assaults from outside
will only leave the advanced party open to the charge of
breaking up a movement that might effect *some* good,
while they themselves are all to do nothing . . . . In fact all
this anxiety to keep us from going 'down to perdition' is
to my mind a proof that ye are helpless and in your help-
lessness strike at a shadow in order to persuade yourselves
that ye are doing something.

Notwithstanding these reprimands Kickham and Devoy were
not at this time in fundamental disagreement on their attitude
towards fenians participating in home rule politics. But,
ironically in view of subsequent developments, Kickham saw
some good in the home rule movement that Devoy had not yet
noticed. Kickham's annoyance may have been aggravated
because Devoy's officious advice came just at the time when
the intransigents on the supreme council were on the point of
doing something about the compromisers. The pressure from
America undoubtedly strengthened this resolve. In any case
the three years' understanding was approaching its conclusion,
and the home rulers on the supreme council also wanted to have
future policy clarified.[47]   In the weeks after his exchange of
letters with Devoy, Kickham travelled to Paris to discuss
matters with John O'Leary — a sure sign of something serious
in the air.[48] He was back in Dublin for a meeting of the supreme
council on 28 May 1876. Here Doran proposed a resolution that
would terminate the policy of co-operation with the home
rulers on the expiry of the three years. This was opposed
strenuously by O'Connor Power and others, and after 'great
discussion' the question was shelved until the next meeting, on
the understanding that Butt would be reminded in the mean-
time of the undertakings about an open convention of
nationalists.[49]   When the supreme council met again on 10
August the prospect of such a conference was no closer and
Doran was adamant that there would have to be a decision this
time. The council voted by a majority of one that:

the countenance which we have hitherto shown to the

home rule movement be from this date and is hereby withdrawn, as three years experience of the working of the movement has proved to us that the revolutionary principles which we profess can be better served by our organisation existing on its own basis pure and simple, and we hereby request that all members of our organisation who may have any connection with the home rule movement will definitely withdraw from it their active co-operation within six months from this date. [50]

O'Connor Power, who would have voted against, missed the meeting due to illness. Kickham was absent, and probably for the same reason: he was at this time suffering from bouts of illness that kept him low for days at a time. [51]   He would certainly have supported the resolution which he had probably helped to draft: in the period from 1875 to early 1878 Doran and himself were accustomed to concert their actions and attitudes on important fenian matters. [52]   In accordance with Kickham's policy, the resolution called a halt to fenian involvement in the home rule movement but without offering any menace. 'Active co-operation' was to end but 'benevolent neutrality' could continue. After the passing of the stipulated six months four members of the supreme council — O'Connor Power, Biggar, John Barry and Patrick Egan — resigned or were expelled because they refused to abandon 'active co-operation'. [53]   Many believed that the breach could be repaired, that a round or two of negotiations and some diplomatic bargaining would lead to compromise and the securing of a comprehensive concept of the IRB. Those who thought that they were reckoning without Kickham. He was quite happy to have discussions, but there would be no compromise on his part. If the others did not submit, there would be nothing for it but 'to part friends after mutual explanation'. [54]   He was determined that, whatever the consequences, the IRB would consist exclusively of men free from attachment to other political bodies. Within a few years the consequences for the strength of his own organisation were to be disastrous, and even as early as 1877 they were serious.

It is significant that few of the effective fenian 'party managers' in Ireland or Britain were on the intransigent side. These were the people who had the ability to recruit members on a large scale, extract subscriptions and service from them, and keep them eager or at least interested. They knew what would and what would not 'sell', and they felt in the mid-1870s that withdrawal from home rule politics would seriously damage the marketability of fenianism. Kickham himself had never been an organiser in that sense. The rank and file of local fenianism had flocked around him in the early 1860s in an instinctive way, not because he had built up any formidable organisational fabric around himself. Even as president of the supreme council he could not bring himself to act as an 'organisation man'; that would have been totally against his instincts.

Was Devoy, the great organiser, not aware that the policy which he was pushing on the supreme council was forcing out the men of managerial calibre? Or, did he know what was happening, and proceed with the intention of getting the management into his own hands or those of his agents while Kickham continued as a figurehead president? The 'compact of agreement' ratified in 1875 had given Clan na Gael certain rights of inspection over the accounts of the IRB. There was more to follow. As early as June 1876 Devoy wrote to Kickham unveiling a plan for the creation of a revolutionary directory with supreme authority over both Clan na Gael, and the IRB. (And Devoy intended to dominate the revolutionary directory.) Kickham did not think the idea was workable and in any case it greatly discouraged him to find this new project being suggested so soon after the conclusion of the long drawn-out debate about the 'compact of agreement'.[55] 'I always regarded this propensity to make radical alterations as a sign of weakness', he declared. Once again the criticism implicit in Devoy's suggestions provoked him to counter-attack:

> Another bad symptom is a mania for criticism . . . . It seems all the fashion nowadays to cover with scorn and ridicule the men who have clung to the old ship and done their best to keep her afloat. You, Rossa, O'Leary, Luby, O'Mahony, 'T.P.' (in the *Democrat*) are in wonderful accord on this subject. Yet I believe it would be very easy to shut you up one and all.

After further rounds of discussion and procrastination the revolutionary directory was set up in 1877, but in practice counted for very little.

This formal linking of the IRB and Clan na Gael was another body-blow for John O'Mahony's Fenian Brotherhood. O'Mahony himself died in poverty on 6 February 1877. Kickham had ever been eager to proclaim his regard for the man, as in his first letter to Devoy: 'I wish ye all thought well of O'Mahony. I believe no Irishman ever had a better claim to the name of patriot than he has.' Now all could show their regard. Following the precedent set at the time of Terence Bellew McManus's funeral in 1861, his remains were brought to Ireland for burial and every opportunity was given to the people to pay their respects and by implication express support for the deceased's ideals. Though it did not make the same impact as McManus's obsequies, O'Mahony's funeral was impressive — a reception at Queenstown, train journey to Dublin, lying-in-state at the Mechanics' Institute and *cortège* to Glasnevin. Although the occasion was ignored by parliamentarians and churchmen, tens of thousands of people turned out to watch the funeral procession on Sunday 4 March.[56] Kickham delivered an oration, prefacing it with a characteristic remark about the unsuitability of a graveside for oratory. He misjudged the pitching of his voice, so that very few heard his speech, but the prepared text was circulated subsequently to the newspapers. O'Mahony's career was briefly summarised and his place in the tradition of Irish resistance indicated. There was some strong symbolism, marking a stage in the evolution of fenian graveside oratory towards its climax in Patrick Pearse's panegyric for O'Donovan Rossa thirty-eight years later:

> No, we have not failed: John O'Mahony has not laboured and lived in vain. And, oh, how he did love Ireland! She was his mother, his queen, his idol, his all the world! And in the long roll of her patriot martyrs and confessors no name will shine with purer lustre than his. Let us dry our tears, and standing round the bier of our dead chief, let us resolve and watch and labour and unite, always trusting in the justice of God, who has implanted this immortal longing for nationhood in the hearts of our people, and hopefully remembering that

'Freedom hath arisen
Oft from prison bars,
Oft from battle flashes,
Oft from patriot's life,
Oftenest from his ashes.'[57]

Kickham's IRB activities in the period we have been considering here necessitated a considerable amount of travelling,
though this was made difficult by his regular bouts of ill-
health and by the poor eyesight which now rendered it
impossible for him to go out alone in unfamiliar surroundings.
Paris was a favourite venue for fenian conferences because
O'Leary and others were prohibited from entering the United
Kingdom. Kickham was there in 1876 and possibly in 1877
also.[58] There are no details of either visit. Most of the journey-
ing was within Ireland. He made a number of trips to the Cork
area, to be near C. G. Doran, then resident at Queenstown. He
stayed with Doran, or more frequently near Cork city at the
house of James F. X. O'Brien, a veteran of the rising of 1867
and president of the supreme council some time before
Kickham took up the office. On at least one occasion Kickham
was in Belfast as the guest of Robert Johnston, supreme council
representative for Ulster. Inevitably there were many journeys
to Dublin, even if, as we have seen, he was not a regular
attender at supreme council meetings.

However, there are also indications of many visits to relations
and family friends that can have had nothing to do with IRB
business. The truth is that the bliss and contentment which
Kickham sought in Mullinahone after his release from prison
were short-lived. Of their nature such idylls are seldom fully
realised. In this case normal disillusionment was aggravated by
the difficulties about property and income already referred
to. Thomas developed a drink problem and was betimes 'going
on' unbearably (in an unspecified way), so much so that Charles
was inhibited from inviting friends to stay in Mullinahone.[59]
However, it was the departure of his nieces for America in
September 1876 that finally undermined his domestic
happiness. In one way or another Kickham during his lifetime lost perhaps half-a-dozen women on whom he leaned, but
he missed none of them more than Annie and Josie Cleary. He

should have been mentally prepared for their leaving. He had warned Thomas in one of his prison letters to keep the little nieces in mind of their eventual emigration to join their parents, but he subsequently forgot to keep himself reminded. In 1876 the girls' step-brother Michael Cleary was sent from America to take them back with him. The task of breaking this news to their uncle was entrusted by the parents to T. P. O'Connor whom they had met during his stay in America. O'Connor's recollection of the event was recorded forty-five years later and so has to be treated very cautiously but, even allowing for colourful exaggeration and the heightening of the occasion by memory, his description shows that Kickham suffered a traumatic shock.[60]   Writing to O'Donovan Rossa, Kickham alluded to 'an accumulation of troubles which at times I fear will prove too much for me. The most crushing of these trials is the parting with my two nieces: I defy you even to *imagine* it'. [61]

In the same letter he asked Rossa about getting paid literary work to do for some American journal or newspaper: 'a little money got by honest work' would spare him 'inconveniences and humiliations'. The inference is that he suffered embarrassment at this stage in obtaining financial support. Alexander's business fortunes had gone from bad to worse. By 1876 his wholesale firm had gone out of business.[62]   No principal had been repaid on the loan of £750 obtained from John T. Hinds and on 22 February 1876 he filed a petition for the sale of the Mullinahone property in the Landed Estates court.[63]   In an effort to maintain the family connection, Charles borrowed enough money to pay off Hinds and had the property transferred back from Alexander to himself.[64]   That was merely solving one problem by creating another. Charles now had to cope with the servicing of a large debt. He kept up the hopeless struggle for more than a year and then bowed to the inevitable; in December 1878 the property was sold to W. P. Lyons of Mullinahone for £900, which apparently just covered the debt including interest and charges.[65]

This sale referred to landlord's interest in twenty or so houses in Mullinahone and did not directly affect the possession of the family residence. However, Kickham had ceased to live there. He had remained on in an almost-empty house after the departure of the Clearys in September 1876. After a few weeks he left for Cork to stay with J. F. X. O'Brien and C. G. Doran for some months.[66] Sometime early in 1877 he went to live at Alexander's residence, 11 Belgrave Square, Dublin.

Chapter Eight

THE INTRANSIGENT

When the purge within the supreme council was taking place in 1876-7 Kickham was certain that the home rule movement had already failed and that this would be universally recognised within a short time.[1] Instead, parliamentary politics gained a new lease of life and popularity from the campaign of obstruction in the house of commons which got into top gear in the spring of 1877.[2] The use of these tactics by Parnell, O'Connor Power and others did not immediately achieve anything positive but it showed that the Irish members need not remain forever a helpless minority. Obstructionism involved a departure from the standards of gentlemanly behaviour traditionally expected of MPs, and this Isaac Butt refused to countenance. As 1877 progressed a deep and bitter division between Butt's supporters and Parnell's became more and more evident. In an attempt to paper over the cracks the Home Rule League decided to hold a conference, which met, after months of infighting, on 14 January 1878.

This was the institution on which some fenians had laid such great store for a number of years in the expectation that they would have a say in its deliberations. When it came, admission was by invitation only, and far from there being any seats going a-begging for 'advanced nationalists' or other interested outsiders, there had been a titanic struggle between the rival factions within the council of the Home Rule League about the allocation of invitations.[3] Exclusion of fenians did not worry Kickham, who wanted nothing to do with the conference, but IRB men still hankering after involvement in the public movement saw a great opportunity being lost. And despite the resignations and expulsions, this way of thinking was still represented on the supreme council, at least in the person of Matt Harris, who had succeeded the expelled O'Connor Power as representative of Connacht.

The *Irishman* of 8 December 1877 carried an open letter from Harris to Kickham on the subject of 'Mr. Butt's conference'. The writer simulated great dismay that Kickham had not been invited to attend. He proposed that Kickham should call an alternative conference and put the resolutions made there to a great public rally. He had much else to say besides. The letter was written without Kickham's fore-knowledge and constituted an unusual mode of communicat-tion between members of the inner circle of a secret conspiracy. Clearly Harris, having failed so far to make headway within the supreme council, was endeavouring to strengthen his hand for the next round by an appeal to the rank and file. He was trying to force Kickham and the supreme council to start some form of public movement. Kickham effectively countered this move with a letter to the editor a week later which included a re-statement of his attitude to the home rule movement and a re-affirmation of his belief that it was not an appropriate forum of endeavour for a fenian.

> So far from being angry with Mr. Butt for shutting me out
> from his 'coming conference', I hereby return to him my
> very sincere thanks for having done so. It quite obviates
> the necessity of protesting instead of, as Mr. Harris seems
> to think, making protest an imperative duty.[4]

Just at this time the supreme council was acquiring a new member who was to advocate an open IRB even more ably than Harris could, and who would not be contained by a well-turned rebuke in the *Irishman*. He was Michael Davitt, who was released on ticket of leave in December 1877 after serving over seven years in penal servitude for fenian activities in England. Almost at once a place was found for him on the supreme council, as representative of the North of England.[5] Davitt and Kickham were opposites in so many ways that an easy relationship could not be anticipated. We have already adverted to the totally different ways in which they each reacted to the adulation heaped on them as released prisoners. Davitt's round of receptions and lectures in December 1877 and in subsequent months scarcely impressed the president of the supreme council. Davitt's personality was outgoing, Kickham was an introvert. Especially in the months after his release, Davitt was searching and probing to find a political and social policy, Kickham was set on a fixed, narrow course. There was a universalist dimension to Davitt's thinking, even on national questions; Kickham measured the world in terms of Irish nationality. In brief, Davitt was flexible and adventurous, Kickham rigid and set in his ways. They shared the burden of physical handicap, but even this raised a bizarre barrier between them. Being by now totally deaf and almost blind, Kickham could exchange ideas directly with someone in his company only by means of the finger alphabet — and of course his interlocutor would have to have learned this manual code. It so happened that the version of the alphabet adopted by Kickham entailed the use of both hands; and Davitt's handicap was that he had only one hand, having lost an arm in a factory accident as a youth.

Given his open-mindedness it was not surprising that Davitt considered the possibility of co-operation between the public and secret national movements. His cogitations might not have been of any great consequence but for the fact that Clan na Gael was revising its policy in this area. Here was a quite amazing turnabout, and it was due largely to the startling political attraction of Parnell. Through the obstruction campaign his charisma as a leader had been revealed and it appealed more immediately to extremists than to moderates. In any case, using that developing tactical skill that gave his charisma full scope, Parnell was making friendly overtures to the 'advanced' men. In August 1877 he had met a close friend of John Devoy, J. J. O'Kelly, who wrote to the Clan na Gael leader in enthusiastic terms about the attractions of Parnell's leadership.[6] Devoy took note and when, some months later, his colleague, Dr. Carroll, crossed the Atlantic as a Clan na Gael envoy, one of the many items on his lengthy agenda was a meeting with Parnell. They met in Dublin in January 1878 and again in London in March and, although nothing definite emerged, Parnell did not say anything to make himself less acceptable.[7] During his Irish tour Carroll had a great deal of contact with Kickham: they spent considerable time together at T. P.

O'Connor's house in Laffana. Kickham must have been aware of the contacts with Parnell; he hardly approved, but we have no evidence that he objected. Carroll remained long enough to carry out a thorough investigation and revamping of the fenian organisation in Ireland and Britain. By his own account he found the IRB in a sorry state and left it a much healthier organisation. Doran (who resigned) was replaced as secretary of the supreme council by a young man named John O'Connor, and a number of serious rifts within the organisation received attention.[8]

In July 1878 Davitt, having gone around the Irish and the Irish-in-Britain lecture circuits earning some money for himself, proceeded to the USA to exploit the market there, and to visit his mother. He met Devoy and they found that their minds were both turning to the same idea (about which they reassured one another), namely, that an active alliance between fenianism and Parnell's parliamentarians was both possible and desirable.[9] On 25 October 1878 Devoy with the minimum of consultation purported to commit the fenians to supporting Parnell, on certain conditions. He launched this 'new departure', as he called it, by means of a dramatic telegram, despatched to the fenian James O'Connor at the office of the *Irishman* in Dublin, with instructions that it be shown to Kickham and, if he approved, passed on to Parnell to whom the main part was addressed.[10]   Therein Parnell was told of the conditions on which he would be supported. These amounted to the adoption of a more nationalist and radical line in parliament.

Whatever the conditions, Kickham could not have approved and it seems that the telegram was not forwarded to Parnell.[11] That did not matter greatly as Devoy at once announced his new departure in the press with banner headlines. He was endeavouring to present Kickham with a *fait accompli* and he probably felt confident that because of the revolutionary directory arrangement and Carroll's re-organisation of the IRB, that body was effectively in his pocket and would have to go along with his initiatives. (Devoy's offer was nominally made on behalf of the Irish-Americans but it was being made implicitly for the IRB also.) He was not allowing for Kickham's single-mindedness and obstinacy. Devoy was indeed dealing very high-handedly with the home organisation and especially with

Kickham. The Clan na Gael man had until quite recently been badgering the IRB about its toleration of members tainted by parliamentarianism, and the supreme council had taken drastic steps to remedy the situation. Now Devoy had performed a *volte face* and he apparently expected the IRB to do likewise. Even if change were thinkable, Kickham could not take it at this pace.

At first Kickham cannot have been certain just what form of support Devoy was offering Parnell. James O'Connor left Dublin for Paris very soon after the arrival of the telegram, presumably to consult O'Leary who had attended the meeting of Parnell and Carroll the previous March. [12] On 8 November O'Leary wrote to Devoy asking pointed questions about the telegram which, he said, was 'only very partially intelligible to me, or apparently, to some of our friends, notably Kickham in Ireland'. [13] The press comments of Devoy and Davitt in the days after the despatch of the telegram made it clear enough what was involved. The proferred 'support' included participation in parliamentary election campaigns and even the sending of fenians to parliament. By all the unwritten rules of political infighting Kickham should have admitted defeat and gone along with the new departure, for the Clan na Gael leader held all the trumps. But, lacking the instincts of the practical politician, Kickham stuck doggedly to his objectives even after they had become unattainable.

The *Irishman* of 9 November carried an unsigned leading article written by Kickham which made an all-out assault on the idea of fenian involvement in parliamentary politics, and on the entire new departure. Having first set out at some length the clear evidence from the American papers that Devoy and Davitt were advocating extremist participation in parliamentary politics, Kickham explained the principles which made this unacceptable.

> Let us consider what all this means. The national party are to send nationalists — that is fenians or members of the revolutionary party — as representatives of Ireland to the English house of commons. But a nationalist must of necessity cease to be a nationalist when he enters the house of commons. He will be assumed to have freely acknowledged the right of England to rule Ireland, since he

will give her government counsel and advice, and enable
them to say that all classes [and] creeds and every variety
and shade of Irish opinion finds free representation and
untrammelled expression in the imperial parliament . . . .
He will have to take an oath of allegiance to Queen
Victoria and will thenceforth be bound in honour to assist
in the preservation of the integrity of the British empire.
It would therefore appear to be impossible that an Irish
nationalist — using the word in its proper signification —
could become a member of parliament without renounc-
ing his national opinions.

And even if it were possible to play the dual role in parliament,
a nationalist could do nothing that the home rulers already in
the commons could not do, Kickham claimed. He saw other
difficulties. Could nationalists be elected in sufficient numbers
to make any impressive demonstration of nationalist feeling?

We doubt it. The franchise is still a packed jury — as it has
always been — in Ireland, and the full volume of the
popular voice in favour of popular candidates cannot
be heard in their favour. Besides, there is a certain hostile
influence of the clergy to be taken into account. On the
whole we think it unlikely that with the present limited
franchise a majority of nationalist representatives at the
elections could be secured. Failure in that respect would
moreover seem to indicate weakness where no such
weakness really exists.

In any case he did not accept that the election even of a large
number of extreme men would be taken as an indication that
the country was in a frenzy of intransigence. On the contrary
it would be assumed that these men had seen the error, or at
least the futility, of their ways and that they had come to
accept the perpetuity of the English connection. As for Parnell
and his obstructionists about whom Devoy and Davitt were
becoming so enraptured, Kickham wished them well, but was
convinced of the futility of their efforts.

Mr. Parnell tells us that with twenty members pledged to
a 'policy of combat' he could do almost anything, and a
home rule organ told us last week that with such a force
the Irish party could 'disrupt' the house of commons —
blow it and all that is in it to metaphorical smithereens.

Well, let them try by all means; we heartily approve, though we are dubious of the success of their enterprise. But for all that we hold to the conviction which has stood the test of lengthened experiment, and has never been controverted, that the English parliament is no place for an Irish patriot — or nationalist — any more than it is for an Irish gentleman.

With Kickham digging in his heels in this fashion there was an obvious need for dialogue within the top echelons of fenianism and arrangements were made for a meeting of the supreme council with Devoy in attendance to be held in Paris. The meeting began on 19 January 1879.[14] In a significant change from earlier practice, Kickham took the chair himself. This was possible because the new secretary of the council, John O'Connor, had gone to the trouble of learning the manual alphabet. As everything that the others said had to be conveyed to Kickham in this way by O'Connor, it is not surprising that the meeting dragged on for four days. [15] This outrageously inefficient means of proceeding served to emphasise the difficulty of influencing Kickham and provided the chairman with unique opportunities of wearing down opposition. After hours of frustration while all the routine items of a supreme council meeting were taken first, the impulsive Davitt apparently tried to communicate directly with Kickham. The chairman became excited and, it seems, withdrew his hand from the possibility of any further interruption while he expounded some basic truths.[16] Eventually Davitt was overcome by annoyance and allegedly rushed sobbing into the streets of Paris. The meeting was resumed next day but only after John Devoy and John O'Leary had mediated between the two handicapped patriots. [17] At the end of the four days Kickham, supported by a majority of the supreme council, was still holding his ground on the principal issues: the IRB would not become involved in parliamentary politics and no IRB member could enter parliament. However, the advocates of the new departure had gained one useful concession: the supreme council would allow individual IRB members who were so minded to participate in election campaigns.[18]

By John Devoy's own account, which cannot be entirely misleading, Kickham and himself got on exceptionally well together in Paris, although their previous correspondence (not to mention Devoy's initiative which was the root of all the fuss) might have raised fears of a less than happy first meeting. Characteristically, Devoy applied himself at once to learning the manual alphabet (which he mastered in twenty-four hours, according to himself), and this would have off-set a great many faults in Kickham's estimation. Devoy accompanied Kickham and John O'Connor as far as Dieppe on their way back to Ireland. [19]

Devoy himself had further business in France. The supreme council had created a difficulty for the 'new departure', but he was still determined to get Parnell working on a political programme that the Clan na Gael could support and influence. He could assume with some justification that he would eventually circumvent the supreme council's opposition; in any event, IRB members had been accorded permission to participate in the forthcoming campaigns. And John O'Leary, as venerable an old fenian as Kickham himself, had become an ardent admirer of Parnell's style and, it seems, almost a personal friend, and heartily approved of fenian co-operation with him. [20]

So Devoy remained on in France for the next stage of his programme, a conference with Parnell to seal their understanding. They met at Boulogne in early March 1879. Devoy came away more convinced than ever of the possibility of 'advanced nationalists' having a working relationship with Parnell, though the astute parliamentarian did not commit himself to anything tangible or specific. [21] Pushing ahead more vigorously than ever, Devoy risked arrest to come to Ireland. Before the middle of April he met Parnell once again, this time in Dublin. During the following three months he travelled through Britain and Ireland revitalising the organisation of the IRB and, no doubt, neutralising the influence of the supreme council on the question of co-operation with parliamentarians. [22] He had yet another meeting with Parnell on 1 June 1879 in Dublin. Davitt was present, and Devoy subsequently claimed that final agreement was reached there on the shape of the new departure. By the end of 1879 Devoy was back in America and, as he had hoped, Ireland was caught up in public agitation led by Parnell and Davitt.

However, it was different from what had been planned at the

beginning of the year in that it was focused on, indeed totally preoccupied with, the land question. Since the autumn of 1877 bad harvests and poor markets had gradually brought on an agricultural depression, especially in Connacht, as a consequence of which many tenants faced financial hardship and even the threat of eviction for inability to pay rents. Davitt saw the possibility of converting this distress into a mass movement on political lines. In 1879 the harvest was again bad and in October Davitt persuaded Parnell to join with him in forming — and to accept the leadership of — the Irish National Land League. The stated objects of the league were to achieve a reduction of rents, and to secure 'the ownership of the soil by the occupiers'.[23] In effect it became the agent of a revolution against landlordism. Kickham initially disapproved of Devoy's 'new departure' proposals because they envisaged IRB involvement in something inappropriate for fenians, namely political agitation, and when the 'new departure' was transformed into the Land League his attitude became even more hostile. Not only did he oppose fenian involvement in the land war as inappropriate, but he denounced the agrarian campaign as being wicked in itself. Some explanation is needed of how a man who had been passionately concerned with the land question since youth could have opposed so vehemently the most effective land agitation seen in Ireland in his lifetime.

Kickham at all times assumed that a satisfactory and final solution to Ireland's agrarian problems would go hand in hand with the vindication of Irish nationhood. To say that he saw land reform as the first item on the agenda of a free Irish government would not convey fully the close link that he perceived between the agrarian and national questions. To Kickham's way of thinking there was a mystical union between the two. Nevertheless, he joined eagerly in the work of the tenant protection societies in the early 1850s, believing that something useful could be accomplished even in advance of political independence. Even after the movement had proved a disappointment he recommended its tactics. In the autumn of 1862 (writing under a pseudonym in the *Irishman*)[24] he advocated self-defence to tenants threatened with eviction on a County Kilkenny estate. He had himself, he said, a particular idea of how 'the life of the country' might be saved, but

Kickham at the age of forty-eight.

pending the implementation of that he was prepared to support action that would gain interim reliefs. What he had in mind, he said, was that people should band together and bargain directly with the landlords to obtain security in their holdings. He was changing emphasis rather than basic policy when he wrote in the *Irish People* of 2 January 1864 that the failure of the tenant right movement of the 1850s proved the futility of hoping for any amelioration 'as long as Ireland continued to be ruled by a foreign government'.

The changed emphasis in 1864 was in accordance with the general policy of the *Irish People*. The fenian leadership had a number of good tactical reasons for insisting that freedom would have to come before land reform. But even if the question had to be put on the long finger, that did not preclude discussion, as numerous leading articles in the *Irish People* demonstrate. These were predominantly anti-landlord. Peasant proprietorship was declared over and over again to be the ideal and inevitable solution.[25] In future the landlords would be emigrating and not the people, was how it was put on one occasion.[26] Because of his well-known concern with rural and agrarian matters, it is sometimes assumed that Kickham was responsible for these articles and so for the land policy enunciated by the *Irish People*. That was not the case. T. C. Luby had conducted a short-lived newspaper [27] in the 1850s that had anticipated the tone of the *Irish People* on the land question. But both Kickham and O'Leary, were unwilling to join during the 1860s, or later, in a blanket denunciation of the country's landlords, or of landlordism.

The notion that Kickham was not opposed to landlordism as such will surprise many people who assume that his support for the tenant protection societies and the accounts of rural suffering and upheaval in his novels prove the opposite. He depicted landlords who inflicted cruel injustice on their tenants, such as Grindem in *Sally Cavanagh*, Somerfield in *Knocknagow* and Perrington in a later work, *For the old land,* but he also had 'good' landlords, and much of the misery that he painted was not inflicted by landlords at all, but by unscrupulous agents acting without the knowledge of the landlords, and by ambitious tenants. Looking at nineteenth-century Irish rural society, Kickham did not see the pattern discerned by other nationalist propagandists — an alien landowning aristocracy exploiting native tenantry. Instead he saw Irishmen (of various social ranks) exploiting other Irishmen because they were permitted, encouraged or even forced to do so by alien and unjust laws.[28] Landlords might be the worst offenders but that was merely because they had the greatest scope. Kickham knew that tenant farmers were quite as diligent and ruthless in clearing labourers and smallholders from the countryside as were the landlords.

In refusing to see landlordism as an evil Kickham differed from the emerging consensus of nationalist mythology, and from the attitudes of John Mitchel, who influenced him so much on other points. He was following instead another strand of Young Ireland tradition, one that owed much to Thomas Davis. Through Davis's writings readers of the *Nation* in the 1840s had been brought into contact with the contemporary English reaction — represented in different ways by Disraeli and Carlyle — against utilitarian industrial society. This involved the glorification of an imaginary, pre-industrial past when all the social orders lived in mutually-beneficial harmony. It was a new version of an old English rhetorical theme that was familiar to a young man steeped in Swift and Goldsmith. Kickham, like John O'Leary, acquired and retained the hankering after a society in which the aristocratic class would be joined in sympathy with the populace and willing to lend its talents and privileges to the pursuit of a common objective. (In *Knocknagow* and elsewhere there is evidence of Kickham's regard for landlords 'of the old stock', such as the Butlers of Ormond, as opposed to recent purchasers of property who looked upon landowning as a commercial venture.) For Davis, Kickham and O'Leary that common objective could only be an independent Irish nation. To give credibility to hopes that the ascendancy would join with the masses in the assertion of Irish nationhood a simplified version of eighteenth-century Irish history was occasionally conjured up; in this the Volunteers of the 1770s and 1780s were depicted as a happy combination of protestant and catholic, landlord and peasant, putting Ireland first and sweeping all before them to establish Grattan's parliament. Kickham resurrected that vision in a ballad published in the early 1860s called 'Eighty years ago' in which the aged

Myles O'Hea speaks the following lines:

> I was a beardless stripling then, but proud as any lord;
> And well I might, in my right hand I grasped a freeman's sword;
> And though an humble peasant's son, proud squires and noble peers
> Would greet me as a comrade — we were the Volunteers. [29]

At the height of the land war Kickham sought to have that ballad re-published in some newspaper or journal with a readership among the landlord class, in an attempt to tell landlords that the attack they were facing was not a true manifestation of Irish nationalism. [30] Kickham's hopes for a repetition of the supposed harmony of the Volunteer era, together with his sympathy for the landlords, had often weakened; the land war caused him to clarify and reassert his basic attitudes. The sight of the president of the IRB defending the place of the landed aristocracy in Irish society is surely something to reflect on.

Not quite so outdated but equally unappreciated in 1880 and 1881, was Kickham's concern for those at the other end of the agrarian social scale. What precisely an *Irish People* leader-writer intended by 'peasant proprietorship' is not always certain. The term may have meant different things to different people. Many fenians undoubtedly believed that those due to become proprietors after a successful national revolution would include many previously landless people. And that could only mean that some existing landholders would have to do with fewer acres. A strong current of anti-farmer feeling ran through fenianism for a considerable period, as was amply demonstrated in the late 1860s when fenian sympathisers effectively crushed a tenant-right campaign that started up about the same time as the amnesty movement. Kickham was fully in tune with the feelings of landless people. Why so much about tenant right and so little about anybody else's right? he asked rhetorically in one of his few editorial comments on the land issue in the *Irish People*. He pointed out that, although the tenant farmers had good reason to complain, their plight was not nearly as bad as that of the 'labourers and mechanics'. [31] Kickham was very far indeed from lacking sympathy with the farmers, but he saw them in the land war making a gigantic grab that paid as little heed to the needs of the landless as it did to the rights of the landlords. (If every existing tenant obtained fee simple overnight, he remarked in 1881, there would still be a land problem.)[32] The politically active 'labourers and mechanics' of rural Ireland did ask of the Land League what was in it for them, but they threw in their lot with the tenants in return for concessions that were mostly in the realm of rhetoric. If they had realised what exactly was happening the story of these years might have been different. But even the greater part of the anti-farmer element in the IRB was carried away by the momentum of the Land League.

One of the conditions stipulated by Devoy in his 'new departure' telegram was 'vigorous agitation of the land question on the basis of a tenant proprietary, while accepting concessions tending to abolish arbitrary eviction'. At the time this attracted little notice from Kickham, whose attention was riveted on the question of fenian co-operation with parliamentarians. The land agitation took him, like almost everyone else outside of the west of Ireland, largely by surprise. In fact so little advance warning was there of the nature of the impending campaign that Kickham and the supreme council gave permission during the first half of 1879 for IRB members to participate in public demonstrations concerned with agrarian distress.[33] But there was no tolerance a year later when Davitt's scheme had emerged in its full colours; and John O'Leary reversed his attitude to the new departure when he saw it transformed into a land war.[34]

Kickham was not opposed to the distressed peasantry in Mayo or elsewhere organising to save themselves from eviction; in fact he heartily approved of this policy in 1879, as he had in 1850 and 1862. When called upon to support the famous campaign against the eviction of the Meaghers of Kilburry (which set the land war ablaze in south Tipperary), he replied that he knew nothing about the case in question, but that if it was one of 'rack-renting tyranny' everyone should give aid to the victims without, however, having recourse to 'Land League balderdash'.[35]

His fundamental objection to the league was that by presuming to seek a *general* solution to the land question prior to independence it challenged his deeply-held conviction that one objective was unattainable without the other. In addition, he rejected the solution being proposed and the means being used to achieve it. At another level, he may have feared that if agrarian discontent was to be substantially allayed the national movement might lose a potential source of valuable support; but, if he did, the thought was quite unconscious, for he could never admit, even to himself, that nationalism might be grounded on mere grievances. Even if he did harbour this calculation (some constitutional nationalists openly proclaimed it later in the century), that did not mean that he was prepared to sacrifice those tenants in actual distress to the nationalist ideal. As we have seen, he advocated that farmers facing demands for exorbitant rents, or the threat of eviction, should band together to resist the landlord aggressor. The Land League, however, as Kickham saw from the start, was not designed simply to help those in dire distress, but was geared to using the distress as an engine to launch a wider campaign — and one of which he thoroughly disapproved. Disapproval quickly developed into disgust when the campaign came to appear as a war against the landlords fought by increasingly indiscriminate methods. His antipathy was heightened by the sight of so many fenians being distracted 'from their own work', and by his personal animosity towards Michael Davitt.

Devoy ensured that Clan na Gael supported the Land League. When J. J. O'Kelly arrived in Europe early in 1880 with funds granted by Clan na Gael for spending on the purchase of arms, Kickham, O'Leary and John O'Connor were obstructive. With the land war gathering momentum they may have had doubts about what use the arms were intended for. O'Kelly, reporting to Devoy, declared that O'Connor had to humour the prejudices of 'the two incapables'; he was particularly annoyed with Kickham, that 'drivelling idiot', as he called him.[36] This bitter hostility between the rigid fenians and the Land Leaguers persisted to the end of Kickham's life (and beyond). Davitt and one or two others were expelled from the supreme council about the middle of 1880.[37] About the same time the council sent O'Leary to America with the overriding task of persuading Clan na Gael to abandon the Land League. Davitt was there to plead his case, and he won.[38] Whether they lived in Ireland or America, the great majority of Irish people interested in public affairs succumbed to the appeal of the league. So did the greater proportion of fenians, leaving a mere remnant loyal to the supreme council.

Anyone antagonistic towards the Land League had no difficulty finding cause for censure in the lawlessness that spread throughout the countryside during 1880 and 1881 as the land war reached its height. Kickham was appalled. He had never condoned agrarian outrages, though he understood how an individual, maddened by injustice, could be moved to violence. The Land League, however, looked to him like organised outrage. He wrote to a friend that he could not find parallels in Ireland 'unless I fix upon Cut Quinlan or "Brennan on the moor". Seriously the thing is at best only Whiteboyism.'[39] He did not disapprove of 'boycotting' as such. It had been utilised by tenant protection societies in the 1850s and the youthful Kickham had celebrated it in verse. Even in 1880 he advocated its use where there was justification, but the landlord 'should be clearly in the wrong' which was not always the case.[40]

Kickham was especially upset by the threat which seemed to be posed to the rights of property by the actions of the League and even more so by the radical talk of some of its supporters.

The *Irish World* wants to abolish credit — no power to recover debts, no interest, no gold or silver currency — merely greenbacks issued by the state. Some may think that this reform may be helped in Ireland by the refusal to pay debts. But people who refuse to pay lawful debts next *take* what they want. The law that is prevailing in case of debts will be equally so in case of robbery. 'Tis no joke to appeal to the lower instincts of an enslaved people. That's what these agitators have been doing all along.[41]

If there was going to be a free-for-all where would the line be drawn?

I am told that feeling is growing very divided among working men in Dublin and elsewhere — that it would be better for them and their families to have spots of land in the country, and they can't see why they shouldn't get them.[42]

The issuing of the 'No rent' manifesto by the leadership of the Land League in October 1881 (when most of them were in

detention in Kilmainham) confirmed Kickham's worst
suspicions. This call for a discontinuation of all payment of
rent he categorised as 'criminal and cowardly'. [43] Kickham had
one word for the evil which he saw the Land League bring upon
the country — communism. [44]

He was annoyed by the growing Parnell cult, especially the
manifestations brought about by the incarceration. The presentation of an elaborately-decorated quilt to the imprisoned
leader with the promise of a couch to follow provoked Kickham
to sarcasm: Would a chamber-pot be next?

> Are the women bent upon making their prophet the
> laughing-stock of the nations? That jewelled quilt bangs
> Banagher; and it seems a couch is in preparation, which I
> suppose will be a bed of peace whose roughest part is but
> the crumbling of the roses. Who knows what's to come
> next? — possibly some Oh-no-we-never-mention-it miracle
> of art. [45]

Parnell and some of his fellow-leaguers launched their own
weekly newspaper, *United Ireland,* in August 1881. In this, too,
Kickham detected a lowering of standards:

> Strange that with all their money . . . they never get a
> decent article, essay, speech or ballad! This paper is shame-
> fully and brazenly dishonest, which is only saying that it
> truly reflects its proprietors. [46]

A rather peremptory summons to attend a league meeting in
Mullinahone in November 1881 gave him an opportunity to
publish another denunciation of the organisation in the press
and to castigate its masters as men 'wanting in those qualities
of head and heart' to be expected in leaders of the Irish people. [47]

In his last years, as he held out against the rush to Parnell
and the Land League, Kickham was more and more isolated. He
wrote of having foes on every side, 'leaguers, skirmishers,
nihilists, repealers, home rulers, whigs, tories and radicals'.
Being in a minority was nothing new to him, but this time there
were differences. The band of faithful disciples had dwindled
alarmingly. Previously he had been the one buoyed up by
enthusiasm for a cause but now it was the others who were
being carried along by an exciting current. Farmers, shopkeepers, many priests, even his own formerly pro-Liberal
relations (especially the womenfolk) had become flaming

enthusiasts, and after a lifetime of setting alight he was pouring cold water.

His worst apprehensions about the Land League proved to be unfounded. The most virulent phase of the land war was already over before his death in August 1882, and the 'final solution' which emerged gradually in subsequent decades did the minimum of violence to the rights of property. In *For the old land,* written in the mid-1870s, Kickham had depicted peasant proprietorship, established through purchase of the landlord's rights on mutually agreeable terms, as an acceptable development (though he did not suggest that it alone would provide the ideal solution). When purchase eventually did take place it failed to establish any significant new rapport between the populace and the old landowners; neither did it do much to benefit Kickham's 'labourers and mechanics'. But it did establish a farming class as near to Kickham's ideal as any man could reasonably expect reality to conform to his dreams — conservative, tenacious, and a bulwark of nationalism.

Chapter Nine

DECLINE AND DEATH

Although his tastes were never expensive, the experience of poverty was a severe trial for Kickham. Not surprisingly, in view of his background and character, he was extremely sensitive about receiving charity. That is well illustrated by the following exchange of letters with the mother of Oscar Wilde, a contributor to the early *Nation* who had presumed to send him a monetary token of respect on his release from prison:

Lady Wilde begs to offer the enclosed small tribute of sympathy for the sad sufferings of the gifted poet, Charles Kickham. Merrion Square, 6 March 1869.

Mr. C. J. Kickham, while sincerely thanking Lady Wilde for her sympathy, is sorry to be obliged to say that Lady Wilde's note has both pained and surprised him. Would Lady Wilde have offered money to any of the '48 convicts in this way? Mr K. thinks he must have been misrepresented to Lady Wilde. He will feel thankful if Lady Wilde will forward the note, which after much hesitation he thinks it right to return, to the general fund for the political prisoners. Dublin, 9 March 1869.[1]

Within months of this display of self-sufficiency he was looking for journalistic and literary work with which to support himself. That was a comedown for a gentleman, but there was worse to follow. After a promising start he failed to gain a regular income from an occupation in which business acumen (which he lacked) counted for at least as much as talent (which he undoubtedly possessed). One commentator remarked that 'he was not ready at turning the coinage of his mind into the mintage

of the realm'.[2] As his financial situation deteriorated he was
reduced to borrowing from friends, including John O'Leary,
Dr. Thomas Crean and Dr. George Sigerson.[3] By 1878 the
parlous condition of the Kickham family finances was becoming
known in nationalist circles. That autumn, just before the
new departure, Dr. William Carroll suggested to John Devoy
that Clan na Gael should look to Kickham's financial security
as soon as Davitt had been properly provided for through his
lecture tour.[4] In the event, help came from the other end of
the nationalist spectrum; on 12 November 1878 the *Freeman's
Journal* carried an editorial notice stating that the writer had
been shocked to hear that Charles J. Kickham stood in danger
of a pauper's doom due to a loss incurred through a relative.
The writer went on to declare that no Irishman, irrespective of
political opinions, would wish to see Kickham in poverty;
the people would be pleased to hear that plans were afoot to
rescue him. The planning was probably done in the office of
the *Freeman's Journal:* the next day's issue carried short letters
from the editor, Edmund Dwyer Gray, and his assistant, William
O'Brien, announcing their donation of ten pounds and one
pound respectively to the 'Kickham fund'. There is no need to
suspect any subtle political motivation such as a desire
politically to neutralise an extremist. For much of the century
popular Irish newspapers made a practice of sponsoring
subscription funds for various causes and personalities.

Kickham's first public reaction appeared in the *Freeman's
Journal* of 14 November. He was obviously shocked and
humiliated that his poverty had been announced to the world.
He was deeply grieved, he said, that he had not been made
aware of the plan in advance, and he suggested that the
organisers might arrange to have *Knocknagow* re-published on
both sides of the Atlantic and so allow him to feel that he was
not getting money for nothing. However, he did not reject the
idea of the fund and the *Freeman* of the following day, 15
November, carried a list of subscriptions and announced the
setting up of a committee. A steady flow of money arrived
over the subsequent weeks and months from various parts of
Ireland, from England, America and Australia. Subscribers
included Parnell, Butt and Gavan Duffy, five bishops, dozens
of parish priests, and a fellow or two of Trinity College, Dublin.

In County Tipperary a number of local committees were
formed. Over £1,200 was collected altogether.

On 21 February 1879 a deputation appointed by the fund
committee met Kickham in Wynn's hotel, Dublin, to ascertain
formally his wishes for the application of the fund.[5] John
O'Connor acted as interpreter and Kickham suggested — no
doubt by prior arrangement — that the money be handed over
to three trustees, namely, himself, James F. X. O'Brien and a
person to be nominated by the committee. The money should
then be invested so as to produce a yearly income and Kickham
should have the disposal of it at his death.[6] The security chosen
was government stock — but American rather than British —
yielding 4 per cent per annum. A deed of trust was signed on
3 February 1881, with Edmund Dwyer Gray as the third
trustee.[7] By then the land war had opened up a deep gulf
between Kickham and most of the organisers and supporters
of his fund, but he never allowed his debt of gratitude to
modify his political attitudes or pronouncements.

One of the earliest subscriptions to the Kickham fund was
£10 from Thomas William Croke, archbishop of Cashel since
1875. In the accompanying letter Croke had this to say:

Having recently had the pleasure of a long, and, in some
respects, memorable interview with Mr. Charles Kickham
in reference to a matter of vital moment to him, at any
rate, and in a minor degree to myself also, I can safely say
that, apart altogether from and independent of his attractions as an Irish poet, scholar and patriot, I take him to be
of all men that I have ever met about the gentlest, the
most amiable, the most truthful, and the most sorely and
searchingly tried, at the same time that I believe our most
holy mother the church has few more dutiful sons than
he, and none more thoroughly devoted to her interests, or
more resolutely and reasonably faithful.[8]

This remarkable letter brings us to the question of Kickham's
relationship with the church during his later years.

The refusal of sacramental absolution to unrepentant fenians
began in an un-coordinated way in the first half of the 1860s
and there is no record of when it first affected Kickham. Much
would depend on whether or not a penitent felt obliged to raise
the subject himself, and on whether or not a confessor felt

obliged to query penitents on the subject. Whatever might happen under more ordinary conditions, it could scarcely be passed over silently if the penitent was in prison on a charge of fenianism. What would happen then, if the fenian refused to renounce his allegiance, would depend on how the priest inter-preted his own responsibilities and the directives of his superiors.[9] Different prison chaplains took different decisions, and at some stage of his prison career Kickham was admitted to the sacraments.[10]   After his release the problem still hung over him. A solution was made more difficult by the papal decree of 12 January 1870 in which the Vatican for the first time condemned fenianism by name.[11] That must have reduced the number of priests willing to be flexible. In any case Kickham had no interest in finding a way out through flexibility or casuistry. If the church refused him the sacraments he would rest confident in his own good conscience. And yet he longed for the sense of security that the sacraments would give him.

Archbishop Croke shared with Kickham an enthusiasm for the romantic concept of nationality and as a student in Paris in the early 1840s he had been closer to the well-springs than the young Kickham.[12]   (In 1848 he and another young priest had offered to take over the running of the *Nation* after the arrest of Charles Gavan Duffy.) [13] But even if he had drunk as deeply, Croke, unlike Kickham, could hide the symptoms. He dissembled his 'advanced' nationalist feelings sufficiently well to climb steadily up the ladder of ecclesiastical preferment, even disarming the suspicions of that scourge of romantic nationalists, Cardinal Cullen, without whose approbation he could hardly have succeeded to the see of Cashel.[14] Safely established as an archbishop, he gradually gained enough self-confidence to display his true colours, though not until early 1878 did Kickham realise that the occupant of the archepiscopal palace in Thurles was a soul-brother. That revela-tion came in a letter from Croke to the *Freeman's Journal* on the subject of the fenian prisoners (including Davitt) released in December 1877. [15]   The letter provoked a rebuke from Cullen,[16] and raised in Kickham's mind the hope that here was a prelate — in his own native diocese — who could appreciate the dilemma in which the catholic fenian was being placed by

the church. On an unrecorded date in the spring or early
summer of 1878 Kickham made his way to Thurles
accompanied by T. P. O'Connor who could use the finger alphabet and was willing to act as interpreter. We have no source of
detailed information on the ensuing encounter except
O'Connor's recollections put on paper many decades later.[17]

Kickham and O'Connor knocked on the archbishop's door
without prior notice. Croke was not available just then, so an
appointment was made for later in the day. The archbishop
himself greeted them on their return and ushered them into
his parlour. They were put sitting at a table containing a collection of books including a copy of *Knocknagow* pointedly set
apart as if just put down. Kickham explained that the object
of his visit was to get the archbishop's permission for him to be
admitted to the sacraments without abandoning his immovable
convictions about the only effective means of winning freedom
for Ireland. He was adamant that he would die without the
sacraments rather than abandon his political views. Croke
offered a defence of the church's ban on secret societies and
questioned the wisdom of the fenians' physical force policy.
Kickham in reply accused Croke of being under the influence
of the archbishop of Dublin and of being an English bishop
rather than an Irish one. Tempers were high on both sides for
a while but in the end the archbishop gave way. He invited
Kickham to nominate a confessor. Kickham suggested two
names, and Croke selected one of them, Archdeacon Quirke of
Cashel, promising to write to him at once giving permission
for Kickham to be admitted to the sacraments.

That resolved the canonical impediment, and Kickham
presumably went to confession to the archdeacon soon after,
but he still had to find a priest who could be something more
than a confessor; he needed a spiritual guide who could fully
sympathise with him. The search for one confirmed Kickham's
disillusionment with the clergy. Writing on literary business to
Matthew Russell, SJ, editor of the *Irish Monthly,* in 1881, he
let fall this *obiter dictum*:

> I have searched pretty diligently and during a good many
> years to find the priest who would take the trouble to
> learn the 'manual alphabet' in order to facilitate my
> religious duties, not to mention giving perhaps a word of

religious comfort; but that priest has not yet turned up, and I have e'en closed my lantern. I know there are priests who can talk with their fingers because it is part of their *drill*. It is routine and conventionality all along the line, from Mount Melleray to Upper Gardiner Street.[18]

Behind that there was the old story of the world's insensitivity to the needs of the handicapped. However, it seems as if Kickham would have been very difficult to please; the complaint quoted above suggests that he required the attention of a priest who had learned the manual alphabet specifically in order to speak to Kickham himself. Russell made tentative arrangements for a fellow-Jesuit to meet Kickham but we do not know if his efforts met with any success.[19] He regretted subsequently that he had not himself taken the trouble of visiting Kickham.[20]

From his correspondence with Russell we can see that Kickham retained to the last his disgust with the clergy's lack of enthusiasm for his brand of nationalism. 'The spirit that slammed the gates of our monasteries in the face of the Irish postulant still lives', he declared truculently in his opening letter.[21] However he was convinced that there would eventually be a change: 'I'd look upon the appearance of anything of mine in an Irish magazine, edited by an Irish Jesuit, as a glimmer of that good and bright time which is so very, very long coming, but which *will* come as sure as God is in heaven.'[22] A two-sentence passage in another letter to Russell encapsulated perfectly Kickham's life-long attitude to the great questions of religion and politics: 'I feel much the same about my Irish faith as I do about my catholic faith. I am very glad and thankful for myself, and very sorry that so many people whom I like are not in the right road with me.' [23] For Kickham there was just one road — and no questioning.

Russell's commemorative sketches of Kickham in the *Irish Monthly*,[24] based largely on their correspondence in 1881, provide almost all of the meagre insight we have into Kickham's private devotional life. His reading does not seem to have extended to devotional books except when he was in prison, and then only fitfully.[25] Even the bible was mentioned principally in connection with prison: he had one presented by Dr. Crean in Kilmainham, and a new testament lent by the chaplain at Mountjoy.[26]   According to Russell, Kickham, when asked about how he prayed in prison, replied that he said the same prayers as when 'out in the world'; [27] that was not very informative but it was consistent with his constant reluctance to reveal that side of himself. When Russell on one occasion suggested that he might try his hand at composing some religious poetry, Kickham's reply showed that he had no desire to share his thoughts and feelings on theological topics with a public audience. 'I believe I have', he wrote, 'too much reverence and too little piety to attempt a purely religious subject; or might I say that I am too much of a believer and too little of an artist.' [28]

If true, the following anecdote — given by Russell — about the day Kickham was convicted in Green Street would shed some light on a dark area.

As he was led away to his cell, something on the ground attracted his notice, and he picked it up. It was a little paper picture of the Blessed Virgin, and he kissed it reverently. 'I was accustomed to have the likeness of the Mother of God morning and evening before my eyes since I was a child', he said to the warder. 'Will you ask the governor if I may keep this?'.[29]

The cloying sentimentality is not untypical of Kickham; however, there is no other evidence that he was devoted to holy pictures and the story may tell less about Kickham's spirituality than it does about Russell's, or that of a young lady named Rose Kavanagh from whom Russell got the incident. It is an improbable story though not an impossible one. What matters is not its truth but the authenticity of the impression which it gives, and no final judgment on that is possible because Kickham successfully veiled that aspect of his life.

Although the trust for Kickham's fund was not formally established until 1881, he began to draw a regular income in 1879. He could henceforth afford to pay a modest rent for his accommodation and he no longer needed to draw on the debt of hospitality owed to him by Alexander. In November 1879 he went to live at the house of James O'Connor, 2 St. John's Terrace (otherwise Montpelier Place), Blackrock, County Dublin, which was to be his last home.[30] O'Connor, a native of Wicklow, had worked on the commercial side of the *Irish*

People and was one of those arrested in September 1865 and subsequently sentenced. After release, at the same time as Kickham, he entered enthusiastically into the work of the IRB and played a major part in establishing the predominance of the supreme council. Very soon after his release he was employed as sub-editor by Richard Pigott, proprietor of the *Irishman*. He was still in that employment in 1879 and co-operating with Kickham in the supreme council's propaganda campaign against the 'new departure'. (His younger brother, John, was secretary of the supreme council.) O'Connor's wife, Molly, had the tact and kindness necessary for dealing amicably with Kickham at close quarters, and she came nearer than anyone else to giving him the considerate female attention that he so patently needed throughout his life, but particularly as his infirmities increased. The company of the O'Connors' young family was another source of contentment for Kickham. St. John's Terrace had the added attraction of being just a few minutes' walk from the sea. Even when he could see little and hear nothing, Kickham never lost that delight in the seaside which (like so many of his contemporaries from south Tipperary) he had developed in his youth at Tramore, County Waterford.

The crowning attraction of the O'Connors' home was their keeping an open house for people with literary and journalistic connections and Kickham's presence naturally increased the number of such callers. For the third time in his career Kickham belonged to a literary coterie, this one looser and more comprehensive than that associated with either the *Celt* or the *Irish People*. Some were old acquaintances, such as Dr. George Sigerson, the noted polymath and translator of Gaelic poetry, who was by now Kickham's doctor as well as a literary friend. His teenage daughters, Hester and Dora, knew Kickham well. They were in due course to become literary figures themselves, members of an interesting if not brilliant generation of Irish women writers. That generation had already arrived with Rosa Mulholland, Katherine Tynan and Rose Kavanagh.

Rose Kavanagh (1859-91) from Killadroy, County Tyrone, had made her way to Dublin by 1879 and was supporting herself there through literary and journalistic work. Like Kickham she found lodgings at 2 St. John's Terrace.[31]   Possessing a sentimental romantic temperament she was excited by the oppor-

tunity of getting to know the fenian veteran who was also the
author of her favourite novel, *Knocknagow*. She learned the
manual alphabet and soon the two were close friends.[32] Rose
Kavanagh as an enthusiastic, vivacious, young lady devoted to
native literature could not fail to appeal to Kickham. She
brought into the life of an infirm and lonely man a new light
and happiness that are captured in his poem 'Rose of
Knockmany'. (One of her earliest published pieces was an ode
to the County Tyrone hilltop of Knockmany). [33]

> For whether I'm strolling
> Where billows are rolling,
> Or sweet bells are tolling o'er Shannon or Lee;
> My wild harp when sweeping,
> Where fountains are leaping
> At lone Gougane Barra or storied Lough Neagh —
> To priest or to peasant,
> No matter who's present,
> In sad hours or pleasant, by mountain or stream,
> To the careless or canny
> To colleen or granny,
> Young Rose of Knockmany is ever my theme.[34]

There was a misunderstanding, however. Rose was worshipping
a venerable figure on a pedestal, while Kickham was forming
another kind of attachment to the girl whose upright form he
could see dimly and whose fingers regularly played on his.
Katherine Tynan, who knew them both, has recorded that
Kickham 'betrayed his feelings', but she was either unwilling
or unable to say in what way. Perhaps he simply made a
proposal of marriage though this is not the most likely explanation. In any case Rose was shocked by the 'betrayal'.[35] Kickham
was thirty-one years older than her. In dealing with the episode
Katherine Tynan laid much stress on Rose's 'boyish' qualities
and speculates on what might have been 'if she had been more
entirely feminine'.[36]

The misunderstanding, whatever form it took, did not lead
to permanent estrangement. Kickham's last poem written in
August 1882 was dedicated to Rose and paid tribute to the
happiness she brought him. It concluded as follows:

Rose Kavanagh

Above: No 2 Montpelier Place (St John's Avenue), Blackrock, Kickham's last residence.

Right: Side view of John Hughes' statue of Kickham.

The bronze statue of Kickham by John Hughes, in Tipperary. The right hand originally held a quill.

FUNERAL OF MR. KICKHAM IN DUBLIN.—TAKING THE COFFIN FROM THE HEARSE AT KING'S-BRIDGE

Kickham's funeral at Kingsbridge: a sketch from *United Ireland*

> Then blessed for aye be that autumn noon
> In the lonely heather glen
> When my heart awoke from its death-like swoon
> And I felt that I lived again.[37]

In the summer or autumn of 1880 Kickham met Charles Gavan Duffy for the first time, almost certainly at George Sigerson's house.[38] For many years Kickham had been critical of Duffy's politics, particularly his abandonment of Irish affairs in 1855, allegedly on the grounds that Ireland was like 'a corpse on the dissecting table'. Since 1855 Duffy had carved out a successful political career for himself in Australia and had received a knighthood. Kickham and himself might not have moved any closer together politically, but at least they could unite in recalling the glories of Young Ireland. The news that Duffy was about to publish an account of Irish nationalist politics in the years 1840-45 based largely on his own extensive and often detailed recollections greatly excited Kickham. He was eager to read an authoritative account of that crucial period, but he was concerned lest the wrong 'moral' might emerge; in other words, he feared that Duffy might take the opportunity to question or disown that romantic nationalist philosophy for the propagation of which (as original proprietor of the *Nation*) he bore so much responsibility.[39] The public renunciation of nationality by the founder of the *Nation* would have been a severe setback. Seeing Kickham's concern, Duffy offered to send him a copy of his book on the understanding that he would record his reactions. By February 1881 Kickham was working his way through the first volume of *Young Ireland: a fragment of Irish history, 1840-45,* and jotting down comments as he went along.[40] The result was a long series of 'Notes on *Young Ireland*' which appeared in the *Irishman* from 26 March to 5 November 1881, and on which we are greatly dependent for information about Kickham's early career.

At Duffy's suggestion Kickham offered the 'notes' in the first instance to the *Irish Monthly* (described by Duffy as 'the only national periodical now living'),[41] only to be informed that a review had already been procured. However the approach was not altogether in vain, as it opened an interesting exchange of letters (already referred to) with the editor, Fr. Matthew Russell, SJ. The *Irish Monthly,* begun by Russell in 1873, survived for over sixty years but was at its best for the first decade and a half when the contributors included Aubrey de Vere, Rosa Mulholland, Ellen O'Leary, Katherine Tynan, Rose Kavanagh and Dora Sigerson. The issue of May 1881 carried a poem of Kickham's, 'A lost picture'. It was, according to the author, the first 'rhyme' of his to have been published 'for many a long year'.[42]

If he had not been publishing verse that was not because he had given up literary work, though he had been concentrating on prose rather than poetry. From the beginning of his work on *Knocknagow* in 1869 until the last day of his life he always had some fiction-writing on hand. In view of his infirmities and his many other troubles he did very well to write three novels in that period of barely thirteen years. *Knocknagow* was completed in 1873 at latest and *For the old land* was finished in 1878.[43] When he was struck by his last illness in 1882 he was just finishing *Elsie Dhuv*[44] (subsequently renamed *The eagle of Garryroe*) which was being serialised in the *Shamrock* (Dublin). *For the old land* was less easy to dispose of and was not published until well after the author's death. *Knocknagow* appeared in a second edition in 1879, this time from the publishing house of Duffy and Sons, which bought the rights for £50 . The author had some difficulty extracting his money and did not receive it until November 1881,[45] although he needed it to pay various debts dating from before the institution of the Kickham fund. Using the fund money to pay off earlier debts would have been improper.

John Devoy has recorded a pathetic incident that occurred in a town in northern France early in 1879 as a group of fenian leaders coming from the supreme council meeting in Paris made their way to Dieppe:

When we went to the cathedral there was a great crowd of children there for their first communion, dressed beautifully as only French mothers know how to deck them out. Though Kickham because of his poor sight could not fully appreciate the beauty of the spectacle, he turned to me and said, 'If the man (pointing to O'Leary) keeps looking at cathedrals and witnesses many scenes like this the grace of

God will strike him sometime or other'. Every head in the church was turned to the man who had spoken so loud in English, but Kickham was unconscious of the fact.[46]

He was totally deaf and, while he caught a glimpse of the array of children, his sight was not good enough to notice the heads turning. Reading was very difficult for him at this stage. Devoy recalled that he had to raise his spectacles towards his forehead, partly shield his eyes with his hands and hold the reading matter a few inches from his face.[47] By 1881 he could read letters only when they were written very clearly, 'as if with a quill pen'.[48] Consequently he had to get most of his incoming mail read by someone who could convey the contents to him by the finger alphabet. At this stage he could not read his own handwriting;[49] it had never been very easy for others to decipher and it now deteriorated further. It was particularly bad when he wrote in bed, as he frequently did in later years — lying on his back, using a pencil, and with a book 'doing duty for a desk turned upside down'.[50]

Kickham did much writing in bed because he was frequently confined there in his final years. From 1875 onwards there were fairly regular references to his being laid up for days at a time. The cause was usually given as stomach upset accompanied by severe headache; for a day or two afterwards he would be very weak.[51] The sufferer himself described his illnesses as 'bilious attacks' and John Devoy used the term 'dyspepsia'.[52] One doctor put it all down to 'mental anxiety'.[53] An apparently unconnected complaint was an occasional intense pain in the limbs and joints that the sufferer likened to 'neuralgia and rheumatism'.[54]

The certainty that the next bout of stomach trouble was at most a few days off cast a gloom even over the good spells. Then there was the perpetual temptation to depression about the sight and hearing. Deafness, one of the most underrated of human afflictions, had for him a pathos all of its own. He told Rose Kavanagh of how much he longed to hear 'the patter of the summer rain among the leaves'.[55] One consolation was that he could 'hear' his own voice when he hummed tunes to himself.[56] But all the time there was disappointment at the want of patience and sympathy on the part of others. 'Have you ever noticed', he complained to Russell, 'that people, cultured and even pious people, are apt to regard afflictions as offences?'[57]

The blindness and deafness which arose out of the accident in his youth contributed to another accident near the end of his life. Sometime towards the end of 1880 he was knocked down and run over by a jaunting car in College Green and received a broken leg. As a consequence he spent the winter and much of the spring in bed.[58] By summer he was up and about and considering the purchase of a new coat (the first in eleven years). For a while he carried dumb-bells in his daily walks around O'Connors' garden with a view to restoring the strength of his muscles.

While walking in the garden just before mid-day on Saturday 19 August 1882 he suffered a paralytic stroke on the left side.[59] Having been helped to bed, he wrote a note to Dr. Sigerson, who came promptly and concluded that the patient's condition was grave but not beyond hope.[60] A priest had already administered the last rites.[61] Sister Mary Patrick Kickham (daughter of James Kickham of the Square, Mullinahone) was summoned from the Mater Hospital where she was superioress, by the patient's request. Molly O'Connor wrote an account of what followed for Ellen O'Leary while the events were still fresh in her mind:

He was greatly excited for some hours after he got the stroke but was quite happy and resigned. He knew he would die; he said it in his letter to Dr. Sigerson. He had a bad night on Saturday, but was better on Sunday. On Monday evening I asked him was he better but he said 'Never, never!'. He had some quiet hours, but about ten minutes before twelve he had a bad turn, and I thought he was going. We were up all night, the doctor giving him a spoonful of brandy every ten minutes, and he lived through the night with an effort. I sent a friend in by the earliest train for Sister Mary Patrick, and to telegraph to his brother at Mullinahone . . . . At twelve o'clock [mid-day] Charles looked up at me . . .and said 'Listen!'. I bent my head but he failed to speak. I said on his right hand 'Do you know I'm Molly?' 'Yes, yes', he said, and put up his hand and patted my cheek. All around the bed were surprised. Then I said, 'Try and tell me what you wish for'. 'Happy, happy', he said distinctly. Later on he looked up at me again and tried to speak, but could not. I said to him: 'Won't you try and tell me what you wish?' 'Merciful Jesus', was all he said. These were his last words on earth. A few hours before he died he had the crucifix in his hand, and he was writing on the quilt. I slipped it out of his hand and put a pencil in its stead, and a sheet of paper on a book, and he wrote a whole lot of dis- jointed things which we can't make out, but you will be happy to hear, dear Miss O'Leary, your name is distinct, and Dr. Sigerson's and I think Rose['s]. He died at twenty- five minutes past eleven [p.m.] with his cousin, Sr. Mary Patrick, and his brothers, Dr. Sigerson, James [O'Connor] and some others around saying the litany of the dying.[62]

The date was 22 August, just three and a half months after his fifty-fourth birthday.

First plans were for burial in Dublin,[63] although this was not in accordance with the wish of the deceased. When E. D. Gray in his capacity as trustee of the Kickham fund authorised the disbursement of £60 for funeral expenses, more elaborate obsequies became feasible.[64] The money was paid, not to any member of the family but to James O'Connor, who, apart from being a proven friend of Kickham's, was also an experienced propagandist. By the evening of Friday 25 August arrangements were in hand for a *cortège* through Dublin and interment in Mullinahone.[65] Fenians gathered from all over Ireland and Britain, and helped to marshal the couple of thousand marchers that accompanied the remains from Blackrock to Kingsbridge railway station on Sunday 27 August.[66] The procession was very far from being confined to those who had supported Kickham to the last. (Even James O'Connor had defected to the Land League in 1881.) A number of the three dozen or so carriages following the hearse carried home rule MPs, including John Dillon, T. D. Sullivan and T. M. Healy [67]: the absorption of Kickham into a unified nationalist tradition was already under way. Eleven bands took part, mostly those of the various Dublin trades (the butchers, bakers, tailors and so on); [68] they would have been available for any solemn popular occasion. At Kingsbridge prayers were recited by a number of priests and the remains were put on a train for Thurles.[69]

In Thurles the character of the funeral changed noticeably, for there was much more popular involvement, and direction was much less evident. A belated and peremptory request was made to have the coffin admitted overnight to the cathedral. The practice of automatically receiving the remains of the catholic dead in church had not yet been fully established in Ireland. Therefore, a refusal did not amount to denial of an accepted right — as later commentators have assumed, being accustomed to seeing every catholic rest overnight in the church before burial. In effect, a privilege with obvious political overtones was being sought for Kickham.

Archbishop Croke was out of the country in the last weeks of August 1882, so the decision about honouring Kickham's remains in the cathedral in Thurles rested with the administrator of the parish, Father James Cantwell. He firmly refused, pleading — not altogether convincingly — that he could not give permission in the absence of the archbishop. Which or whether, Cantwell's decision accorded with a strong political prejudice that he shared with a large number of priests in the archdiocese who remembered all the trouble they had had with Kickham's fenian supporters down the years. Cantwell had indeed contributed a pound to the Kickham fund but his accompanying letter was decidedly cool. [70] The archbishop, of course, had been enthusiastic about the fund, and in the same spirit he wrote to Alexander Kickham on 31 August 1882 offering his condolences on Charles's death and saying that if he had been at home when the remains reached Thurles he would have paid them all due honour.[71] He did not say explicitly that he would have allowed them to rest in the cathedral, but that would have been a comparatively mild gesture by comparison with some of his extremist political exploits earlier in the same year. At the time of Kickham's death Croke was on an extended visit to England, though a later legend held that he was in Rome briefing the pope about Ireland's rights and wrongs.

Kickham's remains rested in Kirwans' house in Thurles on the night of Sunday 27 August and next morning the final stage of the funeral began — the journey by road to Mullinahone. Even by Irish standards the turn-out of people was most impressive. [72] In Mullinahone the difficulty with the clergy took a new twist, for not alone was the church shut, but the gate to the churchyard and cemetery was locked (as was customary on weekdays), and there was no priest waiting.[73] The lock was quickly forced. At the graveside there was an awkward pause at the stage where the religious service would normally begin, until Alexander Kickham ordered that the burial should proceed. Tradition has it that a clerical student led the crowd in a recitation of the 'De profundis' and that the local curate made his appearance before the grave was fully closed. Afterwards John Daly of Limerick, one of the small band of Kickham's faithful IRB followers, gave a short oration.[74]

The locked gate and the lack of burial service must be blamed on Kickham's old adversary, Father Thomas Hickey PP, rather than on any diocesan conspiracy, and even at that it cannot be definitely put down to the parish priest's undoubted anti-fenian *animus*. Father Hickey had less than a year to live and during the preceding twenty years had been frequently absent from his parochial duties in Mullinahone on the plea of ill-health. He was even absent on one occasion when Archbishop Leahy (Croke's predecessor) visited the parish to take up a collection for the cathedral then a-building in Thurles — possibly the ultimate dereliction of duty for a parish priest![75] We can hardly hope to discover if his ignoring of Kickham's funeral was a deliberate snub or simply another instance of habitual negligence, or a combination of the two. In fairness to him, it has never been claimed that he had been given notice of the funeral by the deceased's family or friends.

For the most part the nationalist press either ignored the contretemps at Mullinahone or passed over it lightly. It was but an extra element in the problem that Kickham posed for them as agents of the dominant Parnellite movement, which felt the need to identify with the dead Kickham, and so with the fenian tradition, but without giving the real fenians an opportunity to point out just what Kickham did think of Parnellites and Land Leaguers. Any reminder that Kickham had not accepted the agrarian-nationalist consensus of the early 1880s had to be played down, and nothing would serve to revive unwelcome memories more vividly than an airing of trouble between clergy and fenians.

IRB diehards could not prevent home rulers from joining in Kickham's funeral procession, or from praising his career lavishly, if selectively, in their newspapers, but they could make trouble for any home ruler or Land Leaguer (especially an ex-IRB man) attempting to speak publicly at the funeral. James O'Connor, ex-IRB, and MP-in-the-making, did intend to deliver an oration at the graveside. It may have been prudence rather than illness, as alleged, that caused him to stay away and leave the speechmaking to John Daly.

The decision to invest the entire Kickham fund so as to give an income for life meant that it would be available for bequeathal at death. At the end of 1879 or early in 1880 Kickham turned his attention to the making of a will, taking J. F. X. O'Brien and nobody else into his confidence. The only provision on which he was firmly decided was that £1,000 should be divided between Annie and Josie Cleary.[76] Shortly afterwards he offended O'Brien by not backing him in a newspaper controversy with T. P. O'Connor about the Tipperary by-elections of a decade earlier. The Corkman continued to act as a trustee for the fund, but cordial relations were not resumed and the discussion of testamentary matters was discontinued. When Kickham died intestate O'Brien revealed the deceased's intentions but, naturally, the surviving Kickham brothers were not easily convinced that they should pass up a fortune which was now legally theirs.[77] The estate amounted to over £1,500.[78] George Fottrell and Sons, the firm of solicitors that had handled the Kickham fund — very efficiently — since 1879, dealt with his affairs after death with commendable tact. In 1885 the members of the immediate family waived their claim to the portion of the estate still unadministered at that date in favour of the two Clearys, who then received the sum of £858 between them.[79]

Kickham once remarked that the adage about no man being a prophet in his own country had been reversed in his case.[80] He was referring to the fact that some of the largest contributions to the Kickham fund had come from the parishes of south Tipperary, and the largest of all from Mullinahone. That was irrefutable evidence of his local popularity, a popularity that was not dissipated by his opposition to the Land League in subsequent years. The affection in which his neighbours held 'Master Charles' from his youth was immortalised by his rise to fame, so that almost a century after his death he is still regarded in his own locality with an esteem quite out of proportion to his nationwide reputation, and such as is accorded to very few national figures in their native places. In his own extravagantly sentimental fashion Kickham would probably look upon this 'living on in the hearts of his neighbours' as the best of all monuments.

Within weeks of his death moves were afoot to collect money for a conventional monument, but the project did not materialise until 1898 when it was carried to a successful conclusion by the tide of enthusiasm and activity which marked the celebration of the centenary of 1798.[81] The memorial took the form of a statue of Kickham and it was erected in Tipperary town. The excellent bronze figure by John Hughes was unveiled on 27 November 1898. Significantly, it depicted Kickham seated with pen in hand, because by then he was remembered as a literary man who had been secondarily a political activist. The final chapter of this book examines Kickham's literary legacy, but before coming to that we must analyse his contribution to Irish political history.

Chapter Ten

THE POLITICAL LEGACY

Fenianism is rightly credited with contributing to the evolution of church-state relations in modern Ireland.[1] Section eighteen of the IRB constitution of 1873 decreed as follows:

> In the Irish Republic there shall be no state religion, but every citizen shall be free to worship God according to his conscience, and perfect freedom of worship shall be guaranteed as a right and not granted as a privilege.[2]

While he wholeheartedly accepted this, Kickham would scarcely have phrased it in such doctrinaire terms. Faith and fatherland were too closely linked in his feelings for him to take any intellectual pleasure in the principle of separation of church and state. One has to look to other leaders for the headlines that fenianism set in this area.

In reference to the related though distinct question of 'priests in politics', Kickham is sometimes said to have exerted an important influence over the development of Irish nationalism by his challenge to the clergy's claim to dictate to the catholic laity in purely political affairs. Too much must not be made of this. The church in modern Ireland has indeed wielded very considerable political power, but the relationship between religion and politics was never such as to give ecclesiastics control over the general direction of nationalist public opinion. They could sometimes lead the laity in political matters, but only in a direction in which the laity wanted to go. Kickham's campaign in the *Irish People* was called forth by the necessity of getting the fenians to stand up to the clergy on their own: if they had won widespread support from among catholics of all classes, they need not have worried about clerical opposition. The articulation by the fenian newspaper of the principle that the people need not accept clerical dictation on politics was novel and striking, but the principle was widely, if silently, taken for granted at all times. It follows that later republicans in their disputes with ecclesiastical authority were not dependent on the example set by the fenians and the *Irish People,* even if some of them were aware of it.

If Kickham has to be denied credit for great innovation in the sphere where it is often accorded to him, the position is reversed in another area. For, while he has usually been seen as adhering doggedly to an established fenian tradition of intransigence in refusing to become involved with home rule politics or the Land League, the truth is that Kickham himself created this tradition in the years 1876-80, in contravention of the spirit and letter of the 1873 constitution of the IRB. Even John O'Leary was prepared to do business with Parnell for a few months in 1879, but Kickham never relented. Kickham derived the conviction — transcending mere strategic considerations — that Irish freedom could be won only by men unpolluted by contact with British parliamentary institutions from the apocalyptic teachings of John Mitchel. James Stephens, too, admired Mitchel and Mitchel's guide and mentor, Thomas Carlyle, but his aversion to parliamentarians was primarily a matter of strategy. It was Kickham who tried to turn the IRB into a conventicle of the pure. Like Mitchel, Kickham was at his polemical best when proclaiming the policy of intransigence, as in the parable of the scoobeen players, cleverly incorporated into his notes on Young Ireland:

> One May morning I was staring at and listening to the sights and sounds of the fair green with the superhuman delight of a schoolboy who has got 'leave for the fair' . . . . My attention was called suddenly by hearing close to me the words 'Anyone there for the first fifteen or twenty-five?'

> There was a coaxing blandness in the tones in which this question was put, and I should not have had the least hesitation to take my affidavit that the face I beheld on looking around was the happiest and most benevolent and most smiling human countenance I have ever seen or imagined from that day to this. He had planted his table a

little to one side of the entrance to a tent, from which
'The wind that shakes the barley' was issuing even at that
early hour in the morning.

With his hands resting upon the table, upon the middle
of which he had just placed a span-new pack of cards, he
paused for a reply, evidently quite satisfied that his invitation would prove irresistible. He was right. Four old neighbours of mine moved . . . to his table as if they could not
help it. Five 'hands' were dealt out; but instead of the 'first
fifteen' or 'twenty-five', Pat Healy, the slator, directed the
choice of the game by applying his right thumb to his
tongue and oracularly pronouncing the disyllable
'scoobeen'. After a little while the benevolent gambler
dropped out of the game — from sheer kindness of heart it
was evident — and contented himself with holding the
stakes and keeping a penny a deal 'for the use of the table'.
How happy that man was to see everybody winning! And
as for his four clients — their wordless felicity might make
angels envious.

As the sun was going down that blissful day, I visited
the fair green again, having patronised in the interval
both 'Mullins's Pavilion' and 'Clare's Royal Olympic
Theatre', besides two peep shows and cheap John the
lottery man . . . .

The card players . . . were still standing round the little
table. But now there was nothing but scowls and looks of
indignation and suspicion to be seen among them, always
excepting the proprietor of the table whose beaming smile
was as blandly bright as ever. By a curious coincidence two
of the players declared themselves 'broke'. A third pulled
out three halfpence, to show how nearly bankrupt he was,
while Pat Healy held up a solitary copper and prayed that
something dreadful might happen to him if that coin was
not all that was left of seven-and-sixpence with which he
had started to play in the morning. Who was the mean
rascal who wanted to deny his winnings? The party was on
the point of breaking up with a fight, when Pat Healy, who
was rather lost in astonishment than carried away by
passion like the others, said, enquiringly, 'Maybe 'tis the
scoobeen man has it?' That was it. The mystery was

cleared up and they all saw it. The penny a deal all day long solved the difficulty. They moved away, bending their eyes gloomily upon the scoobeen man . . . .

Parliamentary politics, in Kickham's opinion, resembled scoobeen:

The players at that game are intent only on winning as many tricks and drawing as many pennies as possible, being all the time as happy as the day is long. But the moral of my story is that parliamentary scoobeen is a losing game [for] Ireland. The steady draw 'for the use of the table' must go on. And surely you will not need to be reminded that John Bull is the scoobeen man.

The consequences for twentieth-century Ireland of Kickham's implantation deep within the IRB of the doctrine of the untouchability of (British) parliamentary politics have possibly been great, but there is no way of estimating how much less influence this Mitchelite tradition might have had without his work. Purist intransigence suited Kickham's character and also his personal circumstances, especially the infirmities that prevented him from entering into any flexible contact with strangers. Even if he had been so minded, Kickham in the late 1870s would not have had the physical capacity to engage in the politics of the new departure: there were other than moral reasons why wheeling and dealing were impossible for a man who could go nowhere without a guide, who could talk to no stranger without an interpreter, who could read a letter only with difficulty, and who might not be well enough to pen a reply for days at a time.

In his final years he was concerned with the maintenance of an attitude of mind by himself and his fellow IRB members, and had neither the inclination nor the opportunity to do anything.

The only action that he envisaged for the IRB was armed rebellion whenever the occasion would present itself. There was a clear distinction in his mind between 'honourable' warfare and all forms of what may be called 'terrorism', and he deplored the latter almost as vehemently as he lauded the former. Indeed, one of his arguments in favour of fenianism was that it weaned men away from assassination and atrocity by holding out the alternative of clean, organised action in a disciplined army at

Cnoc na nGaba

("KNOCKNAGOW")

———

Cuid a haon.

———

Catal Cicham

Do rgríob an rgéal ra' mbéarla

agus

Míceál Breatnac

("Coir-Fairrge")

Do cuir Gaedilg air.

———

Ar n-a cur amac ag
S. Ó Dubtaig 7 a Cuideactain (Teóranta),
agur ag
Connrad na Gaedilge,
i mBaile áta Cliat.
———
1906.

Adapting Kickham to later cultural nationalism.

some future date. Kickham had occasion to display his dislike of irregular methods at a meeting of the supreme council of the IRB, possibly held in 1873, when consideration was given to a plan proposed by an American maverick, John McCafferty, to kidnap the prince of Wales and hold him hostage for the release of fenian prisoners, or for some other concession to nationalist demands. John Daly who was present recalled later that the discussion 'was telegraphed to Kickham on his fingers. He sat in his chair dreaming his dream but, being stone deaf, could hear nothing of McCafferty's daring proposition, but when he grasped it he sprang to his feet.' Daly summarised the gist of Kickham's animated comments in these words: 'Are we Irish nationalists . . . or are we brigands?'[4] That concluded the discussion.

In 1876 O'Donovan Rossa, in America, launched the policy which he called 'skirmishing' and which was the first serious introduction of urban guerilla warfare into Anglo-Irish relations; it was to involve dynamite and 'Greek fire' attacks on targets in British cities. The supreme council and its president would have nothing to do with 'skirmishing' and despite his enduring conviction of Rossa's good faith Kickham conceded that the business was 'ignorant, stupid and insane'.[5] Just over three months before Kickham's death the Phoenix Park assassinations of Lord Cavendish and T. H. Burke were perpetrated. Before the responsibility of a small group called the Irish Invincibles was established, suspicion was naturally directed towards the IRB. Barry O'Brien has recorded Kickham's reported reply to the suggestion that fenians might have been involved. Though it may not constitute his actual words, it neatly sums up Kickham's attitude both to the assassinations and the Land League:

'Had the fenians anything to do with it?' a correspondent of an American paper asked Kickham. 'I don't know', was the answer, 'but if they had, they were fenians seduced by the Land League'.[6]

Kickham, then, was opposed to assassination, bombing, kidnapping, and all the devices of terrorism. But discussion of his attitude to violence can scarcely be left at that. His emphasis on the difference between regular and irregular violence does credit to his moral sense and his nobility of mind, but may betray a certain naivety. While the moral case for 'honourable' warfare was undoubtedly easier to make, Kickham seems to have missed the point that this could readily deteriorate into violence of the other kind. Even more seriously, he seems to have given no thought to the suffering that inevitably accompanies any kind of warfare. His lack of sensitivity in this regard was displayed glaringly in his cavalier comment on seeing the men in uniform mingling with the crowds in New York during the Civil War.[7] Kickham's cult of physical force (albeit in regular form) when taken together with his political intransigence could easily be extended by less morally sensitive souls to justify resort to virtually any form of atrocity in aid of 'the cause'.

Any assessment of Kickham's political legacy that is confined to consideration of his concrete achievements and of his contribution to nationalist doctrine, will underestimate him. He is a particularly interesting figure because, over and above actions or doctrines, he epitomises both in his person and in his writings the essentials of popular Irish national feeling. For, though Irish nationalism is closely linked with catholicism, and proclaims its attachment to republicanism, in the last analysis the nation is not guided by the tenets of either creed — or of any creed — but by the dictates of a national sentiment that transcends mere doctrine. Nobody has personified this more fully than Kickham, and few have contributed as much as he has to its dissemination. The preoccupation of his life was nationalist *sentiment,* rather than any particular doctrine, action or objective. Feeling was everything. He conveyed it all succinctly in one striking imprecation: 'Glory to God in the highest, and on earth *enthusiasm.*'[8] That was written not in the first flush of youth but in the year before his death.

Kickham's centrality is not diminished by the fact that he never acquired certain attitudes which subsequently became standard in nationalist circles. He did not have an automatic antipathy to landlords; the Gaelic League came too late for him, and he never became a language revivalist; though in fenian theory he was for years 'president of the Irish Republic', he never did display the slightest trace of that attachment to republican symbols and forms that became virtually the test of nationalism over a generation after his death, and there is no reason to doubt that, like John O'Leary, he would have been willing to accept a constitutional monarchy in an Ireland separated from Britain.[9] Yet, no plan-of-campaign man, no *gaelgeoir,* no 'sea-green incorruptible' would wish to criticise Kickham, because that would be to disown the essential popular nationalist sentiment on which all particular patriotic causes are grounded.

The Gaelic Athletic Association was founded within a couple of years of Kickham's death, and brought a whole new area of life within the realm of nationalism. Kickham had anticipated this development. He had a keen, if not fully articulated, awareness of the political significance of organised sport, and especially its affinity to the processes that go to make a nationalist movement. As Kickham saw it, the fellowship and sense of community created by sports and pastimes formed an integral part of patriotic feeling. However, games could also give rise to riots, disorder and broken heads, and so, in the interests of social discipline and a quiet life, priests and police in the nineteenth-century often actively discouraged sports gatherings. Predictably, Kickham could not see their point of view and sensed an attack on the things that he held dear. In an article in the *Irish People* entitled 'National sports' he protested against these restrictions and declared that 'our fathers and grandfathers hurled and leaped and danced, and we cannot see why we should not do the same'.[10] Under his direction fenian activity in Mullinahone in the mid-1860s seems to have consisted largely of organised pastimes. Due to the historic deficiency of local institutions the catholic parish acquired by default a paramount civic role in much of rural Ireland in the nineteenth century. Though most of Kickham's published criticism of the clergy was couched in political terms, his deepest disagreement with them centred on the anti-pastime bias of the social regime that they felt obliged to enforce in their parishes. The assimilation of the GAA by the parish that took place — after much tension and conflict — in the generation after his death was at least the partial fulfilment of one of Kickham's dreams.

The GAA was the answer to a need of which Kickham had been keenly aware, and in due course it acquired a political dimension that he would have seen as inevitable and desirable.

The association was successful because it worked up a sense of
local loyalty and here, too, Kickham had been feeling the way
ahead. Mat the Thrasher in *Knocknagow* competing against
Captain French at sledge-throwing is the epitome of local pride
in sporting prowess:

> Turning round quickly the thatched roof of the hamlet
> caught his eye. And, strange to say, those old mud walls
> and thatched roofs roused him as nothing else could. His
> breast heaved, as with glistening eyes, and that soft
> plaintive smile of his, he uttered the words 'For the credit
> of the little village' in a tone of deepest tenderness. [11]

The citation of Tipperary in the sub-title of *Knocknagow* is
an instance of that sense of county 'patriotism' which was not
at all prevalent in Kickham's lifetime, though in sporting
matters at least it has since flourished. In the cult of county, as
in other respects, Kickham anticipated the work and the style of
the GAA. If, as appears to be the case, the author of
Knocknagow has more hurling and football clubs named after
him than any other figure in the national pantheon, that is only
appropriate. The GAA is, even more than the IRB was, an
organisation after Kickham's heart. Indeed, the nearest
approach to the incarnation of Kickham's idea of nationality is
not any institution of government or administration, but all-
Ireland hurling or football final day at the association's
significantly-named headquarters, Croke Park.

Chapter Eleven

THE LITERARY LEGACY

THE BALLADS

James Maher in *The valley near Slievenamon* presents forty of Kickham's poems, some of them previously unpublished. He omits two particularly biting stanzas of 'Soggarth Aroon' (see page 73) and in a few other cases there is some question about whether or not he has obtained the original versions. Verses written for almanacs he eschews entirely. Otherwise his collection comes as close to completeness as could be expected. There could be no certainty of having a definitive collection as Kickham contributed verses under various pseudonyms to a wide variety of journals and left no list.

Maher does not put the various poems and ballads in chronological order and therefore his anthology is not as illuminating as it might be about the progress of Kickham's poetical career. In fact that falls largely into three well-separated productive periods: 1849-50, 1857-64 and 1881-2. Of the four best-remembered items two appeared in 1857 and two in 1859. Whatever patterns may be discerned, they are not those of progressive development or maturation. 'The altar', written in 1849, can be compared favourably with anything he composed later in life. And in the late 1850s and early 1860s he was still contributing verses (under a pseudonym) to *Old Moore's Almanac*[1]. The almanac was a generations-old forum for the exchange of versified wit (often in Ireland of a bucolic type) in the form of enigmas, charades and other 'puzzling poems'. Kickham's involvement in this sub-literary underworld is a sharp reminder of the extent to which he was still a villager,

albeit a well-read one, until he went to work for the *Irish
People.*

As a disciple of Young Ireland Kickham saw in poetry a
means to national regeneration. In particular he wished for a
new supply of morally and nationally uplifting ballads that
would wean the populace from vulgar ditties such as 'Barney
Bralligan' and 'Brennan on the moor'.[2] That kind of moral
purpose could be expected to produce didactic pieces and many
of Kickham's verses do seek to point a lesson, but the lesson is
usually submerged in an exposition of the author's basic and
predominant sentiment about rural Ireland or, rather, the
'valley near Slievenamon', as a naturally blissful place into
which, however, the serpent has entered. The restoration of
pristine felicity is linked intimately with the assertion of nationhood (not, be it noted, with any specific measures that might
follow). The principal manifestations of evil are insecurity of
tenure ('Clearing', 'Awaking', 'A lost picture', 'Patrick Sheehan'
etc.) and, above all, emigration ('Home longings', 'The Irish
peasant girl', 'A remonstrance', 'The exile's plea' and many
others).

A distinct though frequently associated theme is celebration
of place. Slievenamon, the valley near Slievenamon, the Anner
river and Carraigmoclear are all enshrined in well-remembered
Kickham verses. The sense of devotion comes across strongly
but detailed description occurs only in occasional flashes. Even
the poem apparently most wholly dedicated to a single place,
'Carraigmoclear', is an ode rather than a descriptive piece,
though it does open with a striking evocation of the well-
rounded promontories of the nearby mountain as seen from the
rock:

> Oh! sweet Slievenamon, you're my darling and pride,
> With your soft swelling bosom and mien like a bride.

The third stanza of 'Carraigmoclear' runs as follows:

> Yet a maiden might sleep the rough granite between,
> On the flower-spangled sward, 'tis so sunny and green;
> 'Tis thus you will find in the stormiest breast,
> Some spot fresh and warm, where love might be guest;

And how like a bless'd dream did one autumn eve glide
With my first and my only love there by my side!
Ah! no wonder, no wonder, I gaze with a tear
On the rocks and the flowers of old Carraigmoclear.

This introduction of a personal subject is quite typical of Kickham, and almost invariably the topic is his regard or his regret for some girl. A number of the poems are devoted exclusively to such matters (for example 'Rose of Knockmany', 'An autumn noon', 'Susan', 'The last dream', 'Fanny'), and altogether in his poems Kickham addresses or mentions a dozen different females. These range from the admired but ungrateful Bessie Blunden in 'The last dream' to a newly-born niece for whom he composes a lullaby, 'My Annie'. What part some of the others had in his life and affections it is difficult to tell. In poetry or out of it, there is much ambiguity about Kickham's relationships with women.

'The Irish peasant girl' (*alias* 'She lived beside the Anner') is regarded by many as Kickham's best poem and it is certainly one of his most popular. It is also among the most representative, dealing as it does with the subjects of place, emigration, loss of a loved one, and patriotism, and having a simple, touching story. The cloying sentimentality just about held in check here floods over elsewhere in his verses and frequently reaches the level of mawkishness. That is partly a reflection of authentic personal feeling, and partly an inevitable feature of less-than-first-rate work within the conventions of romantic poetry.

Kickham can scarcely be blamed for lacking the innate talent which makes a first-rate poet; but he must be faulted for the obvious verbal flaws that mar many of his verses. This defect is all the more surprising in view of the admirable felicity of his prose diction. But many of his verses are made to scan or rhyme by the introduction of such well-worn archaisms as 'clomb', 'I trow', 'for aye', 'a-near', 'methinks' and 'melting ruth'. 'Oh!'s and 'Ah!'s are liberally distributed throughout. However, Kickham has left a good half-dozen or so poems that deserve to be noticed on their own merits as poetry and without reference to their historical or biographical significance. Such selections are notoriously difficult to secure agreement about, but the following would have to be seriously considered: 'The Irish peasant girl', 'St John's Eve', 'Carraigmoclear', 'Rose of Knockmany', 'The altar', 'Gone with a vengeance' and 'Susan'.

Such a list would not include most of his popular compositions, but in fairness to both Kickham and his admirers it must be pointed out that virtually all his verses were written to be sung rather than spoken or read. That followed from his ambition for the provision of popular songs. Very little Young Ireland verse would be remembered if it had not been put to music, and the same is true of Tom Moore's Irish melodies. In Kickham's young days the closest approximation to cultural nationalism among the politically nationalist, catholic middle classes was the cult of these famous melodies (and even where the political nationalism was hesitant Tom Moore was lionised). Kickham held Moore in the highest regard both as a man and a composer, and from his novels it is obvious that he greatly desired to see the wives and daughters (convent-educated) of the gentleman farmers of Tipperary adopting the melodies for singing in the parlour to the accompaniment of their newly-purchased pianos. Kickham never attempted to emulate Moore's exquisite refinement of language — the populace needed something more robust in any case — but otherwise he saw himself doing much as the author of the melodies had done. He made no attempt to compose original airs, but wrote verses with some well-known music in mind, often a tune already used by Moore. He was particularly grateful to the 'national poet' for rescuing from oblivion so many excellent Irish airs. Kickham's popular songs are often nowadays rendered to melodies other than those envisaged by the author. He would have been appalled at the thought of anything of his being played at waltz tempo, as some now are.

Not surprisingly, a number of Kickham's songs are in ballad form, including 'Rory of the hill' and 'Myles O'Hea'. With one exception they are undisguised 'literary' ballads. The exception is 'Patrick Sheehan', which reads and sounds like an authentic example of the anonymous 'popular' or 'folk' ballad in English that was flourishing in the country from at least the beginning of the century. By good fortune the inspiration and composition of this unique song have been recorded. On 28 September 1857 the following item appeared in the *Freeman's Journal*:

Dublin police, Saturday; College Street station. A young man named Patrick Sheehan was brought up in custody of police-constable Lynam (46 B) charged with causing an obstruction to the thoroughfare in Grafton Street. The constable stated that the prisoner was loitering in Grafton Street for the purpose of begging, having a placard on his breast setting forth that he had served in the Crimea in the fifty-fifth regiment, that he had lost his sight in the trenches before Sebastopol, and that he was discharged on a pension of sixpence per day for nine months and that this period being now expired he was obliged to have recourse to begging to support himself. A Crimean medal was found on his person. Sergeant Thomas, fifty-fifth regiment, gave evidence which corroborated the statement of Sheehan as to his having served in the fifty-fifth regiment before Sebastopol and his being discharged from physical incapacity. The prisoner was committed for seven days for begging.

Kickham read this report on 3 October 1859 (probably as reprinted in the *Weekly Freeman*) and the *Kilkenny Journal* of Wednesday 7 October has the following from him:

I send you a few verses. The *Freeman* of Saturday supplied the subject. Poor Patrick Sheehan! I read the report of the case till my blood boiled and my eyes grew moist. On Saturday night in bed I composed these verses – and on this morning (Sunday) I commit them to paper lest they should pass from my memory. Print them in the next *Journal* if you think them worthy of a place therein, that they may be a lesson and a warning to the young men of our time who may have a taste for 'sogering'. This could be sung as a street ballad to one of the 'lamentation' airs, and heaven knows, never was there a fitter subject for lamentation. I could give them a better polish if I liked; but such is not my object. I wrote them rough and vigorous, such as the old ballads of the people used to be, that they may seize on the popular ear and produce the intended effect on the popular heart and mind and spirit of the country. And for this object there is nothing like a rough but racy street-ballad, the defects of which I have imitated rather than avoided.

On the basis of the *Freeman*'s report Kickham constructed the
pathetic story of a young man forced by necessity to enlist in
the army, blinded in the trenches, and condemned to
mendicancy and prison. The element of compulsion in the
enlistment was essential to Kickham's view of the business: if
Sheehan were a willing recruit, moral indignation at his fate
would be undermined and so, an eviction, poverty, unemploy-
ment and the workhouse were introduced as background to his
enlistment. The newspaper report gave no indication of
Sheehan's place of origin; Kickham assigned him to the
mellifluous-sounding and easily-rhyming Glen of Aherlow.

In later years it was claimed that Kickham's ballad shamed
the authorities into giving the unfortunate Sheehan a pension
for life. That unproven and highly unlikely story is at least an
indication of the impact of 'Patrick Sheehan' on the popular
mind. Within a few years of its composition it was a standard
item in cheap song-books, ballad sheets and the repertoires of
street singers. By the middle 1860s a few other Kickham songs
had attained similar status. They included 'Rory of the hill',
'The Irish peasant girl' and his version of 'The shan van vocht'.
Ever since, there have always been a few of his songs, but not
always the same ones, in the popular repertoire. If Kickham had
avoided all political involvements and had never published a
sentence of prose, he would still have won himself a place in the
songbooks.

THE TALES AND SALLY CAVANAGH

Unlike his verse work, Kickham's prose follows a recognisable
pattern of development. The *Celt* provided him with his first
opportunity for publication of prose, apart from leading
articles, and in availing himself of the chance he did not depart
very far from the spirit of the political editorial. He selected
events and episodes illustrative of the socio-political life of the
countryside, re-told them in literate form, and drew political
lessons. The first, 'Poor Mary Maher' was published in
November, 1857; it is a typical 1798 atrocity story, the title-
character having been in Kickham's youth an old demented
beggar-woman whose poverty and insanity were both attributed
to the persecution of her family by the yeomanry. The second
story, 'Annie O'Brien', tells of another helpless female victim

of tyranny. In this case the cruelty is perpetrated by the land-lord who evicts Annie and her widowed mother from their comfortable farm when they are unable to meet the rent. Friends and neighbours, preoccupied with their own insecurity, fail to assist them and when Annie's intended husband returns from America he finds that the mother has died in a wayside hovel and that the daughter is dying in the workhouse. After the worst has come to the worst the young man rejects the temptation to perpetrate an outrage against the landlord and instead returns to the USA to join 'the Irish-American army'.

'Never give up', published in September 1859 demonstrates that the evicting landlord need not necessarily have his own way. It is set in the early 1850s and describes the successful functioning of the tenant protection society in defence of a threatened farmer. The truth that landlords are not universally wicked emerges in 'Joe Lonergan's trip' (October 1859) where we see the hero holding his own in a struggle with the tithe proctor and the justice of the peace, thanks to the aid of his landlord, the Marquis of Ormond. 'The lease in reversion' illustrates how members of the tenant-farmer class could them-selves be the perpetrators of injustice in agrarian relations. This however was published not in the *Celt* but in the *Irish People* of 26 November 1864.

The discontinuation of the *Celt* in 1859 deprived Kickham of a ready outlet for his stories, a situation that was remedied in 1863 by the appearance of the *Irish Harp,* published by the Irish Serial Publication Company. As indicated by the publisher's name, the *Irish Harp* was interested in stories which could be spread over a succession of issues, so Kickham began to write a longer story than anything he had previously penned. His choice was an account of adventure and intrigue set in the second decade of the nineteenth century and involving the notorious 'Corravoth' and 'Shaunavest' factions; its title is the name of one of the protagonists, 'White Humphrey of the Grange'. It was published in three parts and was Kickham's only prose contribution to this short-lived periodical.[3]

Comment by the narrator in all of these stories though small in quantity is clearly intended as political propaganda, and each of the stories appears to be chosen as much for its political content as for any intrinsic appeal. The recital of horrors in

'Poor Mary Maher' and 'Annie O'Brien' is obviously intended to evoke militant emotion, and in the latter a suitable channel for such feeling is suggested by mention of the Irish-American army, an undisguised advocacy of fenianism. 'Never give up' has a number of asides of a propagandist nature: the divine will ('British providence') is forcefully rejected as an explanation of Ireland's miseries and there is a frank admission that the ultimate objective of recalling the episode is 'the good old cause of the good old country'. At the end of the story bearing his name Joe Lonergan is made to remark that 'There is a deal to be done yet', to which the narrator adds this closing remark: 'Which assertion we re-echo, with a prayer that WE may live to see it done, and help to do it.' The reader of 'White Humphrey of the Grange' is asked to believe that faction-fighting is encouraged by the authorities and that it is another of the evils which will disappear only when Ireland is free.

In 1926 these stories with the exception of 'The lease in reversion' (see page 212) were published in one volume edited by William Murphy, under the title *Tales of Tipperary*. The use of the term 'tales' could be misleading. These are not in the same category as, for example, Gerald Griffin's *Tales of the Munster festivals,* fairly considerable essays in literature. Kickham's tales are not literary but simply literate. Neither are they tales in the sense of being inventions of the author's imagination. In each of the five stories there are clear indications that what is being presented is factually true, as for example the opening paragraph of 'Poor Mary Maher'.

> Oh! I remember her sad story well; I was intimate with her in earlier days, and had often heard my mother tell her piteous tale. Strange, too, in despite of all her singular peculiarities, I had a child's love for Mary, she was so sadly gentle, so touchingly kind to everyone. This is her true and unexaggerated story, as gathered from her friends and from her own lips, in those moments when she could be got to speak of the past.

'White Humphrey of the Grange', the longest and most complex of the five is followed by this note from the author:

> Nearly all the incidents in this story really occurred. But we have given fictitious names of places and persons for the real ones. The fate of the traitor as given in the last

chapter — with all the particulars — is strictly a fact . . . .
So that this 'glimpse of Tipperary fifty years ago' such as it is, has the merit of being founded on fact.

In 'Joe Lonergan's trip' there is an account of an alleged visit by the hero to the 'nether regions' which is clearly not 'founded on fact'. But even here the author is not inventing anything: local folklore had just such a story concerning Joe Lawrence of Poulacapple, a contemporary of Kickham's.

Sally Cavanagh (which first appeared in serial form in 1864) is quite different from the tales, and has to be classed as a novel. Its largest constituent element is the story of the ruination of the heroine, her husband and family in a particularly heart-rending example of a pattern familiar in Ireland in the late 1840s. A callous landlord, Grindem, presses for an exorbitant rent during bad times and Sally's husband has no option but to emigrate in search of work and money, having obtained a promise of patience from the landlord. But there is no law to restrain the cruel proprietor and before long he is forcing Sally to sell the oats on which the family must depend for the winter. When mother and children reach the verge of starvation Grindem makes his next move in the following words:

'And now, Sally, . . . I needn't tell you what a regard I always had for you; and to prove it to you I'm after coming over myself to offer you the lodge. You can send the children to the old lady's school. They'll be well-fed and clothed; in fact ye'll want for nothing.'

Sally contemptuously rejects this offer of 'security' in return for sending her children to a proselytising school and becoming herself the landlord's kept woman. However, with no money arriving from America (where her husband is having difficulty getting established) she is eventually forced to abandon the holding and go to the workhouse, always in Kickham's writings an abode of horrors. In accordance with the regulations she is separated from her children and, when after some weeks she discovers that they have died of fever, she becomes demented, runs from the workhouse, and is a physical and mental wreck on the verge of death, living in a graveyard, when her husband eventually returns.

On its own that story would not make *Sally Cavanagh* radically different from Kickham's 'tales'; but there is much more to the book. Sally's plight is observed sympathetically but helplessly by a young man named Brian Purcell, the son of a big farmer. Through Brian the reader is introduced to the middle classes of County Tipperary — the better-off farmers and the lower ranks of the protestant gentry. In this milieu we find bleeding-heart love affairs and amorous intrigues, all conducted along the lines prescribed by literary convention. The study of character and motivation involved in this is an innovation for Kickham.

The ordinary people are not left out. Sally Cavanagh's neighbours are depicted not under conditions of immediate economic distress but in pursuit of their everyday occupations and pastimes. There are many sympathetic, humorous and self-evidently authentic vignettes of Irish life. Here is one example:

Josh Reddy was the parish musician. We say *the* musician. There was Dinny Moloughney, 'the piper', and Billy Devine, the 'fiddler'. But Josh Reddy was the 'musicianer'. The two irregular practitioners were content with what they could do in the way of business among the poorest and most humble, or a chance job of a better sort when Josh Reddy was not to be had. When all three happened to be employed on great occasions like Tom Burke's wedding . . . there was then sure to be discord of the most excruciating sort. For Josh Reddy would perform only such pieces as were beyond the powers of his humble rivals, whose epileptic attempts to accompany him were painful to behold. Billy Devine, stopping to screw up his fiddle, would confidentially 'own' to some sympathising bystander that he couldn't 'compare with him'. But, anon — driven out of his wits by some wonderful effort at fingering on the part of Josh — Billy Devine would rush into the midst of the dancers, and with a screech and a flourish of his bow, inform all whom it might concern that 'he played by *air* and didn't give a damn for any man'.

Kickham had found his forte, though he was never to recognise it fully.

The suggestion has already been made earlier that the move from Mullinahone to Dublin in 1863 gave Kickham the new perspective which enabled him to write a novel based on his native surroundings and way of life. *Sally Cavanagh* was a very great breakthrough for its author, but it was no rare specimen in the Ireland of the 1860s. The concentration of literary critics on the excellent and memorable in literature has led to the almost total neglect of a profuse and lively (if largely undistinguished) tradition of catholic-nationalist literature which flourished from the 1850s onwards. Indeed, its origins go far back into the century and it could claim Griffin and the Banims as precursors. Not quite intentionally, Young Ireland fathered for it a bevy of new recruits. In the period 1850-90 the national-minded Irish (or Irish-American) journalist or political propagandist who did not attempt a 'story of Irish life', past or present, was exceptional. These practitioners were joined in their enthusiasm by a host of dilettantes. Stephen J. Brown's *Ireland in fiction* registers a fraction, but only a fraction, of their total output.[4] Their works figured prominently in the catalogues of Duffy and Sons, M. H. Gill and Son, and other 'catholic' publishers in Ireland, Britain and America, side by side with, and sometimes barely distinguishable from, polemical history and catholic apologetics. In 1861 Charles J. Kickham reviewed a recent Duffy publication entitled *Frank O'Donnell: a tale of Irish life.*[5] The author, D. P. Conyngham from Fethard, was a 'veteran' of 1848, a journalist, and a cousin of Kickham. His book featured episodes and scenes of Tipperary life in the 1840s and 1850s strung together by a not very plausible story line. *Sally Cavanagh* and *Knocknagow* may appear to stand in isolation but the truth is rather that they are remembered from amongst a legion of similar but almost totally forgotten works.

KNOCKNAGOW

At about 75,000 words *Sally Cavanagh* is a book of very manageable proportions. *Knocknagow,* over three times as long, is a poorly organised work, though not markedly worse in this respect than many other books composed originally as serials. It has several sub-plots but they are handled (or neglected) so badly that in the last few chapters a gigantic effort has to be made to tie up the loose ends. The result is so patently artificial that the author is forced to have two of the characters poke some fun at it.[6] The attempted main plot is no laughing matter.

It is the story of the depopulation, through the working of greed and of the land laws, of the fictional village that gives the gook its title. The debt to 'The Deserted Village' of Goldsmith is evident not just in the general theme but in the use of detailed descriptions of the departed rural existence which evoke the sense of loss. Kickham falls down when he tries to do something that Goldsmith did not attempt, that is, to recount in detail the process of destruction. Despite his excellent knowledge of the social issues, Kickham's handling of the plot is inept. That very weakness isolates the attractive features of the book by throwing the emphasis on those areas where Kickham is at his best — scene-painting and the depiction of character and incident.

Many of the pictures of country life and people in *Knocknagow* have an immediacy, an accuracy and a sureness of touch that compel recognition and sympathy from anyone familiar with the ways of rural Ireland. Admittedly, not everything rings true — the parlour conversation of the big farmer's family and friends is dull and unconvincing — but so much does come to life that *Knocknagow* provides a brilliantly successful panorama. The clarity and richness of the pictures may owe something to the author's period of imprisonment, during which he had the opportunity to reconstruct in detail before his mind's eye the way of life he had seen around him in his youth.[7] There is a quite obvious debt (extending even to unacknowledged verbatim quotation) to William Carleton, who more than a generation earlier depicted the peasantry of another part of Ireland with the same kind of first-hand knowledge and appreciation, but greater fictional authority. At first sight a comparison between the irreverent Carleton and Kickham may seem implausible, but on inspection the same kind of insight into the life and mind of the Irish countryman is evident. Intellectually they had little in common, and they did not inhabit the same moral universe. Nevertheless, the differences in tone in their respective treatments of the Irish peasantry can best be explained not by differences of vision but by the difference in audiences. Kickham addresses himself primarily to Irish catholics — at home and abroad — profoundly sensitive about the respectability of their antecedents and the image of their community. Carleton's expected readership was far more heterogeneous (significantly fewer Irish catholics could read in his heyday) and included only a small minority who would have to feel that those being described were *their* people.

Not just the tone, but the selection of topics in *Knocknagow* reflects the susceptibilities of those to whom Kickham was primarily addressing himself. The more riotous aspects of Irish rural life such as wakes, fairs and faction-fighting are not dealt with. The very first episode in the book, in which the landlord's nephew on a visit to Knocknagow mistakes the banging of the drum for the report of a gun, mocks and rebukes critics who seize on any and every pretext to represent rural Ireland as a violent place. All of that is not to say that Kickham is uncritical of his own, but he finds it easier to criticise them for things that they have in common with the great Anglo-Saxon world rather than for those peculiar Irish failings so often pointed to by outsiders. Take, for instance, the increasingly mercenary attitude of the small farmers towards marriage – a local expression of the Victorian ideal of thrift. To Kickham's way of thinking it is abominable to put money before love in the choice of a partner, and he lambastes what he sees as a new and soul-destroying trend. The union of Ned Brophy and Larry Clancy's daughter is a case in point.

Ned is in love with Norah Hogan, but she has no dowry to offer, and so he abandons her and goes in search of a bride with money. Old Clancy has a saucepan full of gold sovereigns and so Brophy, having first seen them counted out before him, agrees to a match with the daughter. The 'hauling home' is the occasion of the wedding celebrations described in detail by Kickham, but the heart of the affair is hollow. While the neighbours and friends are enjoying themselves feasting and dancing in the barn, the unloved and unloving bride sits sullenly in the kitchen. One of her new neighbours attempts to enliven her spirits.

'This is a pleasant night we have', said Bessy, sitting down next the bride. Mrs Ned looked straight before her and made no reply. . . .

'You'll like this place very much', Bessy continued, 'when you become acquainted with the people. They are very nice and neighbourly.'

Mrs Ned said nothing.

'To be sure one cannot help feeling lonely after leaving one's own home', said Bessy. 'But it must be a great comfort to you to have your family so near you.'

'What soart is the cows?' asked Mrs Ned turning round suddenly, and looking straight into Bessy Morris's face.

'Oh!', she stammered, quite taken by surprise, 'I really don't know.'

'Because', rejoined Mrs Ned, 'I never see such miserable calves as them two that was in the yard when we wor comin' in'.

Kickham's selectivity does not imply distortion, for whatever he depicts is done faithfully. There are ample indications that he felt compelled to give accurate descriptions of the incidents, places and customs featured in his rural panorama. Of course, not even a writer as uninventive as Kickham can compose a work of fiction in which every person and episode has a one-to-one correspondence with originals in everyday life. However, it is possible to pick out large blocks of *Knocknagow* that are basically true-to-life description done very conscientiously by a faithful observer. That makes the book important as a potential mine of information for social historians, for which purpose it has only just begun to be used.

Even at the level of organisation of material for fictional purposes, *Knocknagow* is an extremely derivative work. Debts to Goldsmith and Carleton have already been mentioned and, in fact, it would not be difficult to compile a long list of literary influences on *Knocknagow*. Charles Dickens was Kickham's favourite author. When an enthusiastic reviewer declared that *Knocknagow* was Dickens without his exaggeration and Thackeray without his bitterness, Kickham was highly amused by this 'going beyond the beyonds', but he admitted that 'Dickens with his exaggeration is exactly what I would strive to be, the ideal at which I would aim but could never hope to get within leagues of'.[9] Despite that declaration, obvious instances of debt to the greater Charles are comparatively scarce in *Knocknagow*. No doubt, it is Dickens's example that makes Kickham treat of Christmas Day in Knocknagow, despite the fact that it was clearly not a very remarkable occasion. The most glaring case of an idea borrowed from Dickens is Norah Lahy, the doomed consumptive girl, too good for this life — a disastrous imitation of Little Nell in *The old curiosity shop*.

A contemporary to whom Kickham is even more indebted in *Knocknagow* is George Eliot, whose rural English midlands settings are much closer to Kickham's world than is Dickens's predominantly urban landscape. We know that Kickham read her works avidly as they became available. *Adam Bede*, published in 1859, can be seen as an important influence on *Knocknagow*. The shared talent of the authors for minute description and analysis of the lives, customs and characters of people in the lower ranks of rural society is a coincidental link, but there can be no coincidence about the resemblances between the upright village carpenter Adam Bede, paragon of virtue, who has 'the blood of the peasant in his veins',[10] and Mat the Thrasher, the chivalrous Tipperary farm-labourer of limitless practical and sporting talent, yet humble demeanour. There is nothing in Mat that Kickham has not observed spread over a number of actual Tipperary peasants, but putting it all together to create his greatest character would be beyond his powers of composition without a model to guide him and, without a doubt, Adam Bede is that model. The two have in common an unmistakable 'plaster St Joseph' quality and ponderous, not to say slow-moving, mental processes. But there is no dullness of mind: both are perfectionists in their respective ways and excel at their trades. Both take up study in their spare time in order to improve themselves. The most striking resemblance is in their love lives. Each has a tender, paternalistic affection for a younger girl, but hesitates to express it owing to an extreme sense of responsibility in matters of the heart. In each case the beloved is a coquette, unworthy (either initially or absolutely) of such concerned love, and flirts with a gallant-looking man in uniform, a fact for which the true lover is most reluctant to accept evidence.

The pivotal third part of *Adam Bede* is taken up with a lengthy account of the celebrations for the young squire's coming-of-age. A comparable position in *Knocknagow* is occupied by another occasion for communal feasting and dancing — a rural wedding. Kickham maintains the similarity by having a landlord, admittedly not a very typical one, at the wedding. Given all the other resemblances it is hardly fanciful to see the sledge-throwing contest between Mat the Thrasher

and Captain French as a parallel (conscious or unconscious) of
the more violent confrontation in the grove between Adam
Bede and Captain Donnithorne.

However, there is no slavish copying. Mat's love, Bessie,
turns out to have a heart of gold, unlike Adam's Hetty, who is
blinded by vanity, seduced by the young squire, and driven
by desperation to murder her child. It was a favourite conceit
of catholic-nationalist rhetoric in the second half of the nineteenth century that infanticide was one of the features distinguishing 'pagan' English society from catholic Irish society;
Kickham's readers would not have accepted an Irish Hetty
Sorrel. Misfortune might befall an Irish girl, but only in the
alien atmosphere of Liverpool, New York or Chicago — a moral
attitude that was to remain deeply rooted in Ireland long after
Kickham's time.

Comparison of *Knocknagow* and *Adam Bede* does not, in
fact, bear out the notion of a stronger spiritual sense among
the Irish. All the people of Knocknagow (with the possible
exception of Billy Heffernan, who is, however, merely super-
stitious) seem to wear their religion very lightly by comparison
with the evangelical-minded section of the population in Eliot's
Hayslope. Mat the Thrasher prays before going to bed but,
compared with Adam Bede, he could be the archetype of the
noble savage, or a model of natural religion. His standards of
behaviour are high, but his morality is as free of anxiety as is
his religion. He has no scruples about Sunday observance, and
before his heart fastened on Bessy Morris he 'had his fling'
among the girls of the countryside.

The important respects in which Mat differs from his model
are a reminder that an author may be derivative and yet
original. Kickham's hero is a more rounded and convincing
character than Adam, and possessed of a number of extra
dimensions. Being Kickham's idea of the all-rounder, he has a
talent for music and the dance. The culmination of the wedding
celebrations is a display of dancing by him and his sister that
enthrals the remainder of the company.

> The excitement rose higher and higher as the dance went
> on, and a loud shout followed every brilliantly-executed
> step. After each step the dancers changed places, and,
> moving slowly for a few seconds, commenced another one

which threw the preceding ones quite into the shade, and, as a matter of course, called out a louder 'bravo!' and a wilder 'hurro!' When the enthusiasm was at its height, two men carrying a large door crushed their way through the crowd. Two more quickly followed bearing another large door. And without causing any interruption, the doors were slipped under the feet of the dancers, which now beat an accompaniment to the music, as if a couple of expert drummers had suddenly joined the orchestra.[11]

Mat Donovan is not just the soul of honour and of industry; he is also the Irish Zorba.

Mention of ways in which *Knocknagow* excels, such as the characterisation of rural types or the description of rural scenes, must not go so far as to claim too much for the total quality of the book. The manner in which it falls short of being great literature can be illustrated by continuing the contrast with *Adam Bede* and focusing on the two lengthily-described rural feasts. Both are interesting as social history, and as effective evocations of important communal occasions. However, while Eliot's coming-of-age celebrations are an integral part of her plot, Kickham's wedding has no such function. The poor handling of plot has been referred to already, but it is a weakness that of itself would not prevent a book from attaining the first rank. Far more important is the fact that the description of the *Knocknagow* wedding does not have the ulterior significance, the symbolic overtones, or the charged atmosphere, that mark Eliot's account of Captain Donnithorne's birthday celebrations, culminating in the dramatic irony of Mr Poyser's remark:

It'll serve you to talk on, Hetty, when you're an old woman — how you danced wi' th' young squire the day he come o' age.

There are no such subtleties in *Knocknagow*; it is deficient in the deeper, intangible meanings and tensions of great literature. But for all its flaws, it is a great book and one of enduring value.

THE LATER WORKS

After his release in 1869, and until his death, Kickham devoted himself to writing at least as fully as he did to politics.

Ironically, while his political attitudes were becoming more and more inflexible, he was working industriously and successfully to learn new lessons and acquire new techniques in fiction-writing. Handicapped and impoverished though he was, he managed between 1873 and 1882 to complete two full-length works, each embodying notable advances.

For the old land, completed five years after *Knocknagow,* was probably envisaged as a kind of sequel, dealing as it does with the life of a rural community in the 1860s and 1870s. Like *Knocknagow* it is peopled by characters obviously based on originals encountered by the author in his own locality, and the story lines concern their interrelationships and the struggles of some of them to hold on to their farms despite unfavourable land laws. Again, there is minute description of typical characters and customs, and much source material for the social historian (even rudimentary statistics on the increase in piano-ownership!).[12]   Continuity with *Knocknagow* is explicitly acknowledged by the author's reference to the pleasure he has had in painting elsewhere the 'great hearted "Fr. McMahon",' who is a contrast to the domineering parish priest (given to abusing his office for political purposes) that he has to present here;[13] McMahon is the kindly 'soggarth aroon' of *Knocknagow.*

Kickham's determination to perfect his technique shows most impressively in *For the old land* and makes it, despite the continuity, quite a different kind of work from *Knocknagow.* The handling of plot is immeasurably better, the different sub-plots being dovetailed together with remarkable precision. Every chapter contributes towards a general sense of movement which is greatly heightened by the judicious pruning of the story (or stories) at many points. This new-found control of plot is well illustrated by the manner of dealing with four weddings taking place on the one day: the efforts of a comic character to attend all four are described, and nothing more. For the author of *Knocknagow* to achieve such expertise in the art of controlled fictional narrative, extraordinary effort and self-discipline must have been required. Hand in hand with this discipline came more objective handling of subject matter, and *For the old land* displays a sense of detachment not to be found in anything previously written by Kickham. The change is not unconscious, for the reader is told that 'it is not our own views or opinions we are giving here, or elsewhere in this history'.[14]

Detachment and fluidity of action in *For the old land* are achieved at the expense of features that help to give *Knocknagow* its extraordinary appeal. There is a comparable range of characters, most of them well-drawn and interesting, but none catches the imagination in the way that up to half-a-dozen characters in *Knocknagow* do. Perhaps he has used up his stock of great characters in the earlier work, but in any case the concentrations on other matters would inevitably distract attention from characterisation.

The advances in technique achieved in *For the old land* are sustained in his last work, *The eagle of Garryroe*, though they are not as obvious because of the subject matter. Having run through his own adult years in three books, Kickham now turns to a historical subject — Tipperary in 1798. As in his early tales, he uses traditional stories, but he now handles them very freely and does not hesitate to expand them and link them by means of totally invented episodes. The result is a story that moves well. But, unfortunately, it is not, in the final analysis, a satisfying story. The reason may be that Kickham is unable to break away from the mentality of the sentimental, romantic story-writer. A happy ending with loving couples being united in matrimony, compromised rebels making good their escape to France, and a wayward child making peace with mother church, might constitute a plausible ending, even to a story of 1798, but not to the story that the reader is implicitly promised in the ominous opening chapter of *The eagle of Garryroe*. Kickham could retell an atrocity story, but he was either unable or unwilling to handle creatively the harsh truth about the course and consequences of an actual Irish rebellion.

Never, either in fiction or elsewhere, did Kickham face the brutal realities of the physical combat that he so eloquently advocated. In this respect is is interesting to note the skirmish which occurs in *The eagle of Garryroe*. What promises to be an account of violent and bloody encounter turns out to be mere farce and ends with nobody injured, and one half-comic rebel pursuing an unhorsed Falstaffian sergeant of yeomanry:

'I never though Bullfinch had such speed in him', Chris Carmody remarked, as he watched the race from behind the large rock. 'Shaun'll never ketch him before he comes to the double-ditch, though he's gainin' on him.'

The double-ditch was at least nine feet high, with a wide dyke on either side. If the sergeant could only clear the dyke, and catch a good grip of the ditch with his hands and knees, he felt that he could scramble safely over before the formidable pike could touch him. Two or three times he cast a hurried look over his shoulder, observing with dismay that his pursuer was coming nearer and nearer to him. As he neared the ditch, straining every nerve, and almost frantic with terror, the fat sergeant resolved not to look again, come what might, and, putting on a spurt, he found himself within half a dozen yards of the brink of the dyke and not yet run through the body. He heard the sound of his pursuer's heavy step close behind; but on he rushed.

Heavens! could it be possible that he was safe? A good spring that would carry him across the dyke now, and the chances were all in his favour. The pikeman would not be able to use his weapon quickly enough to spit him against the ditch before he was over.

'Take that!' exclaimed the angry and breathless black-smith Shaun, just as the fat sergeant sprang from the brink of the dyke.

The terrific lunge was given with all the force Shaun Foddha's gigantic frame was possessed of. He felt the ten-foot ashen handle quiver like a rccd in his grasp. But, could he credit his own senses? The fat sergeant had actually flown clean over the double-ditch, as gracefully as an acrobat leaping through a loop. [15]

What Shaun does not know is that the sergeant has armour in the seat of his trousers!

Such trivialisation ruins a potentially fine piece of work. But, like *Knocknagow, The eagle of Garryroe,* though flawed, has some admirable qualities. Because of the period in which it is set there could be little of the authoritative depiction of life and society that distinguishes the earlier work, though there is the ring of authenticity about the descriptions of one aspect of rural life in Tipperary at the end of the eighteenth century, namely the complex social relations between protestants and catholics. It was something that Kickham knew much about from his own family background. But *The eagle of Garryroe* possesses greater claims to consideration. It has a literary quality almost totally lacking in the earlier works, a richness and allusiveness of language such as we expect from authors of the first rank. Benedict Kiely has pointed to 'a rich excitement of anticipation in the moment when the aged eagle comes from his wooden house on the roof of the castle and slowly spreads his wings to their full extent and cries in hunger to the evening'.[16] The eagle and other symbols are handled with a finesse quite beyond anything Kickham had achieved previously.

He acquired, then, most of the skills of the successful novelist, some of them almost automatically with his early education, others by dint of determined effort in later life. Unfortunately, he never succeeded in getting them all together in the creation of one single *opus,* and he left four extended works of fiction, each with serious flaws but possessing some fine qualities. Together they constitute a noteworthy achievement that deserves more careful consideration than is usually accorded to it.

POSTHUMOUS POPULARITY

In the years immediately after his death Kickham's reputation as a writer was quite high in Ireland. When he died *The eagle of Garryroe* was being serialised in the *Shamrock* (under the title *Elsie Dhuv*). Charles Gavan Duffy writing shortly afterwards placed Kickham next after Carleton, Griffin and Banim as 'a delineator of national manners'.[17] In 1886 a weekly journal, the *Irish Fireside,* conducted in its pages a prolonged survey to discover 'the hundred best Irish books', and either *Sally Cavanagh* or *Knocknagow* was to be found near the top in almost every list submitted.[18] In the same year *For the old land* was published for the first time, as a serial in the *Irish Fireside*.[19] It appeared in book form later in the year. In 1887 Duffy and Company launched the third edition (their second) of *Knocknagow.* Four years later W. B. Yeats included a sample of Kickham's work in an anthology of Irish prose and was quite complimentary in his introductory remarks, faulting Kickham merely for imperfect technique.[20] His descriptive power was declared to be 'of a wholly Celtic kind', a fatuous remark, though intended as praise. Yeats's early 'The ballad of the foxhunter' is an attempt to recreate in verse one of the many touching vignettes in *Knocknagow,* the death of the aged Sam Somerfield — of hard-riding gentry stock — who chooses to spend his last hours propped up in a chair on the lawn, with his beloved horse at hand, his restless pack round about, and his huntsman sounding the horn to the expiring master's exhortations of 'Yoix! Tallyho!' and 'Blow, Rody, blow'.

In truth, Kickham had little future as a literary figure if literature was to be judged by the criterion of Celticism. Yeats had already played a major part in launching a new Irish literary movement which was about to put Kickham and his like clean out of fashion. The Irish renaissance, in its concern with ancient mythology and folklore, and above all in its determination to create a new kind of Irish literature, was a rejection of the tradition to which Kickham's novels belonged. These were indeed imbued with a spirit of nationalism, but it was not the Germanic-style, ethnic/cultural nationalism of the Celtic twilight.

The parallel development of the Gaelic League, with its insistence that literature could not be truly Irish unless written in the Irish language, was another blow to Kickham's prestige. In an endeavour to achieve an accommodation, part of *Knocknagow* was translated into Irish in 1906.[21] The task was completed in subsequent years, and *Sally Cavanagh, For the old land* and the tales received similar treatment. When a new generation devoted to 'realism' arose among the heirs of the Celtic twilight, Kickham's 'sentimentalism' was even more out of fashion, and in the past eighty years his work has seldom received serious treatment from literary critics.

Literary historians, as distinct from critics in search of great literature, cannot ignore indefinitely the tradition to which Kickham belongs. The author of a recent book on the Irish literary revival has pointed to the difficulties posed for its exponents by the dominance of the attitudes and tastes of those who 'found *The playboy* unpatriotic, *The Countess Cathleen* irreligious, and *Ulysses* irredeemably obscene'.[22] Dominant they were, not just among the population at large but among the political leaders of the new Ireland, whether in pre-1922 Sinn Féin, Cumann na nGael in the 1920s or Fianna Fáil in the

1930s. Undeniably, many of those who rejected Synge, Yeats and Joyce, and instituted or approved of the draconian censorship of their followers, were philistines, who have been roundly, and rightly, denounced for their narrow-mindedness. However, a great many were not philistines, but sensitive people who judged the new writers by the standards of the older literary tradition which handled their pieties tenderly and accepted the painful need of the Irish catholic community to feel that it was cutting a respectable image before the world Without any worthwhile leadership or direction, it continued to be by the criterion of numerical support the dominant literary tradition in Ireland at least for the first half of the twentieth century. In the decades when the great figures of the Irish renaissance were attaining their finest achievements, the most consistently popular book in Ireland was *Knocknagow*.

Commercial success began with the 1887 edition which was reprinted over and over again for the next half-century or more. In 1949 M. H. Gill and Son took over publication from Duffys and brought out the thirtieth impression; four more impressions followed in the next thirteen years, and sales continued at a steady rate until stocks were exhausted early in 1970.[23] Within a few years second-hand copies were in keen demand and in 1978 Gill and Macmillan published a facsimile edition. As detailed records are not available from Duffys, there is no way of knowing the number of copies of *Knocknagow* that have been published in Ireland, but it cannot be much less than 100,000. In America, also, many editions were produced in the nineteenth and twentieth centuries by a number of publishers.

Other Kickham books, too, sold well on both sides of the Atlantic. Gills kept *For the old land* in print more or less continuously from 1886 to 1942. *Sally Cavanagh* was published by various firms, including, as late as 1948, Duffy and Company. Having brought out a short anthology of Kickham's verses in 1903, William Murphy worked for some years on collecting the tales into one volume and brought the task to completion in 1926 with the publication of *Tales of Tipperary* by the Talbot Press. The same firm re-issued *The eagle of Garryroe* and *Tales of Tipperary* in one volume in 1963. Meanwhile the Educational Company had published in 1931 a collection of Kickham's verse edited by H. L. Doak. In 1942 James

Maher of Mullinahone published *The valley near Slievenamon* sub-titled *A Kickham anthology: the poems, letters, memoirs, essays, diary, addresses, of Charles J. Kickham.*

Knocknagow, of course, outshines everything else with the Kickham signature from the viewpoint of sales. The veneration in which the author was held in Tipperary and elsewhere has been adduced as a reason for the success of *Knocknagow,* but that is a lame explanation — it is more likely that the veneration was to some extent a response to *Knocknagow.* People bought and read *Knocknagow* because of what it had to offer them, not because of Kickham's political career or reputation.

To a degree scarcely paralleled elsewhere in the western world, modern Irish society has been dominated by the ethos and *mores* of an agricultural community. The land war established that community in a very strong position which was to be further strengthened over the next two generations. Many of the priests, shopkeepers, teachers (lay and religious) and (in due course) gardaí síochána, bank clerks and civil servants came directly from the land. Whether on the land or just off it, the typical members of this society found themselves at home with *Knocknagow.* Of course it dealt with a period, the middle of the nineteenth-century, that had almost gone from memory even at the very start of widespread popular interest in the book — the late 1880s — but that was part of the attraction. *Knocknagow* filled the role of a national epic. It depicted a past that possessed the aura of a golden age and was peopled with a goodly number of heroes and heroines. Here a society preoccupied with the ownership of land could presume to see an explanation of its own origins in a struggle against the vicissitude of insecurity of tenure. Most important of all, here, painted in touching and memorable fashion, were the virtues that this society prized, the emotions that it felt, and the values that it exalted.

The literary and intellectual nationalists of the decades following Kickham's death — whether they belonged to the Gaelic League or the 'Anglo-Irish' literary movement — were, like him, influenced by English intellectual reaction against the modern world. But this had acquired a new tone and, adapting that to local conditions, the new breed of Irish nationalists sought their primitive paradise in Celtic legend or among the living inhabitants of the western seaboard. Kickham had had no special admiration for anything west of the Shannon except Archbishop MacHale, and for two or three generations after his death the majority of Irish nationalists assumed with him that Eden was more like Knocknagow than Kiltartan or Rosmuc.

Politicians paid lip-service to the official Gaelic ideal of the new nationalist élite, but they attended also to the instincts of the majority. When, during the Second World War, Eamon de Valera made his celebrated reference to the Ireland of his dreams as a land of virtuous youths and comely maidens, 'the home of a people who valued material wealth only as the basis of right living, of a people who were satisfied with a frugal comfort and devoted their leisure to the things of the spirit',[24] he was virtually paraphrasing *Knocknagow* for people whom he knew to be imbued with its sentiments. (Such rhetoric never inhibited fumbling in 'the greasy till', but it could act as a palliative when the till was empty.)

The spirit of *Knocknagow* probably had even greater appeal during the years of the emergency than at any other time, but for a full appreciation of Irish attitudes at any period in the first half of the twentieth century, acquaintance with Kickham's classic is essential.

Through his propagandist writings, and through the IRB, Kickham exerted some influence over the politico-military theories and strategies of the cadres of the Irish revolution. Through *Knocknagow* he both expressed and nurtured something far more fundamental, much of the basic mentality of the modern Irish nationalist community.

APPENDIX ONE

'The lease in reversion' is the only identified 'tale' of Kickham's that has not been republished since its first appearance, which was in the *Irish People* of 26 November 1864. It is also the shortest of them, though definitely not the least interesting. Although its moral categories are simplistic, it illustrates very effectively and succinctly some of the complexity of the land question in the mid-nineteenth century. The truth which it points up — that the 'plain people' of rural Ireland could exploit one another as ruthlessly as any bad landlord — has often been forgotten, even suppressed, in line with the mythology of the land war. For Kickham, landlords and landlordism were not intrinsically wicked, nor were the people of the countryside uniformly blameless. As the conclusion of 'The lease in reversion' shows, Kickham has his own simplified explanation of the Irish agrarian problem, but it has at least the attraction of being different from the received one. And whatever about questions of analysis, this story is an excellent, if short, lesson in social history. It has been quietly forgotten because it violates certain taboos — see page 202 above. (Editorial changes in punctuation, etc., have been kept to a minimum.)

THE LEASE IN REVERSION
by Charles J. Kickham

I

"I don't like to have anything to do with it," said Ned Brennan to his wife.

"Wisha don't you? An' why so may we ask?" Mrs. Brennan spoke in a tone of the most contemptuous scorn, and her words lost nothing of bitterness when taken in connection with her look.

"For many raisons" her husband replied, quietly. "Wouldn't we want the little ready money we have to fortune off Alley? She's ould enough now for us to think of settling her."

Her mother glanced at the young woman, who was busy making griddle bread at the great kitchen table; and Mrs. Brennan's look was anything but a loving one. Her daughter appeared to feel this, for she smiled sadly as she bent over her work, and, without being observed, hastily brushed the tears from her eyes, with the back of her hand. Now, Mrs. Brennan really did love her daughter; but her son was her idol, and the thought that the girl should be an obstacle in the way of her plans for him, often made the foolish woman talk and look as if she hated his sister.

Ned Brennan was a hardworking man, who by the closest attention to his farm, aided by his wife's "management" had been able to lay by a little money from time to time, and was known to have some five or six hundred pounds in bank. His own wish was to get his daughter well married, and to leave his farm "in good heart" and "well stocked" to his son. But his wife's ambition took a higher flight, as far as her son was concerned, and nothing would satisfy her but to "make a gentleman of him".

"And what" she asked, "do you mean to do for Richard?"

"'Tis time enough to think of that" her husband replied.

"Dick is only a gorsoon yet; an' Alley is three years oulder."

"I towld you of'en enough not to be callin' the boy Dick."

"Well, Richard, Master Richard, as you tell the men to call him."

"An' do you want to keep him in the dhrag all his life? Do you think he hasn't too much sperit to be a poor spalpeen like his father, workin' and slavin' from mornin' till night?"

"He might do worse" said Ned Brennan quietly.

"Well, that's not the thing" resumed his wife, "but are you goin' to agree about the lase? You know the masther is to call to-day, an' I want to know have you your mind med up?"

"Well, if I was left to myse'f I'd rather have nothin' to say to id."

"Now, Ned Brennan, wanst for all let me tell you that if you let such a chance slip, you're a poor, mean-spirited crather."

"Suppose ould Jim Moore lived tin or a dozen years more how would it be?"

"Let him do his best an' he can't hould much longer. He's every day of ninety years if he's an hour."

"An' what about the people that has the land?"

"What about 'em but to sind 'em about their business. Two hundred acres o' the best land in the barony for twenty-five shillings an acre, an' a lase of ninety-nine years — is id mad you'd be not to take such an offer. So don't be a fool."

Master Richard came in at this moment. He was a good looking lad enough, but exceedingly awkward, and evidently wholly uneducated.

"Dick," said his father, "run out an' lend a hand puttin' in that stack, as I'm afeard we're near rain."

"Wisha don't mind killin' yourself, Richard," said his mother, "for I hope you have better prospects afore you thin to be pullin' an' draggin' like your poor slave of a father. Alley, are you forgettin' to feed the pigs?"

Alley had just sat down after finishing two griddles of bread; and now jumped up cheerfully to set about feeding the pigs.

Master Richard lounged across the fields to Molly Brophy's shebeen for half an ounce of tobacco; and after making the purchase, filled his pipe, and sat by the fire to enjoy it, together with the society of Shemus Dhu, the bailiff, who opened a conversation by declaring how much to be envied were all happy mortals like "Master Richard", who "had nothing to trouble 'em." There was some joking, too, on the subject of Biddy Brophy's stout legs. Biddy was niece to old Molly, and was destined to inherit all her aunt's worldly possessions. She was still a virtuous girl (in the ordinary sense of the phrase) but did not scruple to "put in her word" in conversations, which, to say the least of them, were not particularly edifying.

In the society of this blooming fair one and Shemus Dhu, "Master Richard" spent the eventful day upon which his mother had succeeded, to her heart's content, in "making a gentleman of him."

II

Ballycloon was a farm of about two hundred acres. It was sub-let to several tenants in lots varying from five to forty acres. The immediate landlord or middleman was a gentleman named Warren. He paid a rent of fifteen shillings an acre to the head landlord, and received thirty-five shillings from his tenants; so that Ballycloon was worth him two hundred pounds a year. The tenants were pretty comfortable; but were just beginning to feel that sense of insecurity which is so fatal to the Irish tenant, in consequence of the near approach (in all human probability) of the termination of their leases. The leases were all the same, and old Jim Moore was the last life in them. However they had every reason to hope that the landlord would give them new leases without raising the rent. They saw no grounds for suppos-ing "him a worse man than his father before him." But Mr Warren wanted five or six hundred pounds to pay off an old debt, and the most ready way to get it was to offer a lease in reversion of Ballycloon to Ned Brennan.

"Come, Ned," said Mr Warren, "here is the proposal. Have you the money ready?"

"To be sure he has, sir — why wouldn't he," Mrs Brennan replied. Ned feared to offend the landlord. The only way he could decline the proposal was by pretending that he had not enough of money; but his wife took care not to leave him this excuse. The proposal was signed, and Ned Brennan put his name on the back of his deposit receipts, and handed them to the landlord.

Mrs Brennan went out, and climbing to the top of a "double ditch," surveyed Ballycloon with its ten homesteads from end to end.

"I don't say," she observed, "but we might leave the Brians and the Bolans their land if they behave well. That cowlt must be broken in, at wanst for Master Richard. Ho! you ould devil, there you are with your crith on you!" This last observation was directed to an old man bent with age whom she saw crossing a bridge at some distance. This was old Jim Moore, upon whom from that moment Mrs Brennan looked as a deadly enemy.

"I wondher where is Richard," she continued, "till I tell him the news. He must larn to keep a high head now, for he'll shortly be the first rate man in this parish any way."

Richard was just then making his way to the stable, where he was wont to enjoy his pipe while sitting in the manger swinging his long legs in lazy contentment. His mother called to him, and the youth altered his course and approached her.

"Stand up here along side o' me," said his mother.

"Arra for what?" he asked, as if mounting the double ditch appeared to him rather a troublesome feat.

"Come up here till I show you something." The young man scrambled to the top of the ditch.

"Look at all that land, from the stone wall above down to the Curragh."

"I see it," said Richard.

"An' thim tin houses."

"Begor I see thim, too."

"An who duv you think is the landlord o' that snug little property?"

"Isn't it Misther Warren?" asked Richard in some surprise.

"The property — the *property,* you rogue o' the world," continued Mrs Brennan, poking her promising son in the ribs.

"Begob," says the youth, "myself do'n' know what you're comin' at."

"Well to make a long story short *you're* the landlord and they're your tinants; or, what's all the same, they'll be your tinants when ould Jim Moore dies, an' he's ninety if he's one day."

"Ninety-five i' you plase, mam," exclaimed a voice from behind a thorn bush. The mother and son started; and on looking round they saw the grey eyes of Jim Moore himself peering up at them.

"Ninety-five, if it is plasin' to you, mam," the old man repeated and stepping out into the field he whirled his stick over his head and walked off quite in a lively way, notwithstanding the bend in his back.

"Don't mind the ould fool," said Mrs Brennan, descending from the ditch.

"An' now, Richard, avic, you must larn to be a gintleman, and don't put on that corderoy breeches any more. Wear your cassimer every day. An' I won't let your father sell the cowlt, as you'll want him for a ridin' horse. You must keep up wid the quality from this day out Richard achora; and keep yourself clain an' dacent."

They found Alley and her father talking together in the kitchen.

"You idle sthreel," exclaimed Mrs Brennan, "why aren't you milkin' the cows?"

"Don't you see she's not well," said her father.

Alley was very pale. Her father was just after telling her that the match between herself and Tom Phelan should be "broke up," as he could not now afford to give her the necessary "fortune." Mrs Brennan felt something like remorse as she looked at her daughter.

"Well," said she, "an' can't you go take a stretch on the bed; an' I'll help to milk the cows myself. I never see the like of you for wan girl. You'll never tell when any thing is the matter with you."

Poor Alley Brennan retired to her room, to try and tear a long-cherished hope from her heart. She knew Tom Phelan loved her truly. But she knew also that his father and mother would not consent to his marrying any one who could not "bring in a fortune" for his sister. She felt that tears would be a relief to her; but she could not weep. She leant her elbows on the little window of her room, and, with her chin resting on both hands, gazed out at the setting sun.

"God's will be done!" said she. "There's nothing but disappointment in this ugly world. But I must keep up my spirits, for fear of frettin' my poor father."

The "lease in reversion" began to bear fruit early. Here is a young life blighted before the lease in reversion is one day old.

III

Jim Moore, of course, told the first person he met the important piece of news he had accidentally got possession of; and there was consternation and anger in Ballycloon. Ned Brennan met black or scornful looks wherever he turned. This act of Ned Brennan's was by far the worst thing of the kind that happened in the district for generations. The unfortunate man felt like an outcast from society, and the fluttering of a sparrow in the hedge made him shake in his shoes, for he dreaded the vengeance of some of those whom he had injured. Many and many a time Ned Brennan bitterly exclaimed to himself, "I wish to the Lord I never thought of a lase in reversion." This state of mind soon told on his constitution, and people used to remark on looking at him, that Ned Brennan was withering away like a blighted potato-stalk.

Not so his wife, who braved it out, and held her head higher than ever. Indeed, she went the length of calling upon the Brians and the Bolans and talked patronizingly to them. Her whole soul was wrapped up in Masther Richard; and great were the pains she took to make a gentleman of that amiable youth. Ned Brennan soon felt that his worldly means were wasting away, as well as the flesh from his bones. He wondered why the butter firkins were so long filling, and thought the wheat was not as productive as it ought to be. But while ruminating on this subject, as he smoked his pipe by the fire, a glance at Master Richard's boots and spurs, which, when not gracing the heels and legs of the "gentleman", always hung in the kitchen, would seem to enlighten Ned Brennan as to the wheat and butter, particularly when taken in connection with his wife's frequent visits to the market-town. Of course, a gentleman could not go to the hunt, and put up at the hotel, and meet "the quality," without having money in his pocket. And, by-the-by, the quality laughed at and cordially despised Master Richard; but they drank an immense quantity of whiskey at his expense. Mrs Brennan took down the boots, and began polishing them. They were bright enough, but the fond mother always insisted on "giving 'em a rub" before her darling put them on.

"Where is he goin' to-day?" her husband asked.

"Whisht now, Ned," said she looking admiringly at the shining boot into which her arm was thrust, "what good would it do you to know where he's goin'?"

"He didn't come home very sober last night," her husband remarked.

"An' if he didn't itself," she retorted sharply; "many's the time we see yourself takin' a sup. An' sure 'tis what every gintleman does."

"Well," said Ned Brennan standing up, and talking firmly and decidedly, "there's wan thing I won't stand in my house any way, an' you *must* turn away that girl.''

Mrs Brennan reddened up to the roots of her hair, and a look of real pain came into her eyes. Without venturing to reply, she hurried in with the boots and shoes to her son's bedroom.

Richard pulled on his boots and strapped the spurs to them, and then looked out to see whether his horse was ready. His eyes rested upon his sister who was keeping the peace between half a dozen calves which were feeding from a tub in the yard. Poor Alley looked sad enough, and with the skirt of her gown pinned up, and her arms bare, had rather the appearance of a drudge.

"I wish," said her gentleman brother, "you would tell Alley not to speak to me before gentlemen. Young Bagnel and I were at the hotel door last Saturday, and she came up to tell me something about oats at the mill, I was never so ashamed; and I wouldn't mind so much, only for that fellow Phelan was with her.''

"Tom Phelan is a dacent buy," said his mother, "an' they're well off.''

"Oh, he's well enough for a farmer," Mr Richard replied. "But you see he's a bad character, and all the gentlemen have an eye on him.''

"I never h'ard anything agin him before," said Mrs. Brennan.

"Well, I can tell you," said Mr Richard, "that fellow is a Phoenix man. But, there, the horse is saddled at last, and mind tell Alley not to pretend to know me in town any more." And gentleman Richard put on his hat and walked out. The workman who held the horse touched his hat, according to orders, and returned to the barn muttering, "Put a beggar on horseback," &c.

From this slight glimpse of Ned Brennan's household, it may safely be inferred that the visits which we happen to know he makes to the bank pretty often are not for the purpose of *lodging* money. However, thanks to the lease in reversion, he has credit. But if Jim Moore lives many years, and he appears to be growing younger and livelier every day, 'tis up with Ned Brennan, for he is already deeply in debt, and paying heavy interest too.

And how fares it with the families on Ballycloon? They are

all beggared. And why? Because they lost all energy when they found they might be driven from their farms at any moment. Thinking each year would be their last they ceased improving and manuring, and commenced the system of dragging all they could out of the land. The young men and women fled to America. In a few years the soil was so impoverished it could not make the rent. So these ten comfortable, industrious families were scattered and ruined. Ballycloon is Ireland in miniature.

Mr Richard did not think it inconsistent with his gentility to continue his visits to the shebeen house. Why should he, when he had several *"rale* gintlemen" to set him the example? Shemus Dhu, the bailiff, and our gentleman enjoyed their glass of grog together, and joked about Biddy Brophy's stout legs.

But there was a halt to our hero's gallop. It was discovered that the lease in reversion was not worth two-pence. The land was so exhausted no man in his senses would pay the twenty-five shillings an acre for it. So that, if Jim Moore kicked the bucket to-morrow, Ned Brennan could do nothing with "the property." The bank came down upon him, and seized his cows and horses, not sparing even the "gentleman's" riding horse.

Still Mrs Brennan believed in "the property," and attributed all her woes to Jim Moore's longevity. At last Jim died, but Mrs Brennan discovered to her utter bewilderment, that it would not be worth while, even if they could afford it, to go to the expense of ejecting the tenants, for it would require hundreds of pounds to put the land into heart again, and make it worth the rent. The foolish woman still continued pilfering from her husband, to keep Mr. Richard in pocket money. One day, as she sat alone near the kitchen door, Biddy Brophy's stout legs stepping across the yard attracted her attention. Biddy walked in, and placing a bundle in the old woman's lap, walked out again. Mrs. Brennan saw at a glance that the bundle was neither more nor less than a young "gentleman." Being an energetic woman, she hurried after Biddy, and implored her to take back the child, and promised to supply her with money for its support. The unfortunate girl was only too glad of the offer. Mrs. Brennan clasped her hands together and begged of God to forgive her, when she remembered how she connived at her son's immoral conduct, even in her own house.

Ned Brennan and his family were turned out of house and home, owing two year's rent. Alley volunteered to go to America, resolved to send every cent of her earnings to her father and mother. They were barely able to scrape together as much money as would pay her passage; but Mr. Richard invented some plausible story, and induced his mother to steal his sister's passage money for him. The shebeen house was shut against him, and on no terms would he be admitted till he should make Biddy Brophy an honest woman. So our worthy came at poor Mary's passage money, and converted it into his own "marriage money." So Biddy got a gentleman for a husband; but we cannot wish her joy of her bargain.

Poor Alley Brennan earned a day's hire where she could get it, and did her best to keep hunger from the cabin door. They were actually hungry one day, and Mrs. Brennan was forced to apply to her son for a "handful of meal." Mr. Richard was smoking his pipe, after assisting Shemus Dhu to drive Bolan's only cow to pound — the gentleman was regularly installed as the bailiff's assistant — when his mother walked in and told her sad story. He stood up very calmly, and taking her by the shoulder pushed her out of the house. On the whole, it was a gentle push; but it killed her. When she reached the cabin she only said, "Ned, my heart is broke," and lay down on the wisp of straw in the corner. She died that night.

IV

Tom Phelan wasn't the happiest man in the world all this time. He loved Alley Brennan better than ever. For you see Tom was a bad character and a Fenian; and the brave, uncomplaining struggle Alley Brennan made to support her father and mother raised her infinitely in his esteem. What better could you expect from such a fellow? What made his conduct the more reprehensible was the fact, that his married sister had a sister-in-law who made her house too hot for her, and she was most anxious to hand over the troublesome lady to her brother, and so get shut of her. The troublesome lady was very anxious for the exchange herself, and Tom's indifference to her blandishments, and her three hundred pounds, did not tend to sweeten her temper. His father, however, utterly set his face against his son's "marrying a pauper," and Tom Phelan did not well know what to do. One day he happened to call to a neighbouring farmer, to borrow a horse or two, to draw hay off a meadow which was liable to be flooded by the river. It was in harvest, and the farmer had a large number of reapers at work. When Tom went into the field he felt as if a dagger was plunged into his heart, for Alley Brennan, his own Alley, the girl of his heart, was one of the binders. He knew she had been obliged to earn her bread in this way, but he had never seen her so employed before.

"Father," said Tom Phelan, when he reached home, "I have my mind made up. Give the place to Mary and let me go to America. I never cared for any woman but one, and I never will."

They all saw that he was in earnest. His mother and sister threw their arms round him, and begged of him not to leave them.

"Marry her, Tom, marry her," cried his mother, "she's a good girl, and I'll give you my blessing."

"Oh, father," said Mary, "do let him marry Alley Brennan — what matter about me."

Mary was a kind-hearted girl, and, we believe, would have acted generously under any circumstances. But in this instance her brother's marrying a wife without a fortune was just what she wished. For her father had made a match for her with a big farmer from an adjoining parish, and was only waiting till Tom should "bring in a fortune," to name the day. Now Mary detested this big farmer, who only wanted money; while her heart and soul were centered in a certain young man who was ready to take her without a penny, and whose suit her father would never favour if he had a fortune to give her. And so Mary was pleading her own cause as well as her brother's. Well, to make a long story short, Tom Phelan and Alley Brennan were married, and they're now as happy a couple as you'd meet in a day's walk. They brought her father home to live with them. Tom befriended Master Richard, too, in many ways; and Master Richard showed his gratitude by stealing one of Tom's cows on a fine moonlight night. He missed the cow early next morning and started at once for the fair of M———. He just arrived in time to find a "jobber" counting eleven pounds fifteen into Master Richard's hand. Tom Phelan (being a bad character and a Fenian) did not hand over his hopeful brother-in-law to the police. He merely said to him —

"Keep it and be d——d, provided you leave the country before this day week."

The gentleman was too glad to get off so easily. He sailed for Queensland the next week. We have never heard a word about him since; and we hope we never shall.

There are only two houses instead of ten on the lands of Ballycloon. What an amount of misery and crime has been caused by this lease in reversion. But the reader will please to reflect that such things could not happen if Ireland were free.

APPENDIX TWO

KNOCKNAGOW AND CNOICÍN-A-GHABHA

For a generation after his death most accounts of Kickham's career assumed that Mullinahone was his birthplace. Early in this century they began to take note of a Mullinahone tradition that he was born at the home of his maternal grandparents near Cashel, and that the place was known in Irish as Cnoicín-a-ghabha and provided Kickham with the name of the fictional village in his most famous work. Part of that tradition is verified by the recording of his baptism in the Cashel parochial register. But where exactly was Cnoicín-a-ghabha? There is no townland in County Tipperary with a name obviously derived from it (such as 'Knickeenagow' or 'Knocknagow'). In the past fifty years or so it has been identified with Mocklershill, about four miles from Cashel, and a two-storey residence there has been pointed out as the home of the Mahonys and the house where Kickham was born. It so happens that the tithe applotment book for the area was compiled in 1828, the year of his birth, and, sure enough, that records the existence of a landholder named Mahony in Mocklershill. However, he held less than three acres and accordingly was unlikely to be living in a large farmhouse, or to be the father of two daughters sufficiently well endowed financially to marry into the prosperous Kickham family.

The tithe applotment records tell of another Mahony, the holder of nearly sixty acres on the outskirts of Cashel, in a townland called Palmershill, and he is a more likely candidate for the honour of having been Charles J. Kickham's grandfather. Mocklershill and Palmershill could easily have been confused in oral tradition, more especially as there was no Mahony in either townland by 1850.

Neither place has any proven claim to be identified with Cnoicín-a-ghabha. However, there is independent and quite fortuitously preserved evidence that the name was not the invention of somebody trying to explain 'Knocknagow'. Humphrey O'Sullivan, the diarist, writing in Irish, mentioned it briefly as a place near Cashel ('láimh le Caiseal Mumhan') where freak weather conditions were reported to have occurred on 20 July 1835 (see below, note 10 to chapter one).

NOTES TO THE TEXT

CHAPTER ONE

1 The name originated in England where the commonest form is Kirkham, with variants Kirkam and Kerkham.

2 Memorial of an indenture between John Constable and Charles Kickham, 22 Aug. 1796 (Registry of Deed, 519/100/338255); Mr. Frank Murphy of Clonmel recites this charade attributed to C. J. Kickham:

> My first is an insult not easy to bear,
> My second a dish which is prized though not rare.
> Put them together and you will unfold
> The name of a grandsire who worked not in gold.

3 Memorial of an indenture between J. R. Bradshaw and Charles Kickham, 7 Oct. 1810 (Registry of Deeds, 628/485/432880).

4 Memorial of an indenture between Robert Constable and Charles Kickham, 3 May 1815 (Registry of Deeds, 734/175/500510).

5 There is an illuminating summary of family tradition in Patrick Heffernan, *An Irish doctor's memories* (Dublin, 1958), pp. 10-11, though not all the details can be accepted as fully accurate.

6 P. J. Hamell, 'Maynooth students and ordinations, 1795-1895: index' in *Irish Ecclesiastical Record, 5th series,* cx, no. 3 (Sept. 1968), p.176.

7 T. D. O'Dowd, 'The earliest educational work of the Irish Vincentians' in *Proceedings of the Irish Catholic Historical Committee* (1962), pp. 17-22.

8 For the descendants of Charles Kickham (1752-1815) see A. K. White, 'Family of Charles J. Kickham, 1752-1840' in James Maher (ed.), *Romantic Slievenamon* (Mullinahone, 1954), pp. 240-2.

9 Samuel Lewis, *A topographical dictionary of Ireland* (2 vols, London, 1837), ii, 411.

10 Amhlaoibh Ó Súileabháin, *Cinnlae Amhlaoibh Uí Shúileabháin,* ed. Michael McGrath, S.J. (4 vols, Dublin, 1936-7).

11 O'Leary, *Recollections,* i, 264.

12 Kickham, 'Young Ireland', 24 Sept. 1881.

13 John Savage, *Fenian heroes and martyrs* (Boston [1867]), p.379.

14 Kickham, 'Young Ireland', 18 June 1881.

15 Michael Cavanagh, 'In memoriam − C. J. Kickham' in *Celtic Magazine,* i, no. 1 (Jan. 1883), p.323; J. J. Healy, *Life and times of Charles J. Kickham* (Dublin, 1915), pp.12-13.

16 Richard Kelly, *Charles J. Kickham* (Dublin, 1914), p.13 gives this detail obtained from Dr. George Sigerson who attended to Kickham's medical needs in later life.

17   The point is made most bluntly in Richard Pigott, *Recollections of an Irish national journalist* (Dublin and London, 1883), p.129.

18   O'Leary, *Recollections,* i, 265.

19   *Kilkenny Journal,* 7 Aug. 1861.

20   C. J. Kickham to T. P. Kickham, 3 Jan. 1868 (letter in possession of Mr. James Cusack, Clonmel); Kickham, 'Young Ireland', 14 May 1881.

21   Kickham 'Young Ireland', 24 Sept. 1881.

22   O'Leary, *Recollections,* i, 3.

23   Kickham, 'Young Ireland', 24 Sept. 1881.

24   Ibid., 18 June 1881 and 24 Sept. 1881.

25   Ibid., 29 Oct. 1881.

26   Ibid., 29 Oct. 1881.

27   Ibid., 29 Oct. 1881.

28   Ibid., 24 Sept. 1881.

29   Communications to undersecretary, Dublin Castle, July-Aug. 1848 (S.P.O., Outrage papers); *Hue and Cry,* 2 Sept. 1848.

30   *Tipperary Free Press,* 19 July 1848.

31   This account of events in Mullinahone on 25 and 26 July 1848 depends mainly on the following sources: reminiscences of C. J. Kickham published in C. G. Duffy, *Four years of Irish history, 1845-9* (London, 1883), pp.659-62; Patrick O'Donoghue's memoirs of the rising of 1848 (N.L.I., MS 770); and article by D. P. Conyngham (who was present) in *Irish People* (New York), 24 Feb. 1866.

32   William Despard, J. P., to high sheriff of Co. Tipperary, 26 July 1848 (S.P.O., Outrage papers).

33   The statements include those by: Michael Cavanagh, loc. cit., p.327; John Savage, op. cit., p.361; J. J. Healy, op. cit., p.17; and Rev. Matthew Russell's introduction to Kickham, *Knocknagow,* pp.vii-viii.

34   Correspondence of Rev. Daniel Corcoran with officials of Dublin Castle, Aug.-Sept. 1848 (S.P.O., Outrage papers).

35   C. J. Kickham, *Sally Cavanagh, or the untenanted graves* (Dublin, 1869), preface, p.xvii.

36   *Papers relating to proceedings for the relief of the distress, and state of unions and workhouses in Ireland: eighth series,* appendix p.xiv [1042], H. C. 1849, [xlviii, 454]

37   *Comparative view of the census of Ireland in 1841 and 1851 distinguishing the several unions and electoral divisions and showing area and population of those districts respectively,* p.9, H. C. 1852 (373), xvi, 357.

38   *Proceedings of the commissioners for the sale of incumbered estates in Ireland from commencement up to 1 January 1852,* p.11, H.C. 1852 (167), xlvii, 427.

39   John Savage, op. cit., pp.358-9.

40   C. J. Kickham, *Sally Cavanagh* (Dublin, 1869) preface, p.xviii.

CHAPTER TWO

1   Quoted in Matthew Russell, 'Charles Kickham' in *Irish Monthly,* xv, no.9 (Sept. 1887), p.487.

2   Richard Pigott, *Personal recollections of an Irish national journalist* (2nd ed., Dublin and London, 1883), p.129.

3   *Irishman,* 13 Jan. 1866.

4   *Irishman,* 25 Nov. 1865.

5   T. P. O'Connor to William Murphy, 12 Sept. 1912 (letter in possession of Mr Patrick Murphy, Drumcondra).

6   Devoy, *Recollections,* p.314.

7   *Irish People* (New York), 24 Feb. 1866.

8   Ibid., 24 Feb. 1886.

9   T. P. O'Connor to William Murphy, 12 Sept. 1911 (letter in the possession of Mr. Patrick Murphy).

10   Recollections of Bessy Rose Bradshaw (née Blunden), 18 Jan. 1899 (MS in possession of Mrs. Bradshaw, Drangan).

11   See *Valley nr. Slievenamon,* p.166.

12   See ibid., p.165.

13   *Nation,* 20 Oct. 1849 etc.

14   Kickham, 'Young Ireland', 15 Nov. 1881.

15   Ibid.

16   *Valley nr. Slievenamon,* p.115.

17   *Nation,* 10 Nov. 1849.

18   J. H. Whyte, *The independent Irish party, 1850-9,* pp.11-13.

19   *Irishman,* 4 Sept. 1869.

20   Letter of C. G. Duffy to John O'Leary quoted in *Sunday Independent,* 10 Aug. 1913.

21   *Tablet* (Dublin), 1851-2, *passim.*

22   For the general political history of this period see Whyte, op. cit.

23   *Tipperary Leader,* 27 Jan., 24 Feb. 1855.

24   See ibid., 28 Aug. 1855, leading article signed 'A Tipperary democrat'.

25   Ibid.

26   Quoted in *Valley nr. Slievenamon,* pp.143-4.

27   Quoted ibid., pp.122-3.

28   *Irishman,* 16 Mar. 1861.

29   C. G. Duffy, *Four years of Irish history, 1845-9* (London, 1883), pp.144, 241.

30   Michael Cavanagh, 'In memoriam: C. J. Kickham' in *Celtic Magazine,* i, no. 1 (Jan. 1883), p.328.

31   *Irish People* (New York), 24 Feb. 1866.

32   John Power, *Irish periodical publications, chiefly literary* (London, 1866), p.23.

33   P. C. Power, *The story of Anglo-Irish poetry* (Cork, 1967), p.62.

34   John Dunne to Michael Mullally, 1855 (photostat copy in N.L.I., MS 14215).

35   See Brian Ó Cuív, *Irish dialects and Irish-speaking districts* (Dublin, 1967), p.89.

36   Devoy, *Recollections*, p.264.
37   C. J. Kickham, 'White Humphrey of the Grange' in *Tales of Tipperary* (one vol. with C. J. Kickham, *The eagle of Garryroe*, Dublin, 1963), p.30.
38   Ibid.
39   See John Dunne, 'The fenian traditions of Slievenamon' in *Transactions of the Kilkenny Archaeological Society*, i, part 3 (1851), pp.333-62. The statement of Robert Johnston (interviewed in *Irish Press*, Christmas number, 1936), that Kickham shared his own love of Ulster Gaelic traditions and folklore, could be misleading. Immediately afterwards Johnston states that Kickham 'was moved to tears by some of the stories of Antrim and Down' and planned a history of the province. Undoubtedly, what interested Kickham was the Ulster material corresponding to his own tales — traditions of '98 and the like.

CHAPTER THREE

1   'A retrospect' in *Irish People* (Dublin), 2 Jan. 1864.
2   *Tipperary Leader*, 17 Nov. 1855.
3   Ibid., 23 Feb. 1856.
4   Kickham, 'Young Ireland', 29 Oct. 1881.
5   Ibid., 9 Apr. 1881.
6   *Irish People* (New York), 24 Feb. 1866.
7   On the Irish Papal Brigade see G. F.-H. Berkeley, *The Irish battalion in the papal army of 1860* (Dublin and Cork, 1929).
8.   Details of the Mullinahone reception etc. in *Irishman*, 10, 17 and 24 Nov. 1860.
9   *Kilkenny Journal*, 10 Nov. 1860.
10   Michael Cavanagh, 'In memoriam: Charles Kickham' in *Celtic Magazine*, i, no. 2 (Jan. 1883), p.330.
11   T. C. Luby's recollections of fenian events (N.L.I., MS 331).
12   *Irishman*, 30 Mar. 1861.
13   *Irish People* (Dublin), 2 Apr. 1864.
14   *Irishman*, 11 July 1863.
15   'Sliab-na-mban' [C. J. Kickham] in *Irishman*, 4 Oct. 1862.
16   Copy of report on Slievenamon meeting of 15 Aug. 1863, authorship not clear (S.P.O., Police and crime records, Fenian briefs).
17   Report of M. J. French, R. M., 16 Aug. 1863 (S.P.O., Chief Secretary's Office, Registered papers, 1863/7320).
18   Carlisle to Palmerston, Dublin, 24 Aug. 1863 (London, National Register of Archives, Broadlands MSS, GC/CA 518).
19   *Irishman*, 29 Aug. 1863.
20   *Kilkenny Journal*, 7 Aug. 1861.
21   See article by Hester Sigerson Piatt in *Irish Press*, 9 May 1933.
22   In *Irish People*, 12 Dec. 1863 — 2 Apr. 1864.

23 *Proceedings of the first national convention of the Fenian Brotherhood held in Chicago, Illinois,* (Philadelphia, 1863), p.8.
24 Ibid., pp.38-9.
25 Account by an inside observer of the progress of fenianism to 1868 (N.L.I., Larcom papers, MS 7517), p.111.

CHAPTER FOUR

1 Kickham to E. J. Ryan, 14 Dec. 1861 (S.P.O., Police and crime records, Fenian briefs).
2 *Irishman,* 10 May 1862.
3 These contributions were pseudonymous but are reprinted under Kickham's name in *Irishman,* 24 Apr. 1869 and ff.
4 E.g.: 'The happy land — "agitation" again', 26 July; 'A word of warning', 16 Aug.; 'A Roman sacrifice', 30 Aug.
5 O'Leary, *Recollections,* i, 227-8.
6 Printed copy of a statement by Pierce Nagle, 1865 (O'Connell Schools, Dublin, Willis papers).
7 J. Wright [James Stephens] to an anonymous friend [T. C. Luby], [1863] (S.P.O., Police and crime records, Fenian briefs, item 182).
8 James Stephens to John O'Mahony, 14 Oct. 1863 (New York Public Library, O'Donovan Rossa papers).
9 As note 7 above.
10 *Irish People,* 12 Dec. 1863.
11 C. J. Kickham, *Sally Cavanagh, or the untenanted graves* (Dublin, 1869), preface, p. ix.
12 T. C. Luby's recollections of fenian events (N.L.I., MS 331).
13 O'Leary, *Recollections,* i, 252.
14 As note 11 above.
15 For a comprehensive account of the *Irish People* and its personnel see Marcus Bourke, *John O'Leary: a study in Irish separatism* (Tralee, 1967), pp.50 84.
16 See P. J. Corish, 'Political problems, 1860-78' in P. J. Corish (ed.), *A history of Irish catholicism* (Dublin and Melbourne, 1967-71), v, fascicule 3, pp.6-23.
17 O'Leary, *Recollections,* ii, 114-5.
18 Kickham to John O'Mahony, 1865 (Washington, Catholic University of America, Fenian papers).
19 *Irish People,* 26 Dec. 1863.
20 Ibid., 26 Dec. 1863.
21 See O'Leary, *Recollections,* ii, 193-4.
22 Ibid.
23 'Archbishop Cullen's pastoral' in *Irish People,* 7 May 1864.
24 'Ecclesiastical authority' in *Irish People,* 9 Apr. 1864.
25 See Donal McCartney, 'The Church and the fenians' in *University Review,* iv, no.3, (Winter 1967), and Tomás Ó Fiaich, 'The Clergy and fenianism 1860-70' in *Irish Ecclesiastical Record,* fifth series, cix, no.2 (Feb. 1968), pp.81-103.

26   *Irishman,* 27 Feb. 1864.
27   O'Leary, *Recollections,* ii, 8-9.
28   T. P. O'Connor (of Laffana) to William Murphy, 12 Sept. 1911 (MS in the possession of Mr. Patrick Murphy).
29   T. C. Luby's recollections concerning the *Irish People* (N.L.I., MS 333) refer to the problem, *passim.*
30   O'Leary, *Recollections,* ii, 23.
31   MS 331.

CHAPTER FIVE

1   Latest edition of *Nation,* 16 Sept. 1865
2   *Nation,* 13 Jan. 1866.
3   Supplement to *Irishman,* 7 Oct. 1865.
4   Ibid., 7 Oct. 1865.
5   Ibid., 7 Oct. 1865.
6   Major O'Doherty, Paris, to Kickham, 21 Oct. 1863 (S.P.O., Police and crime records, Fenian briefs).
7   Transcript of the trial of Charles J. Kickham before the special commission (Dublin, Oireachtas Library, MS 9 D9).
8   Index to registered papers, 1863 and 1864 (S.P.O., Chief Secretary's Office).
9   Desmond Ryan, *The fenian chief: a biography of James Stephens* (Dublin and Sydney, 1967), pp.210-12.
10   *Nation,* 13 Jan. 1866.
11   Kickham to O'Mahony, [Dublin], [Sept.-Nov. 1865] (Washington, Catholic University of America, Fenian papers).
12   *Irishman,* 18 Nov. 1865.
13   *Freeman's Journal,* 13 Nov. 1865.
14   The proceedings of 14-15 Nov. are reported fully in *Irishman,* 18 Nov. 1865.
15   Ryan, op. cit., pp.215-6.
16   See, for instance, the *Irish People,* 2 Jan. 1864.
17   See, for instance, the *Irish People,* 26 Mar. 1864.
18   *Report of the proceedings at the first sitting of the special commission for the county of the city of Dublin . . . commencing on 27 November 1865* (Dublin, 1865), pp.3-5.
19   Ibid., p.841.
20   See note 7 above.
21   See note 18 above, pp.841 ff.
22   It was referred to at a later stage of the trial and is recorded in the transcript (see note 7 above).
23   Seán Ó Luing, *Ó Donnabháin Rosa I* (Baile Átha Cliath, 1969), pp.236-55.
24   Devoy, *Recollections,* p.309.
25   *Nation,* 13 Jan. 1866.
26   See note 7 above; this is the fullest available description of the trial and is the main source for the account given here.

27 Address of John Pope Hennessy, M.P., quoted in *Irishman*, 12 Oct. 1866.
28 *Irishman*, 21 April 1866.
29 *Irishman*, 25 May 1867.
30 *Irishman*, 17 Feb. 1866.
31 MS in possession of Mr. James Cusack, Clonmel; quoted in *Valley nr. Slievenamon*, pp.244-5.
32 *Irishman*, 13 Apr. 1867.
33 *Irishman*, 20 Mar. 1869.
34 C. J. Kickham to T. P. Kickham, 18 May 1866 (see note 31 above: pp. 245-7).
35 *Irishman*, 13 April 1867.
36 C. J. Kickham to T. P. Kickham, 2 Aug. 1866 (as note 31 above: pp.247-8).
37 Convict prisons records, quarter ending 30 June 1866 (London, P.R.O., H.O. 8/168).
38 Convict prisons records, quarter ending 30 Sept. 1866 (P.R.O., H.O. 8/169).
39 C. J. Kickham to T. P. Kickham, 6 Dec. 1866 (note 31 above: pp.249-50).
40 *Irishman*, 20 Mar., 22 May 1869.
41 *Irishman*, 6 July 1867.
42 Convict prisons records, 1866 (P.R.O., H.O. 8/167-70).
43 C. J. Kickham to T. P. Kickham, 6 Mar. 1867 (As note 31 above: pp.250-53).
44 *Irishman*, 6 July 1867.
45 Interview quoted in *Irishman*, 22 May 1869.
46 Letter to editor, *Irishman*, 23 Oct. 1869.
47 Nine of his prison letters have survived and are in the possession of Mr. James Cusack, Clonmel; they are published in *Valley nr. Slievenamon*, pp.244-68.
48 *Irishman*, 21 Apr., 25 Aug., 16 Oct. 1866.
49 *Irishman*, 6 July 1867.
50 *Evening Mail* quoted in *Irishman*, 13 Oct. 1866.
51 *Irishman*, 13 Apr. 1867.
52 *Report of the commissioners appointed by the Home Department to inquire into the treatment of certain treason-felony convicts in the English convict prisons* [3880], H.C. 1867 (xxxv), 673-98; after Kickham's release a much more thorough and impartial investigation was carried out by a commission under the chairmanship of the Earl of Devon.
53 E.g., *Irishman*, 7 Sept. 1867, 22 Feb. 1868.
54 *Hansard 3*, CXCV, cd.159 (22 Feb. 1869).
55 *Hansard 3*, CXCIX, col.97 (8 Feb. 1870).
56 *Irishman*, 20 Mar. 1869.
57 Ibid., 20 Mar. 1869.
58 Ibid., 20 Mar. 1869.
59 Ibid., 20 Mar. 1869.
60 C. J. Kickham to T. P. Kickham, [Salisbury], 4 Mar. [1869] (As note 31 above: pp.269-70).
61 *Irishman*, 13 Mar. 1869.
62 *Irishman*, 20 Mar. 1869.
63 Quotation from letter of Mrs. Annie White in article by Hester Sigerson Piatt in *Irish Press*, 9 May 1933.

CHAPTER SIX

1   T. P. O'Connor to William Murphy, 12 Sept. 1911 (MS in the possession of Mr. Patrick Murphy).
2   Mentioned in memorial of an indenture between A. F. Kickham and J. T. Hinds, 28 Mar. 1868 (Dublin, Registry of Deeds, 1866/11/26).
3   Ibid.
4   Newscutting, 13 Nov. 1865 (Dublin, O'Connell Schools Library, Willis papers).
5   See *Irishman,* 26 Mar. 1864.
6   *Irishman,* 6 Dec. 1865 and ff.
7   C. J. Kickham to T. P. Kickham, 2 Aug. 1866 (MS in possession of Mr. James Cusack; quoted in *Valley nr. Slievenamon,* pp.247-8.)
8   C. J. Kickham, *Sally Cavanagh, or the untenanted graves* (Dublin, 1869), preface, p.vii.
9   Ibid., xvi.
10   Ibid., xvi.
11   See, *Irishman,* 15 and 29 May 1869.
12   See *Daily News* notice quoted in *Irishman,* 11 Dec. 1869.
13   Reprint of New York *Tablet* review of *Sally Cavanagh, or the untenanted graves* (Boston, 1870) in *Emerald* (New York), 29 Jan. 1870.
14   *Shamrock,* 19 Feb. 1870.
15   *Irishman,* 24 Apr. 1869 to 12 Feb. 1870.
16   *Emerald,* 4 Dec. 1869 to 1 Jan. 1870.
17   Kickham to John O'Mahony, 28 Sept. 1869 (Washington, Catholic University of America, Fenian papers).
18   Ibid.
19   *Shamrock* (Dublin), 10 Sept. 1870.
20   Ibid., 10 Sept. 1870.
21   *Emerald,* 12 Mar. 1870.
22   *Shamrock,* 19 Mar. 1870 and ff.
23   *Shamrock,* 10 Sept. 1870.
24   Ibid., 10 Sept. 1870.
25   Ibid., 10 Sept. 1870.
26   Ibid., 10 Sept. 1870.
27   T. J. Crean to Kickham, [Dec. 1868 or Jan. 1869] (MS in possession of Mr. James Cusack; quoted in *Valley nr. Slievenamon,* pp.264-6).
28   *Tipperary People,* 2 Dec. 1898.
29   C. J. Kickham to T. P. Kickham, 4 Mar. 1869 (MS in possession of Mr. James Cusack; quoted in *Valley nr. Slievenamon,* pp.269-70).
30   Kickham to the editor of *Irishman,* 11 Dec. 1869.
31   Police report, 20 Dec. 1869 (S.P.O., Police and crime records, F papers, 5334R).
32   *Irishman,* 9 Sept. 1869.
33   *Irishman,* 21 Aug. 1869.
34   *Limerick Reporter and Tipperary Vindicator,* 22 and 29 Oct. 1869.
35   *Irishman,* 27 Nov. 1869.

36 *Irishman,* 4 Dec. 1869.
37 *Hansard 3,* cxcix, col.122.
38 *Irishman,* 29 Jan. 1870.
39 T. P. O'Connor to William Murphy, 12 Sept. 1911 (MS in possession of Mr. Patrick Murphy).
40 Luby's recollections of the *Irish People* (NLI., MS 333).
41 *Irishman,* 26 Feb. 1870.
42 See note 39 above.
43 For example, *Irishman,* 5 Mar. 1870.
44 Ibid., 5 Mar. 1870.
45 *Irishman,* 26 Feb. 1870.
46 See note 39 above.
47 Ibid., *Irishman,* 4 June 1870.
48 *Irishman,* 12 Feb. and 5 Mar. 1870.
49 *Irishman,* 26 Feb. 1870.
50 T. P. O'Connor to William Murphy, 25 Nov. 1912 (MS in possession of Mr. Patrick Murphy).
51 *Irishman,* 5 Mar. and 4 June 1870.
52 *Irishman,* 5 Mar. 1870.
53 Ibid., 5 Mar. 1870.
54 *Irishman,* 9 Apr. 1870.
55 *Irishman,* 4 June 1870.
56 *Freeman's Journal,* 31 Jan. 1874.
57 *Irishman,* 29 Nov. 1869 and ff.
58 *Nation,* 28 Sept. 1872.
59 *Irishman,* 31 Jan. 1874; Devoy, *Recollections,* p.312.
60 *Sally Cavanagh* (Dublin, 1869), preface, p.xv.
61 Ibid., p.xv.   62 Ibid., p.xv.
63 T. P. O'Connor to William Murphy, 12 Sept. 1912 (MS in possession of Mr. Patrick Murphy).
64 Annie Cleary (Mrs. White) quoted in *Irish Press,* 9 May 1933.
65 This was the impression gained by the police in 1869: 'Fenianism: index of names', p.463 (S.P.O., Police and crime records) and police report, 25 June 1869 (ibid., F papers, 4406R).

CHAPTER SEVEN

1 The emergence of the supreme council is examined in detail in R. V. Comerford, 'Irish nationalist politics, 1858-70' (Ph.D. thesis, T.C.D., 1977).
2 *Irishman,* 5 Dec. 1868.
3 Kickham to O'Mahony, 28 Sept. 1869 (Washington, Catholic University of America, Fenian papers).
4 James Stephens to his wife, 5 Sept. 1877 (N.L.I., Stephens letters, MS 10491).
5 *Tipperary People,* 2 Dec. 1898.

6   T. W. Moody and Leon Ó Broin, 'Select documents: the I.R.B. supreme council, 1868-78' in *Irish Historical Studies*, xix, no. 75 (Mar. 1975), p.304 (hereafter referred to as 'Select documents: supreme council').

7   Ibid., p.316.

8   *Irish Freedom*, Mar. 1913.

9   Ibid., May 1913.

10   'Select documents: supreme council', p.318.

11   Ibid., p.292.

12   Ibid., pp.317-22.

13   Ibid.; John Daly's recollections in *Irish Freedom*, Apr. 1913.

14   Ibid., Mar. 1913.

15   Devoy, *Recollections*, p.304.

16   *Irishman*, 7 Jan. 1871.

17   Constabulary report, Apr. or May 1870 (S.P.O., Police and crime records, F papers, 6344 R).

18   A. M. Sullivan, *New Ireland* (popular edition), p.344.

19   See David Thornley, *Isaac Butt and home rule* (London, 1964), pp.161-2.

20   Ibid., pp.164-5.

21   'Select documents: supreme council', p.314.

22   Ibid., p.329.

23   Kickham, 'Young Ireland', 4 June 1881.

24   *Irishman*, 31 Jan. 1874.

25   See his article 'John Mitchel on organisation' in *Irishman*, 31 July 1869.

26   *Irishman*, 7 Feb. 1874.

27   Ibid., 14, 21 Feb. 1874.

28   Ibid., 13 Feb. 1875; William Dillon, *Life of John Mitchel* (2 vols, London, 1888), ii, 288.

29   Ibid., ii, p.288.

30   *Irishman*, 13 Feb. 1875.

31   Ibid., 13 Feb. 1875.

32   Ibid., 20 Feb. 1875.

33   Ibid., 20 Feb. 1875.

34   Ibid., 27 Feb. 1875.

35   William Dillon, *Life of John Mitchel*, ii, 294.

36   Fr. Richard Galvin to Fr. Thomas Hickey, 23 Mar. 1875 (Doran papers in possession of Mr. John Elliott).

37   R. F. Foster, *Charles Stewart Parnell: the man and his family* (London, 1976), p.141.

38   Ibid., p.141.

39   Kickham to Thomas Crean, 23 Nov. 1881 (quoted in *Valley nr. Slievenamon*, p.299).

40   See note 37 above.

41   C. G. Doran to John Devoy, 30 June 1875 (William O'Brien and Desmond Ryan (ed.), *Devoy's post bag* (2 vols., Dublin, 1948 and 1953), i, 114-5).

42   William Carroll to John Devoy, 8 Feb. 1876 (*Devoy's post bag*, i, 133-5).

43   Editorial note in *Devoy's post bag*, i, 76.

44 William Carroll to John Devoy, 8 Feb. 1876 (*Devoy's post bag,* i, 133-5).
45 Kickham to Devoy, 29 Apr. 1876 (*Devoy's post bag,* i, 162-5).
46 Ibid.
47 'Select documents: supreme council', p.320 and p.329, note 23.
48 William Carroll to John Devoy, 26 May 1876 (*Devoy's post bag,* i, 170-71).
49 'Select documents: supreme council', p.321.
50 Ibid., p.294.
51 Kickham to C. G. Doran, 6 Aug. 1875 (Doran papers).
52 This is clear from the letters of Kickham preserved among the Doran papers.
53 Leon Ó Broin, *Revolutionary underground: the story of the Irish Republican Brotherhood, 1858-1924* (Dublin, 1976), p.11.
54 Kickham to C. G. Doran, 28 Feb. 1878 (Doran papers).
55 Kickham to Devoy, 6 July 1876 (*Devoy's post bag,* i, 191-3).
56 *The Irish Times,* 5 Mar. 1877; *Irishman,* 10 Mar. 1877.
57 Quoted in Michael Cavanagh, 'In memoriam: Charles J. Kickham', in *Celtic Magazine,* i, no. 2 (Feb. 1883), pp.425-6; also in *Irishman,* 10 Mar. 1877.
58 Fenian police reports: memoranda of government files, 1876-80 (S.P.O., Police and crime records).
59 Kickham to C. G. Doran, 11 Nov. 1875 (Doran papers).
60 T. P. O'Connor to William Murphy, 12 Sept. 1912 (MS in possession of Mr. Patrick Murphy).
61 Kickham to O'Donovan Rossa, 4 Sept. 1876 (*Devoy's post bag,* i, 201).
62 It appeared in *Thom's Directory* from 1869 to 1875 inclusive, but not subsequently.
63 Records of proceedings, Landed Estates Court, Jan. 1875-Apr. 1876 (Dublin, Public Record Office), p.433.
64 Memorial of an indenture between A. F. Kickham and C. J. Kickham, 9 Mar. 1877 (Dublin, Registry of Deeds, 1877/11/139).
65 Record of Conveyances, Landed Estates Court, Jan. 1878-Dec. 1879 (Dublin, Public Record Office), p.52.
66 Fragment of letter from Kickham, addressee unknown, late 1881 (MS in possession of Mr. Patrick Murphy).

CHAPTER EIGHT

1 Kickham to John Devoy, 6 July 1876 (*Devoy's post bag,* i, 191-3).
2 David Thornley, *Isaac Butt and home rule,* pp.305 ff.
3 Ibid., pp.341-2.
4 *Irishman,* 15 Dec. 1877.
5 T. W. Moody, 'The new departure in Irish politics, 1878-9', in H. A. Cronne and others (ed.), *Essays in British and Irish history in honour of James Eadie Todd* (London, 1949), p.315.
6 F. S. L. Lyons, *Charles Stewart Parnell* (London, 1977), p.71.
7 Moody, loc. cit., p. 312.

8   Leon Ó Broin, *Revolutionary underground: the story of the Irish Republican Brotherhood, 1858-1924* (Dublin, 1976), pp.21-3.

9.   F. S. L. Lyons, *Ireland since the famine* (Dublin, 1971), p.154.

10   Postmaster-general, London, to under-secretary, Dublin Castle, 15 Nov. 1878 (S.P.O., Police and crime records, A files, no. 550).

11   Lyons, *Parnell,* p.80.

12   Police report, 5 Nov. 1878 (S.P.O., Police and crime records, A files, no. 550).

13   O'Leary to Devoy, 8 Nov. 1878 (*Devoy's post bag,* i, 373-4).

14   Moody, loc. cit., p.326.

15   Devoy, *Recollections,* p.313.

16   *Irish Freedom,* June 1914.

17   Devoy, *Recollections,* pp.313-4.

18   Ibid., p.313.

19   Ibid., p.314.

20   Marcus Bourke, *John O'Leary: a study in Irish separatism* (Tralee, 1967), pp.158-9.

21   Lyons, *Parnell,* p.88.

22   Ó Broin, *Revolutionary Underground,* p.23.

23   Lyons, *Parnell,* pp.97-8.

24   *Irishman,* 6 Sept., 4 Oct. 1862.

25   See *Irish Monthly,* 7 May, 25 June, 2 and 30 July, 13 Aug. 1864, 8 Apr. 1865.

26   *Irish Monthly,* 25 June 1864.

27   *Tribune* (Dublin), 1855-6.

28   See 'Never give up' in C. J. Kickham, *Tales of Tipperary* (Dublin, 1963), pp.65-6.

29   *Valley nr. Slievenamon,* p.361.

30   Kickham to C. G. Duffy [1881] (N.L.I., C. G. Duffy papers, MS 8005).

31   1 Apr. 1865.

32   Kickham, 'Young Ireland', 25 May 1881.

33   Lyons, *Parnell,* p.89.

34   Bourke, op. cit., p.160.

35   Kickham to P. J. Quinn, 27 May 1882 (N.L.I., P. J. Quinn letters, MS 5930).

36   O'Kelly to Devoy, 11 Feb. 1880 (*Devoy's post bag,* i, p.488-90).

37   Davitt to Devoy, 5 Oct. 1880 (*Devoy's post bag,* i, p.555).

38   Bourke, op. cit., pp.163-6.

39   Kickham to Thomas Crean, 1881 (*Valley nr. Slievenamon,* pp.295-7).

40   Kickham to J. F. X. O'Brien, no date (N.L.I., J. F. X. O'Brien papers, MSS 13418-77).

41   See note 38 above.

42   Ibid.

43   Kickham to Thomas Crean, 23 Nov. 1881 (*Valley nr. Slievenamon,* pp. 298-9).

44   Ibid.

45   Ibid.

46   Ibid.

47   Quoted in *Freeman's Journal,* 5 Nov. 1881.

CHAPTER NINE

1   Quoted in *Valley nr. Slievenamon,* p.270.

2   *Freeman's Journal,* 23 Aug. 1882.

3   Kickham to George Fottrell, 8 Nov. 1881 (MS in possession of George Fottrell and Sons, Solicitors, Dublin); Kickham to T. J. Crean, 23 Nov. 1881 (quoted in *Valley nr. Slievenamon,* p.298).

4   William Carroll to John Devoy, 11 Aug. 1878 (*Devoy's post bag,* i, 343).

5   Report of deputation appointed by fund committee to wait on C. J. Kickham, 25 Feb. 1879 (MS in possession of G. Fottrell and Sons).

6   Ibid.

7   *Freeman's Journal,* 20 Sept. 1879; deed of trust, 3 Feb. 1881 (MS in possession of G. Fottrell and Sons).

8   *Freeman's Journal,* 15 Nov. 1878.

9   Devoy, *Recollections,* pp.123-4.

10 T. P. O'Connor implied that it was in Mountjoy (see note 17 below), Devoy, *Recollections,* p.316 that it was in Woking.

11 See P. J. Corish, 'Political problems, 1860-78' in P. J. Corish (ed.), *A history of Irish catholicism* (Dublin, 1967-71), v, fasc. 3, pp.43-4.

12 Mark Tierney, *Croke of Cashel: the life of Archbishop Thomas William Croke, 1823-1902* (Dublin, 1976), pp.7-8.

13 Ibid., p.15.

14 Ibid., p.73.

15 *Freeman's Journal,* 25 Jan. 1878.

16 Tierney, *Croke,* p.91.

17 T. P. O'Connor to William Murphy, 4 Aug. 1911 (MS in possession of Mr. Patrick Murphy); T. P. O'Connor, 'My friend Charles Kickham' in *Gaelic American,* 4 Apr. 1925.

18 Quoted in Matthew Russell, 'Charles Kickham: a sketch with some letters' in *Irish Monthly,* xv, no.9 (Sept. 1887), pp.483-98.

19 Ibid., pp.494-5.

20 Ibid., p.498.

21 Ibid., p.489.

22 Ibid., p.489.

23 Ibid., p.495.

24 Ibid. and 'A few more relics of Charles Kickham' in vol. xvi, no.3 (Mar. 1888), pp.131-7.

25 *Irish Monthly,* xv, no.9, p.493.

26 Ibid., p.493.

27 Ibid., p.485.

28 Ibid., p.492.

29 Ibid., p.485.

30 Kickham to George Fottrell, 3 Apr. 1881 (MS in possession of G. Fottrell and Sons).

31 Matthew Russell, *Rose Kavanagh and her verses* (Dublin, 1909), pp.5-6; Katharine Tynan, *Memories* (London, 1924), pp.165-7.

32 Ibid.

33 Matthew Russell, *Rose Kavanagh,* p.5.

34   Full text in *Valley nr. Slievenamon*, pp.95-6.
35   Katharine Tynan, *Memories*, pp.165-7.
36   Ibid.
37   'An autumn moon', quoted in *Valley nr. Slievenamon*, p.97.
38   *Irishman*, 26 Mar. 1881.
39   Ibid., 26 Mar. 1881.
40   Kickham to Duffy, 6 Feb. 1881 (N.L.I., C. G. Duffy papers, MS 8005).
41   Duffy to Kickham (quoted in *Irish Monthly*, vol. xv, no. 9, p.488).
42   Ibid., p.493.
43   *Freeman's Journal*, 14 Nov. 1878.
44   *United Ireland*, 2 Sept. 1882.
45   Kickham to George Fottrell, 8 Nov. 1881 and again 15 Nov. 1881, and
Patrick O'Byrne to Kickham, 15 Nov. 1881 (MSS in possession of G. Fottrell and
Sons).
46   Devoy, *Recollections*, pp.314-5.
47   Ibid., p.306.
48   Kickham to Matthew Russell, 25 Feb. 1881 (quoted in *Irish Monthly*, xv,
no. 9, p.489).
49   Ibid.
50   Ibid.
51   Kickham to C. G. Doran, 6 Aug. 1875 (Doran papers); Kickham to John
Devoy, 29 Apr. 1876 (*Devoy's post bag*, i, 162); Devoy, *Recollections*, p.314;
Kickham to Matthew Russell, Feb. 1881 (quoted in *Irish Monthly*, xv, no. 9 (Sept.
1887), p.494); Kickham to George Fottrell, 8 Nov. 1881 (MS in possession of G.
Fottrell and Sons).
52   Devoy, *Recollections*, p.314.
53   Kickham to C. G. Doran, 6 Aug. 1875 (Doran papers).
54   Quoted in *Irish Monthly*, xv, no. 9 (Sept. 1887), p.494.
55   Ibid., p.488.
56   Ibid., pp.496-7.
57   Ibid., p.489.
58   Ibid., p.494; Michael Cavanagh, 'In memoriam: C. J. Kickham', in *Celtic
Magazine*, i, no.3 (Mar. 1888), p.504.
59   Molly O'Connor to Ellen O'Leary, 24 Aug. 1882 (quoted in *Irish
Monthly*, xvi, no.3 (Mar. 1888), pp.136-7).
60   George Sigerson to George Fottrell, 19 Aug. 1882 (MS in possession of
George Fottrell and Sons).
61   See note 59 above.
62   Ibid.
63   *Freeman's Journal*, 25 Aug. 1882.
64   E. D. Gray to George Fottrell, 25 Aug. 1882 (MS in possession of G. Fottrell
and Sons).
65   *Freeman's Journal*, 26 Aug. 1882.
66   Mark Ryan, *Fenian memories* (Dublin, 1945), p.80; Devoy, *Recollections*,
p.317.
67   *Freeman's Journal*, 28 Aug. 1882.
68   For a factual description of the *cortége* see relevant police report, 27 Aug.
1882 (S.P.O., Chief secretary's office, Registered papers, 1882/36204).

69   *United Ireland,* 2 Sept. 1882.
70   See *Valley nr. Slievenamon,* p.303.
71   Ibid., p.56.
72   *United Ireland,* 2 Sept. 1882; *Tipperary People,* 1 Sept. 1882.
73   Ibid.
74   Ibid.
75   Fr. Walter Skehan's index of Cashel clergy (Thurles, Cashel archdiocesan archives).
76   Draft of letter from J. F. X. O'Brien to Alexander Kickham, Sept 1882 (N.L.I., J. F. X. O'Brien papers, MSS 13418-77).
77   Alexander Kickham to J. F. X. O'Brien, 5 Sept. 1882 (ibid.).
78   Certified copy of administration, 24 Nov. 1882 (MS in possession of G. Fottrell and Sons).
79   Entry in register of wills administrations, 20 Aug. 1885 (Dublin, Public Record Office of Ireland).
80   Kickham to E. Dwyer Grey, 19 Sept. 1879, in *Freeman's Journal,* 20 Sept. 1879.
81   Alexander Sullivan to John Devoy, 6 Sept. 1882 (*Devoy's post bag,* ii, 134); Marcus Bourke, *John O'Leary, p.219.*

CHAPTER TEN

1   See Donal McCartney, 'The church and the fenians' in *University Review,* iv, no. 3 (Winter 1967).
2   'Select documents: supreme council', p.317.
3   Kickham, 'Young Ireland', 17 Sept. 1881.
4   *Irish Freedom,* April 1913.
5   Quoted in *Irish Monthly,* xv, no. 9 (Sept. 1887), p.492.
6   R. B. O'Brien, *The Life of Charles Stewart Parnell* (London, 1898), p.355.
7   Quoted in *Valley nr. Slievenamon,* p.210.
8   Kickham, 'Young Ireland', 16 Apr. 1881.
9   Marcus Bourke, *John O'Leary,* p.166.
10   15 October 1864.
11   C. J. Kickham, *Knocknagow,* p.453.

CHAPTER ELEVEN

1   Extracts from Irish almanacs, with notes by John McCall (MS in possession of Mr. B. P. Bowen, Dublin; on microfilm in N.L.I.).
2   Kickham, 'Young Ireland', 9 Apr. 1881.
3   *Irish Harp,* nos. 2-4 (Apr. 1863, Jan. 1864, Mar. 1864).
4   S. J. Brown, *Ireland in fiction I* (2nd ed., London and Dublin, 1919).
5   *Irishman,* 30 Nov. 1861.

6   C. J. Kickham, *Knocknagow* (1959 ed.), pp.564-5.

7   This point was suggested to me by Rt. Rev. Maurice Browne, who, under the *nom-de-plume* Joseph Brady, scored remarkable success with a fictionalised family and local history in the *Knocknagow* vein, i.e. *The big sycamore* (Dublin, 1958).

8   *Knocknagow*, pp.236-7.

9   Matthew Russell 'A few more relics of Charles Kickham' in *Irish Monthly*, xvi (Mar. 1888), pp.131-2.

10   George Eliot, *Adam Bede* (Everyman edition, 1977), p.160.

11   *Knocknagow*, p.242.

12   C. J. Kickham, *For the old land* (1931 ed., Dublin), pp.32-3.

13   Ibid., p.247.

14   Ibid., p.210.

15   C. J. Kickham, *The eagle of Garryroe* (in one vol. with *Tales of Tipperary*, Dublin, 1963), pp.63-4.

16   'The place of Charles Kickham' in James Maher (ed.), *Sing a song of Kickham* (Dublin, 1965).

17   C. G. Duffy, *Four years of Irish history* (London, 1883), p.659, note.

18   See *Irish Fireside*, 6 Mar., 3 and 24 Apr. 1886.

19   Ibid., 2 Jan. – 24 Apr. 1886.

20   W. B. Yeats, *Representative Irish tales: second series* (London and New York, 1891), pp.243-5, 249-80.

21   Micheál Ó Breathnach, *Cnoc na nGabha, cuid I* (Baile Atha Cliath, 1906).

22   Richard Fallis, *The Irish renaissance: an introduction to Anglo-Irish literature* (Dublin, 1978).

23   Information kindly supplied by Michael Gill.

24   See J. A. Murphy, *Ireland in the twentieth century* (Dublin, 1975), p.84.

BIBLIOGRAPHY

SYNOPSIS

Primary Sources

PRIMARY SOURCES

I Institutional archives, state papers and public records
CASHEL DIOCESAN ARCHIVES, THURLES
Archbishop Croke papers (on microfilm in N.L.I.)
Fr. Walter Skehan's index of Cashel clergy
CASHEL CATHOLIC PAROCHIAL RECORDS
Register of baptisms 1793-1831
Register of marriages 1793-1831
MULLINAHONE CATHOLIC PAROCHIAL RECORDS
Register of baptisms, 1809-80
Register of marriages, 1810-80
OIREACHTAS LIBRARY, DUBLIN
Transcripts of the trial of C. J. Kickham before the special commission, January 1866: MS 9 D9 (on microfilm in N.L.I.)
PUBLIC RECORD OFFICE, DUBLIN
Tithe applotment books
Records of the Commissioners of National Education
Indexes to wills and administrations
Records of Landed Estates Court
Notebooks of Mr Justice William Keogh

PUBLIC RECORD OFFICE, LONDON
Home Office papers, 1866-9
REGISTRY OF DEEDS, DUBLIN
Memorials of registered deeds
STATE PAPER OFFICE, DUBLIN CASTLE
Chief Secretary's Office, registered papers
Outrage papers
Police and crime records: Fenian papers

II   Private papers and manuscripts
Bessy Rose Bradshaw's recollections and last testament, 18 January 1899 (in posses-
sion of Mrs Bradshaw, Drangan)
Broadlands MSS: letters of seventh earl of Carlisle, 1857-64 (temporarily at National
Register of Archives) (by permission of the Trustees of the Broadlands Archives)
C. G. Doran papers: correspondence of C. J. Kickham (in possession of Mr John
Elliott, Dublin)
C. G. Duffy letters (N.L.I., MS 8005)
John Dunne papers (photostat in N.L.I., MS 14215)
Fenian papers (Washington, Catholic University of America; on microfilm in N.L.I.)
George Fottrell and Sons, Solicitors, Dublin: client file on C. J. Kickham, 1879-82
W. E. Gladstone papers: correspondence and cabinet minutes, 1868-70 (British
Library)
C. J. Kickham letters in possession of Mr James Cusack, Clonmel
C. J. Kickham MSS in possession of Mr. A. F. Swaine, Dublin
Sir Thomas Larcom papers (N.L.I., MS 7517)
T. C. Luby's recollections of fenianism and the *Irish People* (N.I.L., MSS 331-3)
John McCall's extracts from Irish almanacs (in possession of Mr B. P. Bowen, Dublin;
microfilm in N.L.I.)
William Murphy's collection of papers concerning the life and work of C. J. Kickham
(in possession of Mr Patrick Murphy, Dublin)
Norton family's papers and scrapbooks (in possession of Miss Nora Norton,
Mullinahone)
J. F. X. O'Brien papers (N.L.I., MSS 13418-77)
Patrick O'Donohue's memoir of the rising of July 1848 (N.L.I., MS 770).
O'Donovan Rossa papers (New York Public Library; microfilm in N.L.I.)
O'Mahony and Mandeville papers in possession of Mrs Hanrahan, Ballycurkeen,
Carrick-on-Suir
P. J. Quinn letters (N.L.I., MS 5930)
Thomas Willis's collection of fenian documents (in library of O'Connell's School,
Dublin, under the care of Brother Allen)

III   Published collections of documents
Letters of John O'Mahony in James Maher (ed.), *Chief of the Comeraghs: a John
O'Mahony anthology* (Mullinahone, 1957), pp.77-124.
William O'Brien and Desmond Ryan (ed.), *Devoy's post bag* (2 vols, Dublin, 1948
and 1953).
T. W. Moody and Leon Ó Broin, 'Select documents: XXXII, The I.R.B. supreme
council, 1868-78' in *Irish Historical Studies*, xix, no.75 (Mar. 1975), pp.286-332.
Peadar Mac Suibhne, *Paul Cullen and his contemporaries* (5 vols, Naas, 1961-77).

IV Works of C. J. Kickham published in book form
(No notice is taken here of the many popular ballad collections and songbooks which have featured Kickham items.)
Sally Cavanagh, or the untenanted graves (1st ed., Dublin and London, 1869; many subsequent editions).
Knocknagow, or the homes of Tipperary (1st ed., Dublin, 1873; numerous subsequent editions).
For the old land: a tale of twenty years ago (1st ed., Dublin, 1886; many subsequent editions).
'The pig-driving peelers' in W. B. Yeats (ed.), *Representative Irish tales,* 2nd series (New York and London, 1891), pp.249-80; (an extract from *For the old land*)
The eagle of Garryroe (1st ed., Dublin, 1920; a few subsequent editions).
Tales of Tipperary (Dublin, 1926; reprinted 1963 in one vol. with *The eagle of Garryroe*).
H. L. Doak (ed.), *Poems of Charles Joseph Kickham with a life and notes* (Dublin, 1931).
James Maher (ed.), *The valley near Slievenamon: a Kickham anthology* (Mullinahone, 1942).
James Maher (ed.), *Sing a song of Kickham: songs of Charles J. Kickham with Gaelic versions and musical notations* (Dublin, 1965).

V Articles and reviews attributable to C. J. Kickham
As the vast majority of Kickham's leading articles were published anonymously or under pen-names there is little hope of identifying them all. A key letter after each of the items below indicates the source of the evidence for Kickham's authorship. In a few instances conflicting evidence has had to be weighed.

A = Original MS extant in Kickham's hand
B = Authorship acknowledged by Kickham
C = Republished under Kickham's name in *Irishman,* 1869-70
D = T. C. Luby's recollections of the *Irish People* (N.L.I., MS 333)
E = John O'Leary, in *Recollections of fenians and fenianism* (2 vols, London, 1896), or elsewhere (Here I am indebted to Mr Marcus Bourke.)
F = Compelling internal evidence (wording, etc.)
G = *Nom de plume* used elsewhere by Kickham, supported by suggestive internal indication

Tipperary Leader

25 Aug.	1855	The 'labouring man'	C
23 Feb.	1856	Why Irishmen should be armed	C

Irishman

30 Nov.	1861	Notice of *Frank O'Donnell: a tale of Irish life*	G
18 Jan.	1862	Notice of *Duffy's Hibernian Magazine*	G
5 July	1862	Our exiled brothers	C
12 July	1862	Our protestant patriots . . .	C
19 July	1862	The banquet to The O'Donoghue	C
26 July	1862	The happy land — 'agitation' again	C
16 Aug.	1862	A word of warning	C

30 Aug.	1862	A Roman sacrifice	C
6 Sept.	1862	A threatening letter with a vengeance	C
4 Oct.	1862	Standing at bay	C
18 Oct.	1862	Lancashire distress and Irish gentility	C
15 Nov.	1862	Our patriot prelate	C
22 Nov.	1862	Notice of *The old mountain home, or the eviction*	G
13 Dec.	1862	Lancashire distress . . . Clonmel again	C
18 Apr.	1863	What can poor Ireland do?	C
2 May	1863	Independent opposition — What is it?	C

Irish People

12 Dec.	1863	Two sets of principles	E
19 Dec.	1863	Two sets of principles	E
26 Dec.	1863	Irish doctrinaires	C
26 Dec.	1863	A retrospect	C
2 Jan.	1864	A retrospect	C
9 Jan.	1864	A retrospect	C
16 Jan.	1864	A retrospect	C
16 Jan.	1864	General Corcoran	C
23 Jan.	1864	Liberty or destruction	C
23 Jan.	1864	The élite of property	C
30 Jan.	1864	Making known our grievance	E
30 Jan.	1864	Shrovetide	C
6 Feb.	1864	A retrospect	C
13 Feb.	1864	A retrospect	C
13 Feb.	1864	The flax panacea	C
20 Feb.	1864	The Chicago fair	C
20 Feb.	1864	The use of arms	C
27 Feb.	1864	The bishop of Chicago and the Chicago fair	E
5 Mar.	1864	Federal enlistment	E
12 Mar.	1864	Silent action	C
19 Mar.	1864	The Chicago fair — denunciations	C
26 Mar.	1864	Ireland united	E
2 Apr.	1864	The national teachers of the anti-national schools	C
9 Apr.	1864	Ecclesiastical authority	C
16 Apr.	1864	Sectarianism	E
16 Apr.	1864	Deeds not words	C
23 Apr.	1864	Pistols and daggers	C
30 Apr.	1864	North and south	C
7 May	1864	Archbishop Cullen's pastoral	C
14 May	1864	The Irish fair in Chicago	C
14 May	1864	The politico-ecclesiastical history of a parish	F
21 May	1864	The bishop of Toronto on emigration	E
28 May	1864	Preparation	C
4 June	1864	Priests and politics	E
18 June	1864	Emigration	F
30 July	1864	Graziers	E
20 Aug.	1864	Dr Cullen's late pastoral	E

24 Sept.	1864	Pulpit denunciations	E
1 Oct.	1864	Clerical calumniators	E
15 Oct.	1864	National Sports	F
5 Nov.	1864	The women of Ireland	F
5 Nov.	1864	Cappawhite and Mullinahone	F
12 Nov.	1864	The special dispensation	E
26 Nov.	1864	The sins of the *Irish People*	E
10 Dec.	1864	Plain speaking	E
17 Dec.	1864	Going against the priests	E
24 Dec	1861	Tralee and Skibbereen	E
31 Dec.	1864	Priests in politics	D
7 Jan.	1865	The new agitation	E
7 Jan.	1865	The enemy's press	E
21 Jan.	1865	Public delinquents	E
4 Feb.	1865	The new association pastoral	E
11 Feb.	1865	Temporal v spiritual	E
18 Feb.	1865	Priests and politicians	E
25 Mar.	1865	Archbishop Purcell's 'card'	E
1 Apr.	1865	Non-electors and elections	E
15 Apr.	1865	The Louth election	A
22 Apr.	1865	Peace in America	B
29 Apr.	1865	The 'national association'	A
6 May	1865	Our clerical correspondents	A
20 May	1865	Review of poetry of William Allingham	A
3 June	1865	An electioneering dodge	E
17 June	1865	Fenianism metamorphosed	E
24 June	1865	The new association	A
1 July	1865	Pulling the wires	E
15 July	1865	An ex-rebel up for Tipperary	A
29 July	1865	The elections	E
12 Aug.	1865	Popularity	A
19 Aug.	1865	The affray at Dangan	A
26 Aug.	1865	Cattle before men	A
16 Sept.	1865	Priests in politics	E

Irishman

| 9 Nov. | 1878 | 'Fenians' in parliament | B |

From 26 Mar. to 5 Nov. 1881 the *Irishman* carried Kickham's 'Notes on Young Ireland' under his own name. This series was an extended commentary on C. G. Duffy, *Young Ireland: a fragment of Irish history, 1840-45.*

VI Published memoirs and other works written by contemporaries
Michael Cavanagh, 'In memoriam: Charles J. Kickham' in *Celtic Magazine,* i, nos. 1, 2 and 3 (Jan.-Mar. 1883)
Michael Davitt, *The fall of feudalism in Ireland* (London and New York, 1904)

Joseph Denieffe, *A personal narrative of the Irish revolutionary brotherhood* (New York, 1906)

John Devoy, *Recollections of an Irish rebel* (New York, 1929)

Charles Gavan Duffy, *Young Ireland* (final edition, London, 1896)

Charles Gavan Duffy, *Four years of Irish history, 1845-9* (London, 1883)

George Eliot, *Adam Bede* (London, 1859)

Robert Johnston, Interview in *Irish Press*, Christmas number, 1936.

T. P. O'Connor, 'My friend Charles Kickham' in *Gaelic American*, 4 Apr. 1925

Jeremiah O'Donovan Rossa, *Irish rebels in English prisons* (New York, 1882)

John O'Leary, *Recollections of fenians and fenianism* (2 vols, London, 1896)

Amhlaoibh Ó Súileabháin, *Cinnlae Amhlaoibh Uí Shúileabháin*, ed. Michael McGrath (4 vols, Dublin, 1936-7)

Richard Pigott, *Recollections of an Irish national journalist* (2nd ed., Dublin, 1883)

Proceedings of the first national convention of the Fenian Brotherhood held in Chicago, Illinois (Philadelphia, 1863)

Mark Ryan, *Fenian memories* (Dublin, 1945)

Rev Matthew Russell, 'Charles Kickham' in *Irish Monthly*, xv, no.9 (Sept. 1887)

Rev Matthew Russell, 'A few more relics of Charles Kickham' in *Irish Monthly*, xvi, no.3 (Mar. 1886)

Rev Matthew Russell, Introduction to C. J. Kickham, *Knocknagow, or the homes of Tipperary* (3rd ed., Dublin, 1879)

John Savage, *Fenian heroes and martyrs* (Boston, 1868)

Hester Sigerson, Personal recollections of C. J. Kickham in *Irish Press*, 9 May 1933.

A. M. Sullivan, *New Ireland* (14th ed., Glasgow, 1882)

Katharine Tynan, *Memories* (London, 1924)

Annie Kickham White, 'The family of Charles Kickham, 1752-1940' in James Maher (ed.), *Romantic Slievenamon* (Mullinahone, 1954)

VII   Parliamentary and other official publications

Second report of the commissioners of Irish education enquiry, H.C. 1826-7 (12), xii

Copies or extracts of correspondence relating to the state of union workhouses in Ireland: second series, H.C. 1847 (790), lv

Sir Richard Griffith, *General valuation of rateable property in Ireland* (Dublin, 1847-64)

Papers relating to the proceedings for the relief of the distress, and state of unions and workhouses in Ireland: eighth series, H.C. 1849 (1042), xlviii

Comparative view of the census of Ireland in 1841 and 1851, distinguishing the several unions and electoral divisions, and showing area and population of those areas respectively, H.C. 1852 (373), xlvi

Proceedings of the commissioners for the sale of incumbered estates in Ireland from commencement up to 1 January 1852, H.C. 1852 (167), xlviii

Census of Ireland for the year 1861: province of Munster [3204] H.C. 1863, liv

Report of the proceedings at the first sitting of the special commission for the county of the city of Dublin, held at Green Street, Dublin, for the trial of Thomas Clarke Luby and others for treason felony ... commencing on 27 November 1865 (Dublin, 1866)

Report of the commissioners appointed by the Home Department to inquire into the treatment of certain treason-felony convicts in the English convict prisons [3880], H.C. 1867, xxxv

Report of the commissioners appointed to inquire into the treatment of treason-felony convicts in English prisons, together with appendix and minutes of evidence [C 319], H.C. 1871, xxxii.

Special commission act, 1888: reprint of the shorthand notes of the speeches, proceedings and evidence taken before the commissioners (12 vols, London, 1890)

Hansard's parliamentary debates, third series

VIII   Newspapers and periodicals: contemporary or quoting contemporaries

Celt (Dublin), 1857-9
Duffy's Hibernian Magazine (Dublin), 1864
Emerald (New York), 1869-70
Freeman's Journal (Dublin)
Hue and Cry (Dublin), 1848
Irish Fireside (Dublin), 1886
Irish Freedom (Dublin), 1913
Irish Harp (Dublin), 1863-4
Irishman (Dublin)
Irish Monthly (Dublin), 1881-7
Irish People (Dublin), 1863-5
Irish People (New York), 1886
Irish Press (Dublin), 1933, 1936
Irish Times (Dublin)
Kilkenny Journal (Kilkenny), 1857-65
Nation (Dublin)
Shamrock (Dublin), 1869-70
Sunday Independent (Dublin), 1913
Tablet (Dublin), 1850-52
Times (London)
Tipperary Examiner (Clonmel), 1858-9
Tipperary Free Press (Clonmel)
Tipperary Leader (Thurles), 1855-6
Tipperary People (Tipperary), 1898
Transactions of the Kilkenny Archaeological Society (Dublin)
Tribune (Dublin), 1855-6
United Ireland (Dublin)
Young Ireland (Dublin), 1875-8

IX   Works of reference

S. J. Brown, *Ireland in fiction I* (2nd ed., Dublin and London, 1919)
Dictionary of national biography (22 vols, London, 1908-9)
P. J. Hamell, 'Maynooth students and ordinations, 1795-1895: index' in *Irish Ecclesiastical Record:* 5th series, cix, no.1 (Jan.1968) to cx, no.6 (Dec. 1968)
Irish Catholic Directory
Samuel Lewis, *Topographical dictionary of Ireland* (2 vols, London, 1837)
D. J. O'Donoghue, *The poets of Ireland: a biographical dictionary* (London, 1892-3)

John Power, *Irish periodical publications, mainly literary* (London, 1866)
Thom's directory

SECONDARY SOURCES

X   Principal later writings referring to C. J. Kickham
J. J. Healy, *Life and times of Charles J. Kickham* (Dublin, 1915)
Patrick Heffernan, *An Irish doctor's memories* (Dublin, 1958)
Richard Kelly, *Charles J. Kickham* (Dublin, 1914)
James Maher, 'Slievenamon and Kickham' in James Maher (ed.), *Romantic Slievenamon* (Mullinahone, 1954)
Mullinahone Macra na Tuaithe, *Charles Joseph Kickham and his native parish of Mullinahone* (Mullinahone, 1974)
William Murphy, *Charles J. Kickham, patriot, novelist, poet* (Dublin, 1903)
P. S. O'Hegarty, 'Kickham's novels' in *Irish Booklover*, xxvi (1938), pp.41-3.

XI   Biographies of Kickham's contemporaries and special subjects
G. F.-H. Berkeley, *The Irish battalion in the papal army of 1860* (Dublin and Cork, 1929)
Marcus Bourke, *John O'Leary: a study in Irish separatism* (Tralee, 1967)
P. J. Corish, 'Political problems, 1860-78' in P. J. Corish (ed.), *A history of Irish catholicism* (Dublin, 1967-73)
William D'Arcy, *The fenian movement in the United States, 1858-86* (Washington, 1947)
William Dillon, *Life of John Mitchel* (2 vols, London, 1888)
R. Dudley Edwards (ed.), *Ireland and the Italian risorgimento* (Dublin, 1962)
Richard Fallis, *The Irish renaissance: an introduction to Anglo-Irish literature* (Dublin, 1978)
R. F. Foster, *Charles Stewart Parnell: the man and his family* (London, 1976)
Denis Gwynn, *Young Ireland and 1848* (Cork, 1949)
Mary Leo, 'The influence of the fenians and their press on public opinion in Ireland, 1863-70' (M. Litt. thesis, Trinity College, Dublin, 1976)
David Leonard, 'John Mitchel, Charles Gavan Duffy and the legacy of Young Ireland' (Ph.D. thesis, University of Sheffield, 1975)
F. S. L. Lyons, *Charles Stewart Parnell* (London, 1977)
Donal McCartney, 'The church and fenianism' in *University Review*, iv (Winter 1967)
T. W. Moody, 'The new departure in Irish politics, 1878-9' in J. A. Cronne and others (ed.), *Essays in British and Irish history in honour of James Eadie Todd* (London, 1949)
T. W. Moody, *The fenian movement* (Cork, 1968)
E. R. Norman, *The catholic church and Ireland in the age of rebellion, 1859-73* (London, 1965)
R. B. O'Brien, *The life of Charles Stewart Parnell* (2 vols, London, 1898)
Leon Ó Broin, *Revolutionary underground: the story of the Irish Republican Brotherhood, 1858-1924* (Dublin, 1976)
Brian Ó Cuiv, *Irish dialects and Irish-speaking districts* (Dublin, 1967)
T. D. O'Dowd, 'The earliest educational work of the Irish Vincentians' in *Proceedings of the Catholic Historial Committee, 1962.*

Christopher O'Dwyer, 'Archbishop Leahy of Cashel, 1806-75' (M.A. thesis, N.U.I., 1971)

Tomás Ó Fiaich, 'The clergy and fenianism, 1860-70' in *Irish Ecclesiastical Record,* fifth series, cix, no.2 (Feb. 1968), pp.81-103

Seán Ó Lúing *Ó Donnabháin Rosa I* (Baile Átha Cliath, 1969)

T. P. Ó Néill, *Fiontán Ó Leathlobhair* (Baile Átha Cliath, 1962)

P. C. Power, *The story of Anglo-Irish poetry* (Cork, 1967)

Matthew Russell, *Rose Kavanagh and her songs* (Dublin, 1909)

Desmond Ryan, *The fenian chief: a biography of James Stephens* (Dublin, 1907)

George Sigerson, *Political prisoners at home and abroad* (London, 1890)

David Thornley, *Isaac Butt and home rule* (London, 1964)

Mark Tierney, *Croke of Cashel: the life of Archbishop Thomas William Croke, 1832-1902* (Dublin, 1976)

J. H. Whyte, *The independent Irish party, 1850-9* (London, 1958)

George-Denis Zimmermann, *Songs of Irish rebellion* (Dublin, 1967)

XII   General histories

J. J. Lee, *The modernisation of Irish society, 1848-1918* (Dublin, 1973)

F. S. L. Lyons, *Ireland since the famine* (London, 1971)

J. A. Murphy, *Ireland in the twentieth century* (Dublin, 1975)

P. S. O'Hegarty, *Ireland under the union* (London, 1952)